Katha Pollitt, a winner of two National Magazine Awards, has contributed to *The Nation* since 1975–first as a poet and later as literary editor, film reviewer, contributing editor, associate editor and, since 1994, "Subject to Debate" columnist. Her most recent book is *Pro: Reclaiming Abortion Rights* (2014).

Richard Kreitner is *The Nation*'s assistant editor for special projects.

Who is
HILLARY CLINTON?
Two Decades of Answers From the Left

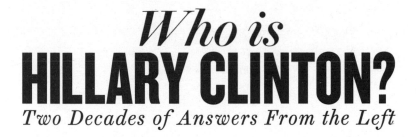

INTRODUCTION BY KATHA POLLITT
EDITED BY RICHARD KREITNER

THE
Nation.

I.B. TAURIS
LONDON · NEW YORK

Published in 2016 by
I.B.Tauris & Co. Ltd / The Nation Company, LLC
London • New York
www.ibtauris.com

Copyright © 2016 The Nation Company, LLC

The right of Richard Kreitner to be identified as the editor
of this work has been asserted by the author in accordance
with the Copyright, Designs and Patents Act 1988.

Every attempt has been made to gain permission for the use of the
images in this book. Any omissions will be rectified in future editions.

References to websites were correct at the time of writing.

ISBN: 978 1 78453 635 0
eISBN: 978 0 85772 875 3

A full CIP record for this book is available from the British Library
A full CIP record is available from the Library of Congress

Library of Congress Catalog Card Number: available

Book design by Omar Rubio
Printed in the United States of America

SFI Certified Sourcing
www.sfiprogram.org
SFI-00453

Table of Contents

HAWK OR HUMANITARIAN?

WHO'S READY?

Introduction

BY KATHA POLLITT

he's a radical feminist. She's just a wife. She's Emma Goldman in a pantsuit. She's a corporate sellout. She's a liberal. She's conservative. She'll move all women forward. Yeah, right: The only woman she cares about is herself.

Some days it feels as if Americans have been debating Hillary Clinton for my entire adult life. It's kind of amazing that a woman who has lived so much of her life in public can still be so... mysterious. She's a Rorschach test of our attitudes—including our unconscious ones—about women, feminism, sex and marriage, to say nothing of the Democratic Party, progressive politics, the United States and capitalism.

How ambitious can a woman be before she attracts scorn from men? From women? Not very. As Arkansas first lady, Hillary Rodham couldn't even keep her own last name. She started a media firestorm in 1992 when she defended her choice to work at the Rose Law Firm with the famous words, "I suppose I could have stayed home and baked cookies and had teas, but what I decided to do was to fulfill my profession, which I entered before my husband was in public life." Fair enough, although conservatives professed to feel grossly offended at the imagined sneer at stay-home mothers. (Hillary was actually referring to the typical hostessy life of a governor's wife.)

The cookies remark was actually the second time Hillary seemed to separate herself from other, less accomplished women. A few months earlier, she and Bill appeared on *60 Minutes* to deny that he had had a long affair with Gennifer Flowers. "You know," Hillary told Steve Kroft, "I'm not sitting here—some little woman standing by my man like Tammy Wynette." Not only did she needlessly insult every woman who stayed with a straying mate, every country-music lover and the great Tammy Wynette, given her husband's proclivities she was either self-deceived (or Bill-deceived) or lying. As the Monica Lewinsky scandal would show, she was not so different from those little women. Only by then the zeitgeist had shifted: By the late 1990s wives who put up with unfaithful men looked like doormats to the sort of people who write op-eds. For pundits, staying with Bill made her either a fake feminist or an opportunist, or both. Her feminist admirers were put in the uncomfortable position of withholding judgment on her loyalty to her marriage, while at the same time her public humiliation increased her popularity with the general public. Why had it taken so long for her to realize that people like women more when they suffer?

The same ambiguity and ambivalence marks her politics and its reception. While much of the country sees Hillary as way left of center—she's a Democrat, a woman, pro-choice, in favor of unions and expanded access to healthcare, or, in other words, a communist—the further you go on the actual left, the more she is perceived as the enemy, a friend to corporate capitalism, the woman who doomed national healthcare, a supporter of welfare reform and a warmonger. John Edwards, briefly the hope of progressives in the 2008 Democratic primary, also voted for the Iraq War, but somehow he escaped the heavy-duty and permanent opprobrium visited on Hillary, even after she attributed her vote to faulty intelligence as she geared up for her primary campaign. Not good enough. (For the real apology, the world would have to wait until her book *Hard Choices* came out in 2014.) Why were those three little words "I was wrong"—not misled, but wrong— so hard to say? John Edwards said them easily enough, and that was the end of the issue as far as public opinion was concerned. You would almost think apologizing canceled out all those dead people. But would that have been the case for Hillary? A man can admit fault and emerge even stronger—it takes a real man to admit he was wrong—but can a woman apologize without being seen as an indecisive flip-flopper, weak-minded and totally unfit to be commander in chief? Would it even have mattered to progressives, who already disliked her? The truth is, the difference between Hillary's foreign policy positions and those of President

Obama's are paper thin. Even during the primary campaign he was talking about bombing Pakistan, and one of his foreign policy advisers was Samantha Power, a major proponent of so-called humanitarian intervention. Yet he was seen as the peace candidate and Hillary as the war candidate—that was why I supported him in 2008—even after the peace candidate made the war candidate his secretary of state.

Similarly, her presence on the Walmart board of directors (1986-1992) comes up again and again, along with her general friendliness to business and Wall Street and big-money donors. You don't have to think these are ideal choices and positions to wonder why she is so strenuously taken to task for them. What do people expect from a mainstream Democratic politician? Barack Obama is pretty much in the same place—how many bankers have gone to prison on his watch for their role in causing the near collapse of the economy in 2008? None. To be fair, progressives regularly point this out. But those charges haven't become part of his public identity, as they have in the case of Hillary.

Why is that? Perhaps it's because the political case against Hillary is tied into common perceptions about her character: She's inauthentic, deceptive, untrustworthy, grasping, ambitious and money mad. This is the picture that underscores and gives life to the many scandals laid at her and her husband's feet—scandals that almost never amounted to much in and of themselves, but provoked a circle-the-wagons reaction that gave them plausibility.

How serious were Whitewater, Morgan Guaranty, Travelgate? In "Hot Water," from 1996, Doug Ireland calls them "ethical and moral breaches...no less troubling than Watergate and Iran/Contra." Hardly, says David Corn that same year: Whitewater was "pathetically low-rent" and Travelgate a defensible decision to fire Republican holdovers who were arguably ethically challenged themselves. What gave the latter scandal staying power, Corn argues, was the prevarication involved in concealing Hillary's role in it. And the reason for that concealment was the White House's obsession with remaking Hillary's image from formidable lawyer into "sweet little wife."

As that example suggests, it is almost impossible to talk about Hillary without talking about gender. Everything about her is inflected by notions and expectations and feelings and stereotypes about women. Even the fact that we call her by her first name is gendered: "Clinton" belongs to her husband. As I write this, sixteen Republicans and five Democrats are running for their party's presidential nomination, but only Hillary has been universally labeled ambitious. As if a politician hoping to win the White House could be anything but! Much of what seems to many people to be ungenuine about her—the many makeovers, the lack of spontaneity in public appearances, the aversion to risk—could well be an attempt to thread the very narrow needle of the public's gender stereotypes: There are many ways for a man to be a successful politician; these days, he can even cry. But a woman politician has to somehow fulfill ideals of femininity that are, at bottom, deferential and power-ceding while simultaneously fulfilling ideals of leadership that are masculine to the core. She has to be warm but not emotional, relatable and likeable but not a people-pleaser, smart but not openly smarter than you. She has to convey competence and authority without being threatening to men—or women. Plus, every single waking minute of every single day she has to look trim and attractive and stylish and younger than her chronological age. None of which will protect her from a staggering array of sexist insults: Lady Macbeth, dragon lady, nutcracker, ice queen, bitch and, my personal favorite, "that buck-tooth witch, Satan." Iron my shirt!

***

Admirers of Hillary will find much to like in these pages. In two pieces, Ellen Chesler makes the case for her as a strong left-of-center feminist leader. In a particularly lively, if almost entirely speculative piece from 1996, Erica Jong imagines the cost of constant political and marital compromise to Hillary's true nature: "Hillary comes across on television as cold and too controlled because that is the truth. She has rejigged her image so often, retailored it so much to please the spin doctors, that it comes across as inauthentic. It is." Andrea Bernstein's solid reporting from the 2000 Senate campaign trail in upstate New York ("Hillary Clinton's 'Smaller Steps'") is mostly critical of Hillary's modest political agenda—the "progressive-icon Hillary—if she ever existed—has gone the way of her headbands and Coke-bottle-bottom glasses"—but fans will appreciate Bernstein's acknowledgment of her oft-disparaged speaking skills: She "can bring crowds to their feet" and "electrified" a crowd of mostly African-American and Latino students. (I welcomed that especially because the times I've heard Hillary speak in person I thought she was terrific, which is not the common view. It's nice to know I'm not alone.)

But the critics of Hillary will probably be happier with this book than the fans. *The Nation* is, after all, a progressive magazine, and no matter how much one wants to promote the cause of women in politics, no matter how willing one is to settle for prudence and pragmatism in an era unfriendly to the left, when you get into the granular details of Hillary's actual positions it can be dispiriting: Bring back those headbands and glasses! Barbara Ehrenreich's "Who Is Hillary Clinton?" is a massive takedown which culminates in a description of Hillary as "a sleek, well-funded, power-seeking machine encased in a gleaming carapace of self-righteousness." Betsy Reed ("Race to the Bottom") astutely analyzes her use of racist dog whistles against Obama. Wendy Kaminer ("Hillary's No Liberal") dismisses her as a "maternalist" feminist hostile to civil liberties and free speech. In a 2012 debate, Bob Dreyfuss calls her a hawk, but—with Hillary there's always a "but"—Barbara Crossette sees her as a superb diplomat who maneuvered adroitly in tight spaces.

Rereading my own contributions (did I really write about Hillary that often?) I note that I was hardest on her as a first lady—

even disparaging her early support for global feminism in light of her support for welfare reform at home. Today that strikes me as a bit unfair. Now I would say global feminism is one of the few shining lights on the international scene, and it was great—and brave—that a first lady took it on as a cause. Also, painful as it is to acknowledge it, welfare reform is a done deal, even among progressives. Advocates for the poor have moved on, with some success, to campaigns around work: higher minimum wages, paid sick leave, paid parental leave. All of which Hillary supports.

Indeed, right now, as she begins her primary campaign, she sounds a lot like the progressive icon Elizabeth Warren, attacking the wealthy and powerful and promising to be a fierce fighter against growing inequality. Her campaign spokespeople say this is what she's always been. The questions is, will people believe her? This collection of *Nation* articles won't answer all the readers' questions, but at the very least it brings the Rorschach blot into clearer focus. ❖

STRANGE
COMPROMISES

The Male Media's Hillary Problem

KATHA POLLITT, MAY 17, 1993

Ted Koppel is not exactly known for in-depth coverage of the issues, but in March he came across a story so big, so urgent, so far-reaching in its implications for democracy that he needed two entire sessions of *Nightline* to reveal its full dimensions to the American people. Atrocities in Angola? One in ten Americans on food stamps? Why Johnny still can't read? Don't be silly. The topic was Hillary Clinton. Does she have too much power, or what?

Having noted for the record that the first lady enjoys healthy approval ratings in the polls, and that two-thirds of the population sees nothing amiss with her chairing the administration's task force on healthcare, and having further noted that most of her critics are white men and Republicans, Koppel devoted the bulk of both shows to conducting a chorus of complaints from members of those overlapping disgruntled minorities. Soundbites from Mickey Kaus, Rush Limbaugh, Robert Novak, Thomas Mann (the Brookings Institution heavy, not the German novelist) and others built up the now familiar media cartoon: Hillary Rodham Clinton as the overbearing wife with a finger in every slice of government pie, a workaholic ideologue accountable to no one but her pussywhipped husband, an "unelected consort" in a "quasi-monarchical relationship," who promotes the hiring of women, like Donna Shalala, from her circle of hyperliberal friends. Kaus noted that her influence is felt even in an "obscure federal agency" like the Resolution Trust Corporation, where people are "scared" of her: "Imagine how strong her influence is on the more obvious agencies!"

"This is not some kind of a woman behind the scenes who's pulling the strings," said Michael Deaver, clearly nostalgic for the astrological management style of his erstwhile employer Nancy Reagan. "This woman's out front pulling the strings."

While Ms. Clinton's attackers were prominent figures, named and given plenty of air time, her defenders were mostly lightweights (the managing editor of *People* or anonymous (a Japanese woman, who said through an interpreter, "I hope I can be like her when I reach her age"). Only two women were quoted more than once: the supremely silly Sally Quinn, herself a power wife of note, and feminist columnist Ellen Goodman, both of whom spoke in generalities about marriage. The whole debate, indeed, was structured as a kind of contest between *Redbook* and *The Wilson Quarterly*, girl talk and fluff versus the threat to the Republic: Should America go down the tubes so that the tea-serving secretaries of Tokyo can have a positive role model? And just in case the viewer might be inclined to say, Sure, why not?, Koppel was quick to sound an ominous note: "When we come back, the question, What if the president thinks the first lady is doing a bad job?" Short of putting her into an insulin coma, the answer was, He's stuck. After all, they're married.

Poor HRC. Perhaps she thought her husband's victory would put paid to the nitpicking and bitchiness and ponderous rumblings about the first lady's "role" which swirled around her during the campaign. All summer long the lifestyle industry churned out articles with titles like "Are We Ready for a first lady as First Partner?" (All right, I admit it, I wrote that one, for *Glamour*. You'd think the election would have answered that question. But no, the media mill grinds on. There was the inaugural hat disaster, the dropping of the strategically assumed adoring gaze at Bill, the readoption of Rodham as a middle name. What with all the head-scratching and thumbsucking that these provoked, you would never know that in the United States today 37 percent of married women do not assume their husband's surname, that 12 percent of the armed forces and 42 percent of law students are women, that 59 percent of married couples have two wage-earners and that in 21 percent of those couples the wife earns more than her husband.

Now that she's actually ensconced in the White House, the first lady has become a quasi-pornographic obsession, exemplified by *Spy*, which put her on its cover in leather with a whip and a manic grin: the First Dominatrix. There are dirty jokes, sexist jokes and sexual rumors galore: HRC is a lesbian, currently conducting an affair with a well-known actress; she's got Bill in some incredible sexual stranglehold. Any doubts that the Clinton administration is the most open in living memory should be assuaged by the fact that *everyone* knows, or thinks he knows, what goes on in the Lincoln Bedroom: the lamp- (or Bible-, or urn-) throwing incident (*Newsweek* actually printed this one), the blackmailing-Bill-with-girlfriends-yet-unknown theory, the no-sex-for-the-past-five-years rumor. It was another mom from my daughter's kindergarten who filled me in on the absence of action in the presidential bed. Talk about six degrees of separation. From the White House to the Lab School, it's more like three.

Now, at this point I must say that I am no fan of Hillary Rodham Clinton's politics. I'm a single-payer healthcare system supporter, myself. I don't like some of the compromises she's made on social issues, either: What kind of children's rights advocate, after all, supports parental notification on abortion? If you pulled out enough of my fingernails, I'd probably admit that I think a wife who takes her husband's name is a wimp, especially if, like Hillary, she does so to make her guy look macho. I'd even admit that there's something sad about the fact that the most powerful woman to emerge from the much-ballyhooed Year of the Woman is a wife. This is the "false feminist" issue raised by Mickey Kaus, who, like most people who raise this objection to Hillary's activism, is no great fan of real feminists. Hillary, by this line, is just piggybacking off Bill instead of relying on her own efforts.

There's no denying that wifehood sometimes confers unfair advantages. But so too does being a husband. Indeed, one of Bill Clinton's likable qualities is that he publicly acknowledges the part his wife's brains and energy have played in his own career. We do not live in a society composed of autonomous monads. In fact, we live in a society that has in very large measure decided to distribute its goods through the family system, whether it's health insurance, Social Security, money or party invitations. (Well, rumor has it that when Isaac Bashevis Singer won the Nobel Prize in Literature, he flew first-class to Stockholm and made his wife fly coach, but you see my point.) But when a man benefits through his wife, we tend to close our eyes; when a woman benefits through her husband, we assume she's otherwise "unqualified." Marty Peretz and Frances Lear both own magazines bought with their spouse's money. But while Lear was ridiculed in the press when she started *Lear's* with her divorce settlement millions (I remember a rather nasty cartoon in these pages)—she was an egomaniac, a greedy alimony queen who knew nothing about magazines, etc., etc.— nobody questioned the validity of Peretz's buying *The New Republic* with his wife's inherited wealth or mocked his ambitions as inappropriate for an academic. As it turns out both magazines are quite successful, but only Lear had to overcome a presumption that her position was illegitimate and that she herself was a fool, perhaps because at some level we still believe that marital money is really the husband's, no matter whose name is on the stocks and bonds, and whatever the community property statutes say.

Hillary's detractors make a great fuss over the fact that she was not elected. That is true. But no one who serves in a presidential administration is elected except the vice president. At least with the Clinton administration the electorate was apprised that Hillary would play some sort of political role, so if people couldn't live with that, they could choose to vote for George and Barbara. With the Reagans, on the other hand, the fact that the first lady would wield considerable power was actively concealed from the people. Why is it so dreadful that Hillary helps Bill make his appointments but not that, say, JFK's father—the ex-bootlegger and Nazi sympathizer—helped him compose his cabinet? (Now, if it had been Rose Kennedy providing the advice, we'd *never* have heard the end of it.) True, JFK took a lot of flak for naming his brother attorney general, and Congress promptly passed the antinepotism law, which Hillary's own position risks flouting. The two cases aren't really comparable—head of the healthcare task force is hardly a cabinet-level position—but taken together they suggest that we rethink the whole subject. Maybe it *isn't* worse to give an administration position to a presidential relative than to a presidential crony or big-money contributor.

Maybe the president should be permitted, as constitutional precedent suggests, to take appropriate counsel from those he sees fit to consult. As for the objection that Bill can't fire Hillary, well, sure he can—although it would doubtless be presented to the public as something else. Certainly nobody thinks that Bill will feel compelled to implement the findings of Hillary's task force if, by some bizarre chance, it comes up with a plan he disdains.

It's funny how those who recoil at Hillary's position in the administration return to the old comic view of marriage, in which any husband more congenial than Genghis Khan is assumed to be putty in the hands of his wife, and any wife less demure than Pat Nixon is assumed to be a shrew. A Republican operative said the Bush campaign planned to show that Bill Clinton is "out of control" and "can't control his zipper, can't control his wife and can't control his waistline." In women, power is always seen as sexual. That's why people can half-believe all the rumors about Hillary, mutually exclusive though they be: let's see, a lamp-throwing lesbian who enslaves her husband by refusing to exercise on his person the amazing sexual power she has over him despite his appetite for other women, with which she is blackmailing him. All this in order to run a policy-wonkery show trial, whose verdict— managed competition, yes!—was in at the start. You'd think the paragon who could pull off this complicated gambit would hold out for secretary of state.

The sexist attack on Hillary Clinton is partly a lazy way to attack her husband, of course. I doubt Rush Limbaugh would be playing "Hail to the Chief" at the mention of the first lady's name

if she were heading up a presidential task force to abolish affirmative action and build a wall on the Mexican border. Similarly,
would Mickey Kaus object to Hillary's interest in the Resolution
Trust Corporation if she did not support the "paleoliberal" notion
that the property belonging to failed S&Ls should be sold off at
modest prices to ordinary people?

From Marie Antoinette to Joy Silverman (whom no less a free
spirit than Bill Kunstler called a "Republican whore"), misogyny
and sexual slurs provide a handy shorthand with which to express
one's hostility to a woman's—or her husband's—politics. But it is
also true that the politics and the image of the Clinton administration are closely bound up with issues of gender: the social shift to
more egalitarian marriages; the growing political power of wom-
en, who voted for Bill Clinton by an eight-point margin, two and a
half times that of male voters; the mainstreaming of a popular you-
can-do-it feminism; and a wellspring of support, disproportionately
female, for renewed government activism in the domestic sphere—
what conservatives, interestingly, like to deride as "the nanny state."
Attacking HRC is a way of attacking these broad social and political transformations without actually making a case against them.
Because, as we saw from the reaction to Marilyn Quayle's speech
about women's "essential nature" and Pat Buchanan's call for a cultural war, that case has already been lost.

The fact is, as even Koppel admitted, HRC is an immensely
popular figure: The January *People* with her picture on the cover out-

sold all issues since last June's "DIANA: Dramatic Excerpts From the Book That Rocked Britain." Even *Ladies' Home Journal* touts her for ushering in the "Age of the Smart Woman." So who has a Hillary problem? The media.

"It makes me sick the way journalists go after Hillary," one male *Newsday* editor told me. "And what's weird about it is they're baby boomers—sophisticated guys who've lived with feminism for twenty years." There's a Freudian explanation for the media's zeal: The Clintons are the first First Family from the boomers' own generation, thus freeing fortysomethings to express their envy and hostility toward those in power: Who do the Clintons think they are? And there's a political explanation: The Reagan/Bush years moved the press in an increasingly rightward direction—the metamorphosis of Joe Klein from sympathetic Woody Guthrie biographer to "family values" harrumpher is the paradigmatic case— which, like the path of an ocean liner, it will take ages to reverse.

And then there's my own pet theory: The anti-Hillary media types, for the most part men, are protecting their turf. (The female snipers are just jealous.) Despite its reputation as *la carriere overte aux talents*, journalism is actually one of the last bastions of old-fashioned irrational male privilege. This year, as in past years, the research project Women, Men & Media found that newspapers and television news programs overwhelmingly featured male reporters, male commentators, male experts and interviewees. The table of contents of virtually every magazine of news and opinion tells the same story. While women have managed to eke out a small preserve in feminist-oriented op-ed columns—Anna Quindlen, Ellen Goodman, Judy Mann and many others—the Big Beats belong to the big boys. There is no female counterpart to the phony-proletarian big-city-ethnic columnists like Jimmy Breslin, Mike Royko, Mike McAlary and Mike Barnicle (although Amy Pagnozzi tries); no female opinionmeister with the week-in, week-out visibility and clout of Joe Klein or Mickey Kaus or Michael Kinsley or John Leo or John Taylor. Journalism, of course, is hardly the only male-dominated profession. But it's the only one that has no official credentialing system by which women can either be kept out (major league sports, the priesthood) or insist on admittance (law, medicine, the Protestant clergy). Journalism degrees are an industry joke; everyone knows all you need is a talent for quick opinions and clever phrases and an ability to meet a deadline, gifts even their most ardent detractors concede women have in spades! There's no good reason that women shouldn't assume the same prominent position in journalism that they now have in the world of books—think of all the important new women novelists, poets, essayists, editors. The more *women* excel in other fields the harder it is to explain their marginality in the press as anything but what it is—sex discrimination.

Could it be that the anti-Hillary pundits and talking heads are motivated by status anxiety and fear for their jobs? She may not have been elected, but what if nobody cares? She's a lot more qualified than most of the people giving her advice in the media. She just *might* usher in that Age of the Smart Woman. And where will the Joe Kleins and Mickey Kauses be then?

Ted Koppel worries about what Bill will do if Hillary does a bad job. He ought to be worrying about what he himself will do if she does a good job, and Cokie Roberts decides she'd like a shot at his. ❖

Hillary & Bill & Harry & Louise

SAM HUSSEINI, DECEMBER 13, 1993

"**I** know you've all seen the ads. You know, the kind of homey kitchen ads where you've got the couple sitting there talking about how the president's plan is going to take away choice and the president's plan is going to narrow options, and then that sort of heartfelt sigh by that woman at the end, 'There must be a better way'—you know, you've seen that, right?

"What you *don't* get told in the ad is that it is paid for by insurance companies. . . . It is time for you and for every American to stand up and say to the insurance industry: 'Enough is enough, we want our healthcare system back!'"

What Hillary Rodham Clinton was referring to in a recent speech was a series of soap opera–style TV ads featuring a woeful couple, "Harry and Louise," and sponsored by the Health Insurance Association of America (HIAA). The first lady positioned herself as a foe of big business; the media played right along.

Tom Brokaw introduced NBC's segment saying, "Hillary

Rodham Clinton today launched a scathing attack on the health insurance industry." Correspondent Andrea Mitchell, working on the basis of anonymous sources, suggested that the administration went after HIAA. because "the White House wanted a scapegoat." On CNN reporters relayed that the administration is "engaged in something close to an all-out war with the health insurance industry," and that "the White House would rather talk about insurance industry profits than the rosy assumptions on which its own plan is based."

A closer look, however, reveals a different sort of deceit on the part of the administration, the TV networks and Senator Edward Kennedy, who joined in the first lady's pseudo-populism, asking the HIAA to "drop the ads and come work with us" on the Clinton health plan. That plan, in fact, serves the interests of the insurance establishment. As Patrick Woodall of Public Citizen says, "The managed competition–style plan the Clintons have chosen virtually guarantees that the five largest health insurance companies—Aetna, Prudential, Met Life, Cigna and The Travelers—will run the show in the healthcare system."

These big companies helped develop Clinton's plan of managed competition, and all but The Travelers paid for much of the research that was done by the Jackson Hole Group, an organization that drew up the original blueprint for managed competition. (The administration tries to obscure this; in rebuttal to the HIAA's ads, the Democratic Party made a commercial saying of the Clinton plan: "The insurance companies may not like it, but the president didn't design it for them—he designed it for you.")

Robert Dreyfuss of Physicians for a National Health Program says, "The Clintons are getting away with murder by portraying themselves as opponents of the insurance industry. It's only the small fry that oppose their plan. Under any managed-competition scheme, the small ones will be pushed out of the market very quickly."

Indeed, the HIAA is made up mostly of small and medium-sized insurers. The five biggest insurers have formed their own organization, the Alliance for Managed Competition, which basically backs the Clinton approach. These big insurers stand to gain from the Clinton plan's increased corporatization of healthcare since they have been rapidly buying HMOs, 45 percent of which are now owned by the eight largest insurance companies. The outlays for advertisements by the big insurers and the HMOs dwarf the money being spent on advocacy ads by the HIAA and either the Democratic or Republican Party.

The compelling question, then, is not who's behind "Harry and Louise" but who's behind Bill and Hillary? ❖

Welfare Rights Are Human Rights

Katha Pollitt, October 9, 1995

"I want to speak up for women in my own country," Hillary Clinton told the UN Conference on Women in Beijing, "women who are raising children on the minimum wage, women who can't afford healthcare or childcare women whose lives are threatened by violence, including violence in their own homes . . . mothers who are fighting for good schools, safe neighborhoods, clean air and clean airwaves . . . and for women everywhere who simply don't have time to do everything they are called upon to do each day." Having delivered herself of this graceful tribute to American women who do too much, Mrs. Clinton went on to denounce genital mutilation, bride burning, female infanticide, forced abortion and the suppression of human rights in China. Then she went home to the White House, where her husband was frantically telepathing to the Senate his fervent wish to sign a "compromise" welfare-reform bill that would end sixty years of federal commitment to poor women and children. No mention of clitoridectomy, though—that's a relief. Well, Mrs. Clinton didn't actually include welfare mothers in her litany of women she was claiming to speak for, did she?

There's something so weird about these UN Conferences on Noble Causes. Governments gather in their colorful native dress to denounce one another's injustices and inequalities, while deploring their own as if they were the weather. Thus, Mrs. Clinton can champion mothers doughtily striving to survive on the minimum wage as if that wage were an act of God, and as if the set of circumstances by which a woman comes to raise children with nothing but $4.25 an hour between herself and the street were not the product of government policies. In the same way, she can "speak up for" battered women even as President Clinton ties his fortunes to welfare changes that will increase family violence by raising the general level of desperation and destitution, reduce services to victims and make it harder for women to disentangle themselves from violent mates.

I'm not pooh-poohing the Beijing conference. "Women's rights are human rights" is a powerful idea, and one that offers real hope for women around the globe, something that could not be said of the idea it is slowly replacing: the religio-nationalist-racialist defense of women's subjection as a "cultural practice." It was thrilling to see so roundly refuted the notion that Third World women don't mind having their genitals sliced off or being stoned to death for "unchastity," don't want family planning, don't care about abortion or sexual harassment. It was satisfying, too, to see feminism acknowledged as the grassroots movement it is, and the Vatican stand revealed as an ideologically rigid, top-down force out of touch with women's lives.

No, what I wish is that the United States would take the UN more seriously. I'm willing to bet no one involved in the welfare-reform game has read the 1989 UN Convention on the Rights of the Child, which our government has finally agreed to sign. Did you know that Article 2 binds signatories not to discriminate against children based on a whole slew of circumstances, including their "birth"? What does that do to the House welfare bill that forbids the dole to young mothers of out-of-wedlock children, and that excludes from welfare children born to mothers already receiving it? Aren't these provisions a form of discrimination between "legitimate" and "illegitimate" children, and between those born before and after Mom goes on the dole? The same Article commits signers not to discriminate against children on the basis of the parents' "status." Since the Article speaks only of the states' duties to "each child within their jurisdiction," does that mean immigration status too? Maybe Proposition 187 makes Pete Wilson an international human rights criminal.[1]

---

1. The 1994 ballot measure in California, backed by Wilson, the sitting Republican governor, would have cut off undocumented immigrants from state services. It passed by a wide margin but was later ruled unconstitutional by a federal court.

The whole document is so kind, common-sensical and humane it's a shock to turn to the recent Luxemburg Income Study report, which demonstrates yet again that US children are worse off than those in just about every other Western industrialized nation, including countries like Italy, where median income is much lower. Generous government policies—childcare, child support, maternity leave, national healthcare, direct payments to mothers—make the sort of child poverty that afflicts one-quarter of American children a rarity, even in Thatcherized Britain and high-unemployment Germany.

All of which, I'm sure, made a deep impression on Barbara Mikulski, Dianne Feinstein, Barbara Boxer and Patty ("mom in tennis shoes") Murray as they cast their votes for the Senate welfare bill. That's every Democratic woman senator but Carol Moseley-Braun—you remember, the ones we voted for to fight for women and children, buck the sexist Congressional leadership and never put their own careers ahead of the public good the way *men* do. It was left to Daniel Patrick Moynihan, old Mr. Benign Neglect himself, to lay blame where it belongs: with the Clinton administration and the timid and co-opted antipoverty advocacy groups.

A few more of these international human rights victories and American women and children may be just about done for. ❖

Slick Hilly?

DAVID CORN, JANUARY 29, 1996

In the future it might be called the Hillary Syndrome: the inability to acknowledge that a smart, accomplished and assertive wife has a role in her husband's career. This condition is partly to blame for one of the latest first lady scandals, in which the release of a confidential memo regarding dismissals at the White House travel office makes Hillary Rodham Clinton a liar. This at an unpropitious time—when her book, *It Takes a Village and Other Lessons Children Teach Us*, is being released, part of the continuing makeover of Bill Clinton's spouse from a super-lawyer/policy heavyweight (remember "two for the price of one"?) to a more traditional presidential wife who politely advocates so-called women's issues: children and breast cancer.

Much of the trouble has arisen because Hillary and the White House have refused to tell the truth about the First Spouse. Before Hillary arrived in Washington, she was an influential lawyer who sometimes worked for shifty businessmen (including S&L man James McDougal, the Clintons' co-partner in the pathetically low-rent Whitewater land deal). She downplayed that portion of the past, instead highlighting her work for the Children's Defense Fund, the Legal Services Corporation and an education reform commission in Arkansas. Now copies of billing records of the Rose Law Firm—inexplicably lost for two years—emerge to show that she spent more time helping McDougal and his pals than she had previously indicated.

When Hillary moved into the White House, the administration assigned her the number-one beat, healthcare reform; but it also strove to counter the impression that she is a Rasputin behind (or beside) the throne. Yet the newly disclosed Travelgate documents show that Hillary exerted political muscle in the White House and was the force behind the firings of the travel-office staff in 1993. As David Watkins, a high-ranking White House official, wrote, "The first lady took interest in having the Travel Office situation resolved quickly, following [her friend and show-biz honcho] Harry Thomason's bringing it to her attention: Thomason [who had an interest in an air-charter brokering firm] briefed the first lady on his suspicions that the Travel Office was improperly funneling business to a single charter company.... The first lady was concerned and desired...the firing of the Travel Office.... There would be hell to pay if...we failed to take swift and decisive action."

There is not much wrong with this scenario. Hillary and other Clintonites viewed the travel office suspiciously, as full of Reagan/Bush holdovers who had functioned practically as campaign staffers. Then Hillary heard from Thomason that the travel office was refusing competitive bids and that there were rumors of financial funny business. She demanded that Chief of Staff Thomas "Mack" McLarty, deputy counsel Vince Foster and Watkins take care of it—immediately.

So far, nothing untoward, though perhaps a bit harsh. The firings were then mishandled—in a PR sense—and the FBI was improperly used. Billy Dale, the head of the office, was acquitted of embezzlement. But media reports noted his office did help reporters bypass customs on international trips, and FBI investigators have told the House that they're convinced Dale cooked the office books. Republican antagonists hint that Hillary orchestrated the dismissals so her cronies could collect the charter business overseen by the travel office. But they offer no proof.

The problem is, Hillary did not disclose her involvement in the episode. When investigators from the General Accounting Office questioned her, she replied in writing that she does "not know the origins of the decision to remove the White House Travel Office employees" and that she "had no role in this decision." And when the White House released its internal review of the Travelgate affair, it did not detail Hillary's participation.

To prevent the current trouble, the White House had only to have been forthcoming in 1993. (In fact, Todd Stern, a White House official who worked on the internal review wrote in his notes, "We need to seriously think about whether or not it won't be better to come clean…even to [the] point of connecting…HRC.") A Capitol Hill Democratic investigator says, "If she had been honest, they wouldn't have any problem. But they had to portray her as just a sweet little wife, not a person calling the shots."

Travelgate, Whitewater—these petty matters hardly compare with the grand sleaze and constitutional questions of Watergate and Iran/contra Yet the public has the right to honesty from the White House. Hillary has prevaricated repeatedly, telling contradictory tales about her $100,000 commodity deal—one of the shadiest chapters of her past. Republicans and conservatives have pummeled her for reasons of political expedience, ideology and psychology (as in the fear of a strong female hand in the White House). But the White House has been so conscious of Hillary's image that it has undermined that image, as she has shifted from a cabinetesque policy adviser to a safe first lady now urging young people to abstain from sex until they are 21. Her lack of candor in several areas prompts a fair question: What's she hiding? Perhaps her biggest secret: who she really is. ✤

Village Idiot

KATHA POLLITT, FEBRUARY 5, 1996

"**S**aint or Sinner?" asks the cover of *Newsweek* about Hillary Clinton. On the *New York Times* op-ed page, Maureen Dowd calls her a hybrid of Earth Mother and Mommie Dearest. I must say, I don't see what all the fuss is about. Don't countless politicians (and their relatives) use their positions to make profitable contacts and advance their friends? And don't they all talk about family, morals, responsibility, children and God? Even if the first lady is guilty of the worst that is alleged against her—and if you can explain exactly what that is, you've probably been up to no good yourself—there's nothing new or exceptional about it: See the careers of Newt Gingrich, Al D'Amato, Bob Dole et al. This is what politics is all about, especially in places like Arkansas, *a k a* The Heartland. "The people you read about in the papers? They all live next door to each other," an Italian journalist told me after a visit to Little Rock. "It's just like Italy!"

Well, there is one new thing: the gender issue. A lot of people still expect the wives of politicians to concentrate on the *Kinder Küche Kirche* side of life, while their husbands go after the bright lights and boodle. HRC has failed to observe this division of labor in her own marriage, for which tradition-minded folk like William Safire cannot forgive her. Now the first lady has written a book, *It Takes a Village and Other Lessons Children Teach Us*, only to land herself in more hot water. In yet another column criticizing HRC, Maureen Dowd took her to task for not acknowledging the ghostly pen of Barbara Feinman, a former researcher and editor for Ben Bradlee, Bob Woodward and Sally Quinn, all now apparently up in arms at this slight to their beloved assistant. Between Whitewater, Madison Guaranty, Travelgate and now Thankyougate, HRC isn't likely to get much time to talk about her book, and since I know how painful that can be, I sat down and read the whole thing. Who knows? I may be the only columnist in America who can make that claim.

The ostensible thesis of *It Takes a Village* is that the well-being of children depends on the whole society. The real message is that HRC is for family values. She prays a lot, alone and *en famille*. She's a good mom. She thinks young people should abstain from sex until they are 21. She opposes divorce: "My strong feelings about divorce and its effects on children have caused me to bite my tongue more than a few times during my own marriage"—I'll bet—"and to think instead about what I could do to be a better wife and partner. My husband has done the same."

I know I'm not supposed to take these notions seriously, any more than I'm meant to gag at the weirdly Pollyannaish tone of the prose, or wonder if Sunday school could really have been her formative intellectual experience. Like her disapproval of television talk shows—thanks to which "we are saturated with stories about priests who molest children" and have become "skeptical of organized religion"—they're just campaign theater, nods to the cultural conservatives that are balanced by other nods, to flexible gender roles, legal abortion (a very small nod), a "modest" rise in the minimum wage. There's no attempt to think anything through: the damage to organized religion versus the damage to children left at risk of molestation, for example, or the kinds of social pressures that would be necessary to produce that bumper crop of 21-year-old virgins. Her opposition to divorce is left characteristically vague: She's "ambivalent" about no-fault divorce (the pet peeve of former White House aide and communitarian William Galston, who proposed abolishing it for couples with children recently on the *Times* op-ed page), but she says nothing about what it would really mean to return to the old system, in which spouses, lawyers and judges colluded in perjury, and wives who strayed could be denied custody and support. It's easy for her to talk: Her husband has obligingly provided her with grounds that would withstand even the most Savonarolaesque reforms.

What else? The first lady is for sex ed that has both an abstinence and, for those youths determined to ruin their lives, a

birth-control component; a free market that's also socially responsible; government that's both smaller and more social-worky. For
every problem she identifies, a study, a foundation, a church, a
business or a government-funded pilot project is already on the
case: teaching poor young mothers how to improve their babies'
cognitive abilities, encouraging fathers to spend time with their
families, involving parents in their children's school. Some of
these programs sound terrific, but none of them are on remotely
the same scale as the problems they confront. If parents are too
poor to afford school uniforms, they've got problems much grav-
er than the community recycling of hand-me-downs can solve.
The first lady is thus a kind of center-liberal version of Arianna
Huffington, who claims that "spirituality" and volunteerism can
replace the welfare state. For HRC the state itself becomes a kind
of pilot project, full of innovation but short on cash, and ever on
the lookout for spongers.

The real irony, of course, is that at the same time HRC is
conceptualizing society as a "village" united in its concern for and
responsibility toward children, her husband is panting to sign the
original Senate welfare bill, which his own administration's figures say would plunge 1.2 million more children into poverty and
render more desperate the condition of those already poor. How
can a self-described child advocate, who goes on and on about the
importance of providing children with enriched parental attention
and quality care from their earliest moments of life, square herself

with policies that would force low-skilled mothers of small children into full-time subminimum-wage jobs, with warehouse care for their kids? Exactly how will permitting states to deny benefits to children born on welfare further those kids' development? And what about the kids at the end of the line when the block grants run out?

After the media figure out Whitewater and insure proper recognition of Ms. Feinman's labors, some enterprising reporter might consider asking the first lady about that. ❖

Hot Water

DOUG IRELAND, FEBRUARY 19, 1996

Too many progressives tend to dismiss Whitewater as little more than the product of Republican electioneering. They take one look at the Clintons' most visible senatorial accusers—sleazoid Al D'Amato, the master of malaprop who is Bob Dole's campaign chair; turncoat Alabaman Richard Shelby; reactionary fuddy-duddy Lauch Faircloth—and, on hearing the antifeminist rhetoric used by some critics of the "twofer" presidency, simply conclude, same-old same-old.

But the Republicans' manifest glee at the findings of House and Senate investigators should not blind one to the mountain of evidence that has dragged the first lady in front of a grand jury, placed her and some of her closest associates under threat of perjury indictments and revealed how the White House has engaged in abuses of power that are, at best, shameful. Consider some of the thornier legal problems:

§ How did Hillary and the Rose Law Firm come to represent

Madison Guaranty, the failed S&L owned by Governor Clinton's onetime top aide and Whitewater business partner Jim McDougal? Under oath, Hillary told Resolution Trust Corporation investigators that Rick Massey, fresh out of law school and only eight months at Rose, "approached me about presenting this proposal to Jim McDougal because he was aware I knew him." But Massey, also under oath, told the Senate, "I don't believe it happened that way" (and added that he was "surprised" and "disappointed" when he learned from the press in 1992 that Hillary and McDougal had been land-deal partners). McDougal himself has told reporters that he put Hillary on retainer because Bill Clinton came "whimpering" to him that the Clintons needed more money—a version supported by a sworn deposition from Madison exec John Latham, who said he'd been ordered to retain Rose because McDougal was a Clinton pal. If, as is likely, McDougal has repeated his story to special prosecutor Kenneth Starr, there are at least three witnesses who could point up Hillary as a perjurer.

§ Madison has been found by federal bank regulators to have been operated by McDougal as a criminal enterprise. One of the scams McDougal ran as he tried to keep the S&L afloat amid the mounting concern of bank examiners was called Castle Grande, essentially a real estate Ponzi scheme on which Madison insiders made nearly $2 million. Among those insiders was Seth Ward, father-in-law of jailed Rose partner and close Clinton friend Webster Hubbell. McDougal used Ward as a front man to acquire most of Castle Grande, which was then carved into parcels and sold using inflated values (McDougal's appraiser has since pleaded guilty to twenty-four counts of land fraud and is cooperating with prosecutor Starr). The recently discovered Rose billing records show that Hillary worked on a number of Castle Grande matters for Madison, including an option to buy back from Ward for $400,000 parcels the RTC later valued at only $47,000. The original purchase documents on this land have mysteriously disappeared. "At the time it assisted Madison Guaranty with the Castle Grande deal," the RTC has found, "Rose Law Finn was aware of regulatory concerns about the soundness of the institution." Lawyers can be subject to both civil and criminal liability in bank frauds, and at the heart of Starr's investigation is the question, What did Hillary know and when did she know it?

§ And then there is the cover-up. Hillary's grand jury appearance was occasioned by the magical rediscovery of her billing records—covered with notes by Vincent Foster—long after they had been subpoenaed by the Senate and Starr. Contrary to Hillary's book-tour assertions, those records starkly contradict her claims that she did little work for Madison and knew nothing of Castle Grande. Rick Massey, the Rose tyro who did Hillary's legal scut work on the S&L, testified that the billings show her work for Madison was "significant." Furthermore, they show fourteen conversations with Castle Grande straw man Seth Ward. Equally explosive is Hillary's newest admission to the RTC that she authorized the shredding—in 1988, she claims—of four of her files on Madison, three of which dealt with Castle Grande and one with Madison's so-called Ward option. (By a late-night release after most reporters' deadlines, the White House escaped national media attention on the importance of the four shredded files—only the CNN Financial Network gave them major next-day play.) Hillary's chief of staff, Maggie Williams, and her political Doberman, Susan Thomases, are already under investigation for their role in the migration of documents from Foster's office to the First Couple's residence in the forty-eight hours following his suicide.

Clinton defenders like to talk of a "cover-up without a crime," choosing to ignore that a cover-up *is* a crime when it involves lying to federal investigators and Congress, destruction or concealment of documents and interference with federal agencies investigating possible wrongdoing, all of which appear to have occurred. These crimes have a name: obstruction of justice. And space does not permit detailing testimony about other administration meddling in probes of Madison matters by the RTC, the FDIC and the Small Business administration, or the moral crimes of Travelgate, in which the White House sicced the FBI and the IRS on seven innocent civil servants and implied they were crooks. (Even the Al Gore chum who wrote the Peat, Marwick management review criticizing some Travel Office bookkeeping practices has now told the House he found no "gross mismanagement" and that, indeed, there was no reason for the mass firing—the first in the history of the nonpolitical office.)

An abuse of power is an abuse of power whether committed by Republicans or Democrats, and corrupt cronyism that loots the public purse is a crime whether committed in a small town like Little Rock where everyone knows everyone or in the anonymity of a big city. The constitutional issues of Watergate and Iran/Contra may not be present in this administration's transgressions, but the ethical and moral breaches are no less troubling. In fact, Whitewater and Travelgate are a litmus test for liberals of their commitment to honesty in government. Do they have one standard, or two? ♣

Sex! Drugs! Spooks! Sleaze!

David Corn, September 9, 1996

Review of Partners in Power: The Clintons and Their
America *by Roger Morris*

eet the most powerful organized crime family
in the United States: the Clintons, Bill and
Hillary.

That's the gist of Roger Morris's excavation into the—gasp!—secret pasts of the first boomers to inhabit 1600 Pennsylvania Avenue. Influence-peddling, political corruption, money-laundering, drug-running, CIA skulduggery, the mob and even murder all appear in this tell-more-than-all account of the Clintons' joint rise to the White House. And, of course, there's plenty of sex. For both of them. More for him, certainly, but she has at least one backdoor lover (guess who).[2] If this book is ever

---

2. It has been rumored that Hillary Clinton had an affair with
Vince Foster, a White House lawyer she had worked with in
Arkansas whose 1993 death was deemed a suicide.

made into a miniseries it would short-circuit the sturdiest V-chip. Think of him as J.R. Ewing with nuclear weapons. She's a cross between Marie Antoinette and Rosalind Shays of *L.A. Law* (you know—the icy bitch of a partner who met her well-deserved conclusion at the bottom of an elevator shaft).

Morris retells a now-familiar tale—always with as negative a spin as possible. Bill is a glad-handing mover born of white trash and bearing emotional scars from a household of alcoholism and abuse. His true hometown is not Hope but Hot Springs, a city "pervasively, hypocritically corrupt," where his uncle was a prominent car dealer who, according to "convincing evidence," had links to organized crime and the Klan. (Morris does not let us in on this evidence.) Hillary, a cold, calculating control freak, was reared by a harsh, unbending and conservative father in a Chicago suburb, where "there were formidable social forces arrayed against honesty and revelation, both within and outside the family." Bill and Hillary formed a partnership in which they talked of doing good but fixated on doing well. But this is more than your run-of-the-mill account of unbridled ambition, compromised principles and whatever-it-takes politics. This power couple has resided in a shadowy netherworld, in which they served (and benefited from) the national intelligence state, drug traffickers and the most shady of financiers.

The trouble with this dishin' book is that too often it prompts a critical reader to ask, Is this stuff for real? Are they *that* corrupt? This is not just because some of the stories are stunners but because the sourcing of the most eye-popping material is often quite weak. Too frequently, Morris employs the phrase "according to an account." Turn to the notes, and it is unclear what account he means. Too often the account, when specified, originated in the hard-to-believe *American Spectator* and London *Sunday Telegraph*, the two most prominent peddlers of anti-Clinton sleaze. Other sources are confidential informants whose relationships to the Clintons, if any, are not described, or persons whose credibility is suspect. Call me old-fashioned, but if you accuse the president of the United States of indulging in sex-and-drug orgies, you ought to possess damned good evidence. Morris does not. He seems part of a disturbing tendency in modern media: If you can get someone to tell you a hot story, you report it, even if you can't prove it.

Let's look at the most sensational of the nonsexual charges in this book: Bill was a snitch for the CIA during his college days, and years later he was a coconspirator in a CIA-ish drugs-and-arms smuggling operation based at an airport in Mena, Arkansas. Morris claims that Bill, who participated in antiwar protests abroad and briefly visited Moscow as a student, spied for the CIA—that is, he might have. For his research, Morris contacted an association of retired intelligence officers, a group full of old boys who generally are not fans of Bill or his national security team. Through this network, Morris unearthed three unnamed sources who maintain Bill was somehow connected to the Company. One says Bill was a full-fledged "asset" who tattled on friends in the peace movement. Another says he once saw Bill's name on a list of informants. A third says Bill had a deal with the CIA to keep himself from being drafted. But another ex-spook told Morris he doubts Bill was on the agency payroll. And still another says it was people close to Bill, not Bill, who had been informants. The upshot? We don't really know. I'm not going to trust a small number of CIA men on this subject—especially when they are contradicted by colleagues. Morris provides no reason to accept one contention over another. The reader is left to believe what he or she wants.

But Clinton's supposed CIA connection is an important matter for Morris, for it leads—hundreds of pages later—to a key section of the book, the chapter on Mena. In the fast-and-loose eighties, a fellow named Barry Seal flew in and out of Mena carrying the traditional commodities of a CIA-backed smuggler: weapons for the *Contras* and drugs for Americans. What does this have to do with our current president? As governor, he suspiciously took little interest in this criminal conspiracy under way in his state. That is true. The reason? Bill was in on it. How does Morris know? L.D. Brown, who was a state trooper on the governor's security detail, says so. As Brown tells it, Bill encouraged him to answer a CIA help-wanted ad. After Brown applied and was interviewed by a CIA recruiter, he was sent to a restaurant where he met Seal, who repeatedly referred to Bill as if he knew him. Brown joined the Seal operation, always keeping the governor posted and discovering that Bill was fully aware and supportive of the nefarious misdeeds in Mena. The governor even told him that the Seal flights were transporting cocaine for Dan Lasater, a bond dealer who was a Clinton associate and campaign backer. Thus Bill is said to be mixed up in the most reprehensible of criminal enterprises and intelligence evildoing. And Hillary, too, for she was "a closet Contra supporter" (according to "some").

Morris swallows Brown's story whole—but supplies us with no proof of the trooper's claims. It is tough to believe that someone who applied for entrance into the CIA through conventional channels would be dispatched on his maiden assignment into such a highly sensitive operation—with no training, no polygraph, no true testing. Morris gained access to thousands of pages of Seal's personal papers. Presumably, none confirmed any relationship between Seal and Bill, since nothing is quoted from these records to back up Brown's allegations.

Much of Morris's salacious material depends on Arkansas state troopers of iffy reliability, most notably Larry Patterson and Roger Perry, favorite sources for *The American Spectator* and conspiracy-mongers of the right. Morris cites this pair in declaring that Hillary and Vince Foster had a passionate affair. But these troopers are proven liars, who once claimed they had evidence that Foster killed himself at the White House. They did not. If they fibbed about that, why should we believe them on the subject of

Bill's and Hillary's extracurricular activities?

Morris aptly guides the reader through the convoluted details of Whitewater. So many of the component deals do stink, especially the arrangement in which the Clintons and their partners bilked senior citizens as part of the land venture. But what engages Morris most is the covert world of the Clintons. He notes that state troopers—there they are again!—procured for Bill countless women and watched as the governor liaisoned with "literally hundreds" of women. He even reports that Bill indulged in "drug orgies"—without providing persuasive evidence. Morris refers to a murder involving "some of the governor's closest supporters," but does not fully explain it. He quotes a convicted drug dealer who claims she saw Bill snort coke at toga parties in Little Rock. He asserts that Clinton pressed the police to drop narcotics charges against his brother. (Clinton later did not interfere when the narcs busted Roger.) He alleges numerous financial improprieties and dozens of political fixes—without fully documenting each one. (A few episodes, such as Hilary's go-go commodities speculating, are well detailed; too many are not.) He accuses Clinton of pocketing money from contributors.

Now much of this may be true (Clinton in a toga!). But in most instances Morris leaves a show-me reader dissatisfied. Yet Morris is a talented and incisive political observer. When he is not depicting the Clintons as worse than Mario Puzo's Corleones, he does a wonderful job of positioning Bill and Hillary in the political firmament. The best and quite worthwhile portions of *Partners in Power* focus on how a corrupt Democratic Party nourished the couple that would come to lead it.

Morris is an effective political anthropologist. He observes that Bill and Hill, while they occasionally took a verbal poke or two at the Establishment, always courted the power structure. In Arkansas, they ran their campaigns with money showered upon them by corporate interests, usually setting state records in money-grubbing. (In a typical rhetorical flourish, Morris writes that Bill "was neither neophyte nor defector in America's money tyranny but one of its more wanton and prodigal offspring.") Hillary may have asked in a 1970 speech, "How much longer can we let corporations run us?" But with little hesitation she became a corporate lawyer who sat on the boards of corporations that disregarded environmental laws and fought unionization efforts—as she was a part-time do-gooder for the Legal Services Corporation and the Children's Defense Fund. Bill could rail against the utilities, and then hand them almost everything they wanted. As Morris puts it, Bill denounced "special interests while leaving their power intact." At times, Morris seems upset that Bill and Hillary did not join the Socialist Workers Party and vow to smash corporate capitalism. But he still manages to present a potent indictment of yuppie liberalism, Clintons-style.

The shame is that trenchant political and sociological observations about the corruptions of Washington, Little Rock and the entire political class drown in the ooze of evidence-shy exposé. The real and provable deeds of the Clintons offer rich enough material for anyone who wants to understand what the book's sub-title calls "their America."

Max Brantley, an Arkansas journalist, once said of the ink-blot couple, "We saw in them what we wanted to believe." The Clintons have always made that easy—especially for journalists. By becoming obsessed with the dark side of the Clintons, Morris has undermined what might have been a valuable work. His book is further proof that the Clintons have a knack for bringing out the worst in their critics. Which is quite a useful talent to have if they're as evil as Roger Morris believes. ✣

Hillary's Husband Re-Elected!

ERICA JONG, NOVEMBER 25, 1996

In a recent e-mail, Jong writes: "Reading over my article on Hillary Clinton, I am enormously impressed by the way she has grown. Her work in the Senate and her triumph as Secretary of State has made her the best prepared candidate for President. She has also gained grace and humor in dealing with her detractors. She gives me hope that all women can do this."

Here we are, two minutes after the last American presidential election in the twentieth century, and Hillary Rodham Clinton is still the most problematic first lady in American history— admired abroad, hated at home, mistrusted by women journalists even though this administration has actually done much good for women. Suspected of being a megalomaniac, embroiled in document-losing, spy-hiring, the suicide of an aide conjectured to be her lover, and possible perjury; pilloried in the press and jeered at in political cartoons; distrusted even by her admirers—can't Hillary do anything right? Why does she get no credit for all the positive things she has done?

The old campaign button that trumpeted "Elect Hillary's Husband in '92" showed a picture of Hillary, not Bill. Indeed, it's hard to remember it now. It's even hard to remember how Hillary flouted the rules decreed for political wives: the obligatory Stepford Wife impersonation, the fake flirtatious flattery that makes wives seem feminine and nonthreatening; the willingness to pretend to be the power behind the throne; the diplomatic surrender to the role of first lady.

The kaleidoscope of Hillary images and the frequently self-destructive behavior of the first lady are particularly regrettable because both the Clinton administration and the Clinton marriage are historic. As a couple, the Clintons raise important issues about both electoral and sexual politics. It is clear that without HRC's participation, Bill Clinton would have gone right down the Gary Hart sewer. Because his wife stood by him in that first Barbara Walters interview in 1992, because he did not exactly deny "causing pain" in the marriage while Hillary held his hand supportively, the first Clinton campaign was able to weather and rise above what had been killing sexual crises for other presidential candidates. Unlike France, America does not coddle public adulterers. Only "the little woman" can save them. She forgives, we forgive.

In those days—the first Clinton campaign—we were still hearing a lot about getting two for the price of one. Elect one, get one free. Hillary was the freebie. Never before in American politics had any couple campaigned this way. The very American ideal of a "power couple" who add up to more than the sum of their parts was put on the ballot in the 1992 election. America was enthusiastic about it then. Indeed, the Clinton candidacy looked bravely feminist compared with the fuddy-duddy aura of Bush and Mrs. Bush. But misogyny was far from dead, as we were soon to see.

The subsequent assault on Hillary demonstrated the entrenched woman-hating both of the American press and the bigoted public it so badly serves. When William Safire of *The New York Times* called HRC "a congenital liar," surely he was subjecting her to a different standard from the one to which he had held other first ladies. Can anyone in the laser glare of the public eye be expected to be candid all the time? Did anyone ask Pat Nixon what she thought of her husband's destruction of evidence? Was Nancy Reagan interrogated about Irangate? Certainly not. But HRC's gene pool was impugned at the drop of a document. With the roasting of Hillary it became clear that when we wish women to fail, we decree for them endless and impossible ordeals, like those that were devised for witches by their inquisitors. If they drown, they are innocent; if they float, they are guilty. This has pretty much been the way America has gotten rid of its cleverest political women, from the feminists Victoria Woodhull and Emma

Goldman to Eleanor Roosevelt and the unsuccessful vice presidential candidate Geraldine Ferraro. And there is no doubt that many people still wish HRC to fail. Even now.

Clinton strategists—including the disgraced Dick Morris—kept Hillary out of the limelight for most of the campaign. She was only seen (but not heard) in proper "helpmeet" photo-ops like the Atlanta Olympics, the Wyoming vacation and the exotic ports of call she visited with First Daughter Chelsea. America preferred—58 percent of men told pollsters that their view of Hillary was unfavorable—the duplicitous Southern charms of Elizabeth Hanford Dole: a driven career woman with no children who claims she is "pro-life," a chief Red Cross administrator who uses her powerful charity as a political tool of the Republican Party, a soft-spoken, flirtatious belle married to an old man, a saccharine public speaker who used the Republican convention in San Diego as an excuse to drown the delegates in treacle. Duplicity in women makes America comfortable; straightforwardness does not. There was even, I learned, heated debate in the White House about whether HRC should speak at the Democratic convention or remain out of sight and earshot. After Liddy Dole's San Diego seduction, it was decided that, however risky, Hillary had to speak. What a far cry from 1992, when Hillary was considered an asset! By the summer of 1996, she was a liability to be hidden. This is what four years of Hillary-hating had accomplished.

The deal of the Clinton marriage fascinates me, and I suspect it fascinates a good portion of the electorate. It reflects our period better than any political marriage I can think of. Clearly Hillary figured out in law school that if the time was not yet ripe for a woman president, it was likely to be ripe for a guy as driven and smart and personable as Bill Clinton. And she could be his chief adviser, patron (she made the money—with no small help from his political position) and disciplinarian. However much she warmed to his Southern charm, no matter how much she loved him, his political ambition turned her on just as much.

Not that there is anything wrong with a marital deal. You might even say that the more things that bind a couple together, the better chance they have of staying together. But theirs is a radical deal for an American political marriage. HRC has never staked out highway beautification as her bailiwick (as did Lyndon Baines Johnson's wife, Lady Bird) or crusaded to put warning labels on rock albums (once the one-woman campaign of Second Lady Tipper Gore). On the contrary, she has claimed center stage with top policy issues—however politically naïve she may have been.

This audacity dazzled at first. But then, why should a first lady stick to so-called women's issues? Hillary was always policy-minded, always loath to be ghettoized ideologically. She was always far more serious than Bill, even in college and law school. He was a people pleaser. She was a woman who put intellect first, which meant automatically that many men—and women—would not be pleased by her. One of the reasons she hooked up with Bill was that he was the first man who seemed not to be afraid of her intellect but rather challenged and attracted by it. He was determined "to get the smartest girl in the class," as an old Arkansas buddy of his told Roger Morris. He was sick of beauty queens. "If it isn't Hillary, it's nobody," he informed his mother, cautioning her to be nice to Hillary before he brought her to meet the family in 1972. Though he apparently had nostalgia—and a use—for those beauty queens after he and Hillary were married, at the time of their courtship Hillary's brains thrilled him more. She excited him. Maybe she still does. After all, many powerful men yearn for the sting of a dominatrix's whip now and then; it seems to be a sovereign tonic for hubris.

One of the difficulties of being a smart, driven woman is finding men who are turned on by brains. Hillary's initial attachment to Bill probably had a lot to do with the excitement of finding such a fearless man. Later, it seems, she had invested so much of herself in the marriage and in the daughter they shared that she wasn't willing to throw it all away even if faced with compulsive, repeated infidelities. The stresses on HRC have been extreme, and one must say that despite them she has proved an exemplary mother. She has protected Chelsea from the media, allowed her the space to grow into womanhood, put her education ahead of politics. As the mother of a teenage daughter, I honor HRC for what she has achieved.

Still, we have to look at the strangeness of the public image put forward by this revolutionary presidential couple: They were

elected as a team but have absolutely refused to make the terms
of their marriage public except to admit that he "caused pain." It
is the inconsistency of this position that has accounted for a great
deal of the trouble. If you vote for a couple, you feel entitled to
know about the bonds that hold them together. But Hillary has
insisted that those bonds are private. People resent her determination to have it both ways. But how on earth could the Clintons
own up to the details of Bill's sex life? The fact that they have
quashed the issue thus far is nothing short of a miracle.

The more you read about Bill Clinton, the more it seems evi-
dent that not only were there affairs but that he used his position
as governor to facilitate them, using state troopers as beards and
panderers, getting them to pick up frilly little gifts at Victoria's
Secret. But I assume that his erotic life is no better and no worse
than any other male politician's. I am, in general, so disillusioned
with male politicians that I actually prefer Bill Clinton the woman-
izer to Bob Dole the deadbeat dad who dumped the first wife who
nursed him through his famous war wounds. (Dole actually got his
political cronies to arrange an "emergency divorce" so he could
jettison the old wife and family more cheaply.) Fucking is fucking,
but failing to pay child support is a real crime. At least Bill Clinton
didn't abandon his wife and child.

Hillary's history is full of paradoxes. A baby boomer who grew
up in a straight-arrow Methodist Republican-registered family in

a white, upwardly mobile suburb of Chicago, she became a left-leaning Democrat at Wellesley College. At Yale Law School she was studious, solitary, solemn, given to wearing flannel shirts and thick glasses, noted for her brilliance and hard work. Her mother, a closet Democrat, had compromised with her life and did not want Hillary to compromise—a familiar mother-daughter story. Her father was stern, unambiguously Republican, tight with money and difficult to please. Imagine a girl like that winning the good ol' boy who has been dating beauty queens! It gives you an idea of how much his "locking in on her" (as one old friend put it) must have meant to her.

Hillary is an appealing figure to me because her life shows the strange compromises gifted women make. She had already changed her politics, drifted away from her parents' reactionary attitudes. What lay ahead were other complete makeovers—looks, name, ideals. Everything would have to change for the greater glory of Bill Clinton and the pillow power he bestowed. If she has often come across as angry and unsettled, as constantly remaking her image, it is because this is the truth. How could she not be angry? Like an ancient Chinese noblewoman with bound feet, she has had to deform even her anatomy to get where she needed to go. She hobbled her own fierce ambitions to transplant herself to Arkansas and defend his. She gave up her end-of-the-sixties indifference to female fashion, her passion for social justice and her native disgust with hypocrisy. Then, while he used her feminism as a shield to cover his philandering, he proceeded to make a mockery of everything she believed in.

Since Bill Clinton had always been clear about his ambition to be a top Arkansas politician and then president, his path never changed. Hers changed constantly—and with it her hair, her eyes, her weight, her name. At some point she must have had to decide that all those changes were worth it. How else can a smart woman justify such a metamorphosis? She had to recommit herself over and over to life with him. No wonder she demanded paybacks, such as running healthcare reform and his public life. She would have felt demolished otherwise. One sympathizes with her strength to make demands. But the power struggle of the marriage inevitably influenced the power politics of the nation, and that is what is so radically new about the Clinton presidency.

George Bush used his first day in the presidency to congratulate "right to life" marchers, even while insinuating that first lady Barbara Bush did not agree with him. No such stand for Bill Clinton. He and Hillary were joined at the hip politically, however much stress their marriage might be under. Their presidency has redefined public and private. Both Clintons' policies are in lockstep, even though their marriage may be chronically on the rocks.

"We cared deeply about a lot of the same things," Hillary told an interviewer for the campaign film *The Man From Hope* in 1992. This revealing quote, edited out of the final film, makes the deal of the marriage clear. "Bill and I really are bound together in part because we believe we have an obligation to give something back and to be part of making life better for other people," she went on (as quoted by Bob Woodward in *The Choice*). The tragedy of their story is that such idealism had to be replaced by a ruthless commitment to politics, and this deformation of principle came much harder to her than to him. Hillary's image problem has several root causes. One is undoubtedly the ineptness of her staff. Another is the undeniable fact that there is no way for a smart woman to be public without being seen as a treacherous Lady Macbeth figure or bitch goddess (our failing, more than Hillary's). But the deepest problem is that Hillary comes across on television as cold and too controlled because that is the truth. She has rejigged her image so often, retailored it so much to please the spin doctors, that it comes across as inauthentic. It is.

The truth is that Bill is what he is—warm, tear-jerkingly populist, dying to please, woo and pander. He's a born salesman, "riding on a smile," in the immortal words of Arthur Miller. Hillary, meanwhile, is a brainy girl trying to look like an Arkansas beauty queen, a corporate lawyer trying to look like a happy housewife, a fierce feminist who has submerged her identity in her husband's ambitions. It doesn't add up—too many contradictions—which is why we don't believe it. The pearls and pink put on for the campaign—as well as the new, practiced smiling—are not totally convincing either. We expect Lady Macbeth to reappear, rubbing the blood from her hands.

We should weep for Hillary Clinton rather than revile her. She is a perfect example of why life is so tough for brainy women. The deformations of her public image reveal the terrible contortions expected of American women. Look pretty but be (secretly) smart. Conform in public; cry in private. Make the money but don't seem to be aggressive. Swallow everything your husband asks you to swallow, but somehow keep your own identity. Hillary shows us just how impossible all these conflicting demands are to fulfill.

For Hillary and her generation, "no single act came to symbolize so vividly her role and sacrifice as the surrender of her maiden name," as Roger Morris points out in *Partners in Power*. Refusing to be submerged in the identity of wife is a burning issue for our generation. A woman can give up on this outwardly and continue to seethe inwardly. As with so many other Hillary transformations, the stress shows. I'm glad it does. It shows that she still has her conscience intact, if not her soul. She is not the consummately smooth performer her husband is.

Besides the constant hair transformations, nothing has shown Hillary's discomfort with her role as much as her choice of Jean Houston and Mary Catherine Bateson as spiritual guides. For all the idiocies of the American press, which cheaply depicted Hillary's spiritual quests as "seances," Houston and Bateson are serious figures. Bateson is a writer and anthropologist who, like her mother, Margaret Mead, is fascinated with the changing roles of twentieth-century women. Like her father, the English-born anthropologist Gregory Bateson, she also has a deep interest in spirituality in the modern world. Houston is a respected spiritual teacher and author. It is to Hillary's credit that she sought guidance from such interesting women. It also shows her deep need for reassurance in the midst of the nonstop Hate Hillary campaign that has been the salient feature of her public life. As Bob Woodward suggests, "Hillary's sessions with Houston reflected a serious inner turmoil that she had not resolved."

Apparently, Houston encouraged Hillary to take heart from her role model, Eleanor Roosevelt, and to use the technique of imaginary conversations with a mentor to confront her own deep hurt about the attacks, jealousy and misunderstanding she has encountered as first lady. This is an ancient technique for building self-knowledge and resolve. It was used during the Italian Renaissance by Machiavelli. Nevertheless, Hillary has been ridiculed as the dupe of seance-mongers for her very human need to reach out for help. This is beyond unkind. It is cruel and unusual punishment. I would rather put my faith in leaders who acknowledge their human need for guidance than in those who will accept none. Hillary remains deeply troubled on many levels; I wish she could open herself to psychological help. But then, of course, she might have to leave Bill!

Hillary herself is in great speaking form these days: passionate, strong, determined. She has even learned to soften political discourse with smiles. Once again her hair has been redesigned, her jewelry is smaller and more "feminine"—the safety of pearls— and some adviser has connived to dress her in pastels. You could say she's on the Dole. She has been Liddyized. She frequently says, "My husband and I believe" or "the president believes," and she allows no public space for those who would divide them. She is poised, cool, in control. The anger does not show. All that is miss- ing is the sense of the real woman underneath the pretty makeup and softly tailored suit.

One wants to say Hillary is the hollow woman—but in fact the opposite is true: She is a seething mass of contradictions, so she dares let none of her feelings show. "Relaxed" is not a word you would use about her even now. She gives off an aura of discipline and ferocious tenacity. It's impossible to glimpse the human being beneath the mask. Yet all those stories of her breaking down in tears or rage in private after this perfect composure in public seem wholly believable. She seems to be holding herself together with hairspray.

What is familiar about this picture? A woman is sacrificed to her husband's ambitions. Her personality is deformed. She takes almost all the flak in the press while he gets away with murder. You might almost say she is taking the punishment for him, and for all women who step outside the lines prescribed for paper- doll political wives—in fact, for all contemporary women. Hil- lary Rodham Clinton looks more to me like Joan of Arc every day. She is burned as a witch week in and week out so that her husband can rise in the polls. She is the scapegoat half of the Clinton duo, the rear end that gets whipped so the smiling Clinton head can triumph. She is Agamemnon's Iphigenia sacrificed for a propitious wind, Euripides' Alcestis going across the Styx instead of her husband.

And this is the way the Clinton presidential couple is conventional rather than revolutionary. Yes, they dared to present themselves as a team. But once again it's the female half that gets trashed while the male half is forgiven for all his transgressions and winds up being president. Bill Clinton owes Hillary. Big. The only difference between him and other guys is that he seems to know it. History has burdened Hillary Clinton with changing the way powerful women are perceived in our culture. But if she can see herself as part of a historical continuum, as a pathfinder opening the way for her daughter's generation, she may be able to rise above the pain of daily crucifixions in the media.

With a second Clinton administration, HRC has the rare opportunity to triumph over her detractors. She has already fulfilled her wish to be an Eleanor Roosevelt for the end of the century. In many ways her mainstreaming of feminism has prepared us to accept a woman president in the twenty-first century. By acting as a lightning rod she has gotten us comfortable with women who talk back in public, don't hide their brains, don't hide their passionate mothering. HRC is the latest incarnation of Miss Liberty.

I'm glad she's a survivor. Her survival means I can survive. If the next Clinton ticket is HRC and Al Gore, I intend to vote for them more happily than I voted for Bill Clinton on Tuesday. ❧

BLOND AMBITION

Hillary for Veep?

ELAINE LAFFERTY, MARCH 8, 1999

I t is, depending on one's perspective, a delicious and redemptive scenario, a terrible nightmare or, if you are the escapist sort that hasn't yet cottoned to the hard reality of Election 2000, an unlikely joke. As the fervor surrounding the idea of Hillary Rodham Clinton running for the Senate from New York reaches a high pitch, Democratic supporters and Hillary loyalists are quick to point out that the whole business of HRC running for office sprang full grown from the forehead of Zeus—either in the form of Representative Charles Rangel or Robert Torricelli, Democratic Senatorial Campaign Committee chairman. Then labor leaders, black leaders, women's leaders, began beating the drums. In Mexico on February 15, President Clinton himself cautioned that the idea of running had not occurred to Mrs. Clinton until "a lot of people started calling."

In fact, Hillary Clinton running for office has been a serious topic of dinner table discussion in the residential quarters of the White House for weeks. "It was Elizabeth Dole on the ticket with

Bush that really got her going," said a source close to the family. And while a Senate run in New York or Illinois was considered a strong possibility, Mrs. Clinton was initially leaning toward becoming Al Gore's running mate. Her concern in those night-time talks was that Mrs. Dole's potential presence on the GOP ticket would erode the gender gap that has been critical for Democratic victories in the past few elections.

The 1996 presidential election was marked by an eleven-point gender gap, the largest ever recorded.[3] Women's votes in 1996 also provided the margin of victory in eight Senate races. In 1994 they won nine Senate races. Republicans have been plagued by an average six- to nine-point gender gap. A woman on the Republican ticket might erase that, so a woman on the Democratic slate could be crucial. Ellen Malcolm, head of EMILY's List, which promotes [liberal] women candidates, says, "We can't afford to lose that advantage with Democratic voters." Still, Malcolm seemed wary about the prospect of Hillary Clinton on the national ticket. "That's hypothetical. There's no point in speculation." Indeed, the prospect of any Clinton on the ticket in 2000 could be unappealing to an electorate eager to forget the name at the center of a thirteen-month scandal. Moreover, the idea of Mrs. Clinton serving as Gore's vice president strains credulity. Hillary has negatives that have been forgotten amid the

---

3. According to some exit polls, the gender gap in the 2012 election was as high as 20 percentage points, with Barack Obama winning over women voters by 12 percent and Mitt Romney winning men by 8 percent.

current lovefest. She is more left wing than most DLC moderates, and she can bring an arrogant, inept political touch to the handling of important issues, such as the ill-fated healthcare reform.

Various scenarios were discussed within the family, which included Mrs. Clinton's brothers and her mother, who has spent much time in Washington lately. Neither Al nor Tipper Gore was involved in these discussions, which were largely confined to family. The intensity of the effort to recruit Hillary Clinton for the New York race has put the prospect of a vice-presidential bid on the back burner for the moment. The urgency is for her to decide about the New York race.

Eleanor Smeal, head of the Feminist Majority, says that she loves the idea of Mrs. Clinton running in New York but adds that her presence on the national ticket would be extraordinary. "Sixty percent of the Democratic vote is female, and Hillary Clinton has about a 15 percent gender gap on her side among women. Women love her. She would energize the Democratic base in a way that they would go wild. That won't happen within the Republican Party for Elizabeth Dole. The Republican base finds her too moderate."

Does she want to run for office? There is conflict between the side of her that wants a quieter, more private life and the side that not only wants to make policy but loves the game of politics. Her usual inclination in this lifelong inner conflict, says a family friend, falls on the side of battle and politics, a willingness in the end to join the political fight. Whatever her decision, it is likely to come sooner rather than later. ❖

Home-Free Hillary,

CHRISTOPHER HITCHENS, JULY 26, 1999

I n her terrible book *It Takes a Village* the first lady gives us an intimate glimpse of the political and decision-making process as it played out *chez* Clinton in the crucial guber-natorial year of 1986. It was beginning to look like a tough race, and the question became—how to break it to Miss Chelsea?

> One night at the dinner table, I told her: "You know, Daddy is going to run for governor again. If he wins, we would keep living in this house, and he would keep try-ing to help people. But first we have to have an election."

Skipping lightly over the remainder of that regurgitation-inducing passage (Mrs. Clinton proposed a "role-playing" dinner-table game whereby her 6-year-old daughter had to play Governor Clinton, and then sit and listen to hypothetical abuse of the candidate until she cried, which she repeatedly did), one notes that the "priorities" and "agenda" haven't altered all that much. First one has to have a house, and then one has to have an election. In between, Daddy—most ably seconded by Mummy—makes like he wants to help people.

In almost two decades of unstinting service to *The Nation*, I have never quite penetrated to the pulsing quick and core of New York liberalism. I understand dimly that Mrs. Clinton must have somewhere to live. I also quite see that she must have something to do, and somewhere to sit. I haven't yet had it convincingly explained to me why this is all up to us, or why a nomination to the United States Senate is not just hers for the asking, but hers even *without* the asking.

Over the Independence Day weekend, I couldn't open a newspaper without being prompted again to wonder if I had or had not missed something. *The New York Times* on July 3 advised me solemnly of the predicament of the soon-to-be-homeless, as it appeared from the vantage of Westchester County:

> The $3.8 million North Salem house that Mrs. Clinton likes is owned by James Kohlberg, of Kohlberg & Company, an investment firm he started with his father, Jerome Kohlberg, a founder of the leveraged buy-out firm Kohlberg Kravis Roberts & Company. Jerome Kohlberg is also a Democratic contributor.

Then, on July 4, *Parade* brought me a carefully posed cover story, in garish color, about the first lady's current squat. Pegged to the bicentennial of the White House and ostensibly written by Mrs. Clinton herself, it was pitched with an affecting folksiness. ("I almost fell off of my chair"; "On my birthday in 1995, I came down the formal staircase to find the entry hall transformed into a 1950s-style living room—replete with plastic-covered divans and rabbit ears on top of a big old TV!") But the grand historical note has also to be struck, even in these pulp pieces:

> No one can enter the Lincoln Bedroom without thinking of President Lincoln drafting the Emancipation Proclamation. Or walk into the Map Room without picturing FDR commanding our forces during World War II.... The president and I know that *we are only short-term tenants*. [Emphasis added.]

Again, one catches that thin, high note of accommodation anxiety. But when the president and Mrs. Clinton were asked whom they had had to stay overnight in the Lincoln Bedroom, they replied that it was nobody's business but their own. It took the Center for Public Integrity several months of intrusive questioning to establish that seventy-five high-tab donors had been entertained there, for as much as $400,000 a night. (It was, however, stipulated that unmarried contributors could not sleep together. Excuse me, but there are still some standards.) The Map Room and the Roosevelt Room were used, "privately" to be sure, to receive Johnny Huang and Roger Tamraz and other cats, who saw Mr. Clinton rather more often than his own cabinet did. (He convened two cabinet meetings last year, both of them devoted to his own self-pitying explanation of the Lewinsky affair.) In the Map Room, he had his blood drawn for the DNA match that showed him a liar. Mrs. Clinton does not say what emotions overwhelm the visitor to the Oval Office, but *Parade* makes up for that reticence by printing a photograph of the president himself in this hallowed room. He is shown embracing his daughter...

I leave to one side the much-hyped question of Mrs. Clinton using military airplanes and reimbursing the taxpayer at a phony rate: After the Travel Office scandal and the ripoffs cited above, one must not strain at swallowing a gnat or two. I think that I hope she runs. I want to ask her several questions, and her backers one question. To her: Was it not your idea to bring back Dick Morris and employ him in the White House under a code name? Was it not your idea to put healthcare into the hands of the HMOs? Do you still maintain that people dislike you because you are "from" Arkansas? Did you watch the NBC interview with Juanita Broaddrick?[4] Did your daughter watch it? What did you think? (And don't dare, after what you have allowed, accuse anyone of "dragging" Chelsea into anything.) How come the Chinese government made out a check, through an intermediary, to your chief of staff? Are you still in favor of sexual abstinence for teenagers? What did you mean when you told Larry King that "there is no left in the Clinton White House"? Have you recently reviewed the client list of Harold Ickes?

Oh, and the question to her New York backers? Why haven't you asked her these questions? Well, I mean to say, after all she's done for us... ♣

---

4.   In the fall of 1998, Broaddrick alleged on television that Bill Clinton, while governor of Arkansas, had raped her two decades earlier.

Hillary's No Liberal

WENDY KAMINER, AUGUST 9, 1999

"**R**un Hillary Run" buttons are in circulation among Democratic elites, the wealthy, well-meaning men and women who actually seem to enjoy writing four- or five-figure checks to the Democratic National Committee, repeatedly. Slaking the party's thirst for soft money, these serial donors remain inexplicably loyal to the Clinton administration and unabashedly proud of their association with it.

Many of the donors Hillary Clinton has cultivated and captivated over the past eight years share Clinton's image of herself as another Eleanor Roosevelt, in modern professional form. They are not just willing but eager to finance her crusade for a Senate seat, anticipating a dramatic "win for women." That view of her as a liberal feminist prevails right and left, or rather right and center, rallying opponents as well as supporters.

Many are convinced that she is more liberal than Bill, although there is little evidence that they differ ideologically. It's fair to judge her by his administration's dubious achievements; she chose not to run for office in her own right twenty years ago and instead sought power most traditionally, through her husband. If his power was hers, at least in part, then so is his record.

On the record Hillary looks less like a meaner, tougher Eleanor Roosevelt than a kinder, gentler Giuliani. Both Clinton and Giuliani support the death penalty, the 1996 welfare reform bill and the administration's putatively tough and essentially racist initiatives on criminal justice—as well as gay rights, reproductive choice and the New York Yankees. Both have little regard for civil liberties, especially free speech. Unleashed, Giuliani might cut out the tongues of people who criticize him. Clinton, I suspect, would commit her critics to re-education camps. She has no apparent concern for freedom of speech on the Internet. The Clinton administration has championed clearly unconstitutional restrictions on online speech, such as the now-defunct Communications Decency Act and its successor, the Child On Line Protection Act, currently being challenged in federal court.

It is easy to imagine Clinton embarking on an anti-vice crusade. She spouts the subtly repressive principles and platitudes of communitarianism, envisioning a majoritarian society in which collective concerns almost always prevail over individual rights. Remember the politics of meaning, her 1993 call for a collective spiritual renewal, her reminder that we are all "creatures of God"? Hillary has always been something of a virtuecrat, expressly focused on infusing society with the values and presumed virtues of religion. It's true that, unlike Giuliani, she has opposed school voucher programs that divert tax dollars to church schools. But I suspect that opposition reflects concern for the votes of public-school teachers more than a commitment to separating church and state. She has yet to speak out against faith-based social service programs, championed by Al Gore (as well as Republican Senator John Ashcroft), which, like vouchers, channel public money to sectarian institutions providing social services.

Clinton seems likely to sacrifice rights—like freedom from religion—to her notion of social goods. Both she and Giuliani exhibit the sanctimony of people who believe they know what's best for the rest of us—less liberty, more order and values imposed by the state or our neighbors.

Is it wishful thinking to suggest that this is not the face of feminism? After all, in the quest for civil rights, feminists have had to seek the intervention of the state, advocating essential legal restrictions on the economic freedoms of others, notably the freedom to discriminate. And, the campaign against sexual violence has made some feminists mistrust classic liberties, like privacy and free speech, while generating support for repressive criminal laws that deny rights to men accused of abusing women. But feminism has also been a movement for civil liberties that depended on First Amendment rights (as all dissident social movements do) and has sought individual autonomy for women.

When Hillary Clinton advocates policies insuring universal healthcare or expanded daycare and various civil rights laws, she does sound like a feminist (and a liberal), but apart from her qualified commitment to abortion rights (she has supported parental notification laws) or her rhetoric abroad, her feminism, like her liberalism, tends to take the form of statism. She is a statist first and a feminist only half-formed—sympathetic to women's demands for civil rights but often indifferent if not hostile to liberty. Clinton, for example, supports laws that restrict the freedom to divorce.

Maternalism wedded to political ambition can be ruthless. Consider Clinton's tacit support for the repressive juvenile justice bill proposed by the Senate in June. It was the vehicle for a few modest restrictions on gun and ammunition sales, passed with enthusiastic administration support by Al Gore's dramatic tiebreaking vote. When Clinton joined her husband (and most Senate Democrats) in celebrating new initiatives to protect kids from guns, she was in effect urging passage of a law that encourages states to prosecute 14-year-olds as adults, loosens restrictions on housing juveniles with adult offenders, relieves states of the obligation to address racial disparities in juvenile justice systems, federalizes more juvenile crime and imposes harsh mandatory sentences on children. Rudy Giuliani himself couldn't have drafted a bill less protective of children.

Laws like this do not represent wins for women (NOW, to its credit, opposes the juvenile justice bill). Democrats who still harbor old-fashioned liberal feminist sympathies ought to acknowledge that they have found no champion in Hillary Clinton, although in the end, some may feel forced to vote for her. It's too bad they won't have had the chance to vote against her in a primary. In this era of nomination by anointment, politics matters much less than celebrity. ❖

Hillary—NY Progressive

ELLEN CHESLER, AUGUST 9, 1999

L et's get beyond the psychobabble that so often passes for informed political analysis these days and take Hillary Rodham Clinton at her word. Perhaps there is no agenda to her Senate candidacy deeper than the challenge she first set for herself and her generation thirty years ago in a Wellesley commencement address that made national headlines: to practice politics as the art of making possible what appears to be impossible.

From this point of view, Hillary Clinton can lay claim to the effective blend of idealism and tenacity that has characterized generations of progressive reformers in New York. And surely these ties should qualify her as a native as much as a lifetime of rooting for the Yankees.

Like Eleanor Roosevelt, with whom she likes to identify, Hillary Clinton has spent the better part of her years as first lady schlepping around the country and the globe, meeting as often with the powerless as with the powerful. There is nothing really new about her much-publicized listening tour of New York except the several hundred reporters who are now part of her entourage. She has visited more schools, daycare centers, hospitals, family planning clinics, model factories, housing projects, parks, micro-enterprises, agricultural cooperatives and the like than her staff can tally. She has boundless energy and enthusiasm for this sort of thing, born of her understanding that what works, and what's therefore to be taken most seriously, is rarely the product of elegant social or economic planning but rather the less predictable outcome of the often messy process of democratic politics, where policy-makers are obligated to respond to myriad interests.

These encounters are reminiscent of those instigated by New York's most fabled progressive reformers, many of them women, who placed great emphasis on the value of individual case management of social welfare by competent, caring professionals. They too traveled extensively, pioneering the kind of firsthand observation and methodical survey research in factories and tenements that we now take for granted as the basis of informed public policy and yet do not always manage to achieve. They built voluntary civic institutions like settlement houses that in turn modeled innovative ways to provide public healthcare, safe water, food and drugs, more accountable institutions of criminal justice, decent housing, parks and recreation, and wage and hour protections, all of which they saw as necessary conditions for nurturing responsible citizenship.

As the tale is often told, these worthy arrangements creat-

ed widespread public demand for activism by the federal government and helped to spawn the modern social welfare state with
its more secure, if still inadequate, sources of funding and more
exacting professional standards for dealing with the poor. But lost
in modern efforts to create formal distance between the state and
its clients in order to protect their rights was the idea of providing
assistance aimed at building personal capacity and self-reliance.
This shortcoming fueled the disenchantment that resulted in the
compromised welfare reforms of the Clinton era.

Redressing those compromises, without going back to failed
policies, is the challenge that must animate Hillary Clinton's bid
to remain in public life. That she has a good chance at winning
on such a platform is clear from election outcomes since 1996,
which have suggested that women especially remain convinced of
the need for federal interventions to help them in their own lives
and to assist those less fortunate.

It will be important for Hillary Clinton to challenge the view
that she is complicit in the abandonment by her husband's administration of the welfare safety net that New Yorkers first wrote into
the New Deal. She can point to the many ways she has worked
in private and public to replace what had become a deeply flawed
system of pitifully inadequate handouts with better integrated
programs of economic subsidy and social support—programs that
aim to help lift families out of poverty and to restore hope and
opportunity where there was once dependency and despair.

Many of these initiatives are already in place, if not yet adequate to the challenges before them. The Clinton administration has had success in increasing the minimum wage, rewarding work through the earned-income tax credit and passing the Family and Medical Leave Act; widening opportunities for education and job training; expanding access to Head Start and daycare; and protecting reproductive choice. Incremental changes in healthcare provision have resulted in a substantial broadening of the population of working families eligible for insurance (though they are not necessarily yet enrolled). Among these advances is CHIP, the Children's Health Insurance Program, which covers young people through the age of 18. The administration has also made low-income working families, not just welfare recipients, eligible for Medicaid, and it has enacted portability legislation that allows workers to hold on to healthcare when they lose their jobs.

Such measures are valuable, but they must be expanded and rigorously enforced. Given her demonstrated interests and commitments, it's easy to imagine that Senator Hillary Rodham Clinton would place such expansion and enforcement at the center of her policy agenda, advocating massive public education and outreach and an effective system of penalties for states and localities that do not enroll a higher percentage of eligible clients into programs like Medicaid. Her extensive knowledge of these issues will assure her a leadership opportunity when Congress reauthorizes the welfare bill in 2001 and 2002, as will her mastery of the minutiae of healthcare policy, now that her idea of building consumer protections into managed care is on the table again.

Legislative service is the logical culmination of Hillary Clinton's lifelong devotion to civic life. Voters should reward her for years of experience at trying, if not always succeeding, to address the widely acknowledged flaws of even the most well-intended of our public policies. And we should help sustain her conviction, in the face of so much evidence to the contrary, that political office is still a respectable platform for this commitment. ❖

Hillary Clinton's 'Smaller Steps'

ANDREA BERNSTEIN, SEPTEMBER 6, 1999

illary Rodham Clinton, poised as ever, is sitting before an expectant crowd on a beautiful July day in Cooperstown in central New York State. In the next ninety or so minutes, she proceeds to hear an array of overwhelming problems: a wife dying of cancer who got the healthcare she needed only after furious efforts on her husband's part; a farmer's son who is uninsured because he can't afford the cost; a frustrated doctor who cannot prescribe needed medications because his patients can't afford them; a nurse who spends the bulk of her time fighting insurance companies.

Hillary Clinton's response, which starts off tongue in cheek but ends up deadly serious, offers a telling insight into the forces that have shaped her political thinking. "You may recall that I have had some thoughts about healthcare and healthcare reform in the past, and certainly coming out of that experience I remain committed to the idea of providing quality, affordable healthcare to every American. I now come from the school of smaller steps."

The school of smaller steps defines Hillary Clinton's politics, 1999-style. Read to your children. Help a tortilla-maker get a loan to buy a new piece of bakery equipment. Fund 100,000 new teachers. Take $1,000 off your taxes for childcare. Prod businesses to train welfare recipients. All are worthy. All barely dent the enormous problems facing working families.

The school of smaller steps is the stunted child of the 1994 healthcare reform campaign. From that battle, both Clintons apparently concluded that large-scale change is impossible. Never mind that Hillary Clinton's healthcare reform plan was hopelessly complicated and inartfully—ineptly—handled. We'll never know if a simple, expertly guided universal healthcare program would have succeeded. Or even if, as now, Americans would have been willing to eschew tax cuts for government programs they like. Instead, the Clintons drew the lessons that Republicans wanted them to draw all along: The era of big government is over; the era of smaller steps is here.

Hillary Clinton's philosophy of government—the current one—hardly seems to bother New York Democrats, who, for the most part, stand to Clinton's left. Harlem Representative Charles Rangel, who has fought bitterly with the president over welfare reform and tax policy, can't say enough good things about the first lady. Nor can Dennis Rivera, the fiery healthcare workers' union chief, who is often at loggerheads with the Clinton administration over attempted cuts in funding for New York's healthcare system.

Or almost any New York Democrat you ask. On or off the record, Democrats are ecstatic about Clinton's all-but-certain run for the Senate from New York.

Part of this is the cult of celebrity: the president's wife! Here, in New York! Part of this is the yearning for the imagined Hillary to emerge from her chrysalis—the one who sat on the board of the Children's Defense Fund, who promoted education reform in Arkansas, who successfully juggled the roles of lawyer, mother, wife and first lady of Arkansas. (But this 1992-model progressive-icon Hillary—if she ever existed—has gone the way of her headbands and Coke-bottle-bottom glasses.)

And part of this enthusiasm stems from ignorance of her positions. In Cooperstown, one local Democratic activist, all agog with Hillary worship, bubbles on about the New York Democratic Party's support of single-payer healthcare—that's the one Hillary Clinton rejected in favor of preserving a for-profit system. "These are the people you will be asking to support your candidacy," he enthuses. "I'd be happy to help."

This activist isn't alone in being gung-ho. Winne Stachelberg, political director of the Human Rights Campaign, insists Clinton supports "gay families" but can't name a single gay issue (second-parent adoption, say) for which she's articulated support, or describe the first lady's position on her husband's don't ask, don't tell policy on gays in the military, or on the Defense of Marriage Act. Even the most knowledgeable New Yorkers, like Ester

Fuchs, director of the Columbia Center for Urban Research and Policy, find themselves surprised to learn, for example, that Hillary Clinton supported the administration's welfare reform bill.

For many Democrats, Hillary mania is pure pragmatism. Bill Lynch, former New York City deputy mayor under David Dinkins and always seen as the left conscience of that administration, says, "As somebody who is seen as a major player—not a minor player or an insurgent—she's very progressive compared with the rest of the players, including Bill. That doesn't mean I agree with her on all positions. I don't agree with her on the death penalty, for example. That doesn't mean I'm going to support Rudy Giuliani or stay home."

If the school of smaller steps is only slightly inspiring, Hillary Clinton herself can bring crowds to their feet. At a commencement address at City College in June, she electrified the crowd of mostly African-American and Latino students with a spirited defense of public education. "We can never lift up our public schools or the students they serve by tearing them down" or "by undermining the public education system that is at the very foundation of the American dream," she said, to thunderous applause. "Run, Hillary, run!" the graduates shouted, reverence in their eyes as they lunged for a handshake as she passed through the crowd. Even in the Republican town of Clinton in July, residents lined the streets, cheering wildly, waiting for hours to see the woman who bears their hamlet's name. They were not disappointed. "It's not what she's done for New York, it's what she's done for America!" said a buoyant Arm Cianfrocco. With just the small gestures—a smile, a wave, signing an autograph, holding a baby, shaking hands—Clinton conveys a genuine warmth.

Despite the overwhelming media fascination with the state of her marriage and her recent discussion of her husband's behavior, few voters—at least in public forums—seem to care, even going so far as to berate reporters for their interest. What they want to know is whether Hillary Clinton can help them get better schools and jobs or more comprehensive healthcare.

And Clinton, always the thorough study, clearly knows the positions that are most likely to help her win a statewide campaign (many closely resembling those of Senator Charles Schumer, who ousted New York Democrats'—and her own—nemesis, Alfonse D'Amato, last November). She favors the death penalty, agreeing with the majority of New Yorkers (but not the overwhelming majority of African-Americans and Latinos). She tells a dairy farmer in Rome, New York, that she's for the Northeast Dairy Compact—price supports for milk. (The compact is opposed by most consumer groups, who feel it helps big farmers at the expense of poor kids. Not even the White House is for it.) She writes in a letter to Orthodox Jewish groups that she believes Jerusalem is the "eternal and indivisible" capital of Israel. (That puts her at odds with her husband and Israeli Prime Minister Ehud

Barak, who think the issue should be part of final-status talks, but not with New York's Orthodox Jewish community.) She's for lower air transportation costs upstate.

Clinton is a political newbie, and the throng of political reporters following her since March has seized on her every policy pronouncement and turned it into news headlines. Still, it took Clinton's summerlong "listening tour"—a series of events featuring five or six speakers with a specific point to make, plus an invited audience of 100 or so citizens—to begin to flesh out just what Senator Hillary Clinton would stand for. The tour, of course, was billed as a listening tour, not a time for the first lady to be rolling out policies of her own, and there is still plenty of time before November 2000 for her to propose measures that bear her stamp. There may be grand gestures yet in store. But whenever the first lady opened a window into her thinking, the school of smaller steps was clearly in view.

Take welfare reform. In the week leading up to the 1996 Democratic National Convention, Bill Clinton signed the welfare reform bill—and the national party feared a revolt from New York Democrats, who overwhelmingly opposed it. Most of those Democrats simply assumed that the former Children's Defense Fund board member agreed with their position and that she had tried to convince the president to get out his veto pen. But at the first stop on the first day of her tour, with vocal "welfare reform" critic Senator

Daniel Patrick Moynihan at her side, the first lady made clear that that had not been the case. "I supported the bill that the president eventually signed," she told a reporter who asked her pointedly if she had betrayed women and children by supporting the bill. "I had strong concerns about some of the issues that were being pushed at that time by the Republican majority in the Congress, for example, when the Republican Congress tried to delink Medicaid from welfare. But eventually the bill was in a state that I felt should be signed, although there were still problems with it that needed to be remedied.... I supported it because I believed the system was so broken and the political conditions were such that we had to make some dramatic changes in order to clear the decks, provide opportunities for people who were able to become independent and self-sufficient and really take a hard look at who was left."

Five days later, one of those very people spoke up in an unexpected fashion at a stop at Westchester Community College. This woman had been chosen as a shining example of a single mother who had moved from welfare to work after completing a certificate program. And she did have good things to say about the program that got her a job. But, taking Team Clinton unawares, she added, "I felt cheated. I have a 3-year-old and of course I wanted to continue after I finished my program which is a year certificate program.... I felt my classmates achieved their degrees, and I'm two semesters away.... There's no evening childcare programs...Once you're going to workfare, they want you to go straight to work," which she did after an unsuccessful struggle with social services officials.

Of course, these are exactly the problems advocates for the poor warned of: It's one thing to "reform" welfare, quite another to provide the childcare and education supports and jobs needed to get and keep people in the workforce.

The first lady clucked sympathetically. "I don't think we've done what we need to do on childcare, and it's not just for people who've gone off welfare, it's for all working families," she said. "We should have a basic bargain with Americans. If you're willing to work and you're working full time, you should be supported in whatever way is cost-effective for you to stay working and to set a good example for your child."

There is hardly a working parent or an advocate for the poor who wouldn't be thrilled to hear that kind of rhetoric—and perhaps Senator Clinton would charge forward on childcare. But the solutions she champions are a long way from universal quality daycare. In January she told a single mother making $35,000 a year who pays $800 a month for childcare—cheap, by New York City standards—"That's why my husband has proposed a $1,000-a-year childcare tax credit." That's great—but where is the mother expected to get the other $8,600? In Westchester, seven months later, Clinton cheered on a human resources professional who talked about her company's employment-skills training for people trying to get off welfare. "It's amazing—you have to start with teaching

them how to shake hands," said the company official. Clinton nod-
ded sympathetically but didn't offer any ideas as to where all the jobs
for these newly trained workers are going to come from.

Microcredit loans are another idea Clinton favors as a way
to help women out of poverty. "I am a very big believer that
increasing access to credit is one of the most important ways to
help generate economic activity, and I've worked for a long time
in creating opportunities for small loans for small business," she
told an audience of senior citizens at a run-down senior center
in Utica. "Maybe you're a small housecleaning service or a small
bakery but you can't get the loan you need to buy a new piece of
equipment because that's only a $1,500 or $2,000 piece of equipment, and you can't afford it, but that size loan isn't profitable for
a bank, so you're caught." (In other venues she substitutes "tortilla
maker" for "baker.") "That's not a progressive policy," snorts one
policy-minded New York Democrat, who, like many people interviewed for this article, didn't want to be quoted publicly criticizing
the first lady. "If you lend a small amount to a few people, some
will be fine. Most will fail. A few people will be helped to do a few
things in a few places."

If in 1994 Clinton was set scurrying, tail between her legs,
off the national healthcare policy stage, she clearly hasn't stopped
thinking about the subject. Almost any healthcare horror tale is
met with deep empathy. Though it's hard to imagine she's ever
had to shout at an HMO bureaucrat about, say, Chelsea's unpaid

doctor's bills, somehow she knows what it's like. "It becomes a kind of roll of the dice," she told the Cooperstown audience. "If you've got a family member who is aggressive and knowledgeable and not put off and never gives up, eventually, probably, the insurance company will say 'OK, we can go ahead and let his wife have it because we know ninety-nine other people we can shut down the first ten times they call.'" Though she clearly mistrusts major corporations—"we can't really find out how much a drug actually costs to develop," she said in Cooperstown. "You have to take the word of the drug manufacturer, so you're really at their mercy"— she also has an underlying faith in the power of the market to sort these things out. "We need to figure out ways to create bigger pools of consumers of health insurance so we could have more people in a pool that could get costs down," she told a farmer who complained of having to pay $6,200 a year on health insurance for her family of three and who said that many farm families are simply going uninsured.

But Clinton's response reflects exactly the theory of the 1994 healthcare plan. And it hasn't worked. If hospitals, which are also huge corporations, can't negotiate with health insurance companies—and that's a theme repeatedly stated on the listening tour— it's not clear how even giant pools of family farmers could do it. If Clinton mistrusts corporations, she is also unwilling to take them out of the healthcare equation, though doctors, patients and hospitals alike complain to her over and over again that it is exactly that—that medicine has become a business—that's the problem. It's not clear from Clinton's comments what responses "the school of smaller steps" would suggest beyond the now-defeated Democratic version of the Patients' Bill of Rights, which she supports. She laments the fact that these issues—the right to see specialists, the right to sue health insurance companies—have to be legislated.

If there is one area where Clinton shines, progressive supporters still believe, it is public education. Randi Weingarten, president of New York's United Federation of Teachers, has known Clinton since the eighties, when, as first lady of Arkansas, she went around the state promoting what Weingarten calls "a very far-reaching education reform plan for Arkansas. It was one of the earliest efforts at education reform." In the White House, Weingarten says, unlike the case with so many other issues, Bill Clinton hasn't wavered. "They're a cohesive team on this issue, and his education plan is a very sound one," Weingarten says. "He's trying to raise the standards for all kids, not just create one pilot program here, one good school there." In listening-tour stops across the state, the author of *It Takes a Village* promoted that plan: federal dollars for more teachers (though the number, 100,000, is barely up to the needs of New York State, let alone the nation), which, she rightly noted, Republicans in Congress approved as the 1998 elections approached but are now trying to sabotage.

Clinton said she also supports federal funds for school construction and modernization to create more classrooms, because "we do have significant evidence that reducing class size in the lower grades is a very important educational initiative." Clinton added, "I'm for universal pre-kindergarten, and I think that would be something the federal government has to fund." She is also for national standards and testing, and "reading thirty minutes every day to your children"—a typical New Democrat, popular, cost-free proposal.

Nor is Clinton bereft of ideas when it comes to higher education. She is for the Schumer bill offering tax deductions for college tuition. A worthy goal, says Frank Mauro of the Fiscal Policy Institute, especially since the Clinton administration has taken steps to help poor kids through Hope scholarships (though, as ever, not enough). But, notes Mauro, a tax deduction is skewed to help the well-off more than the poor, because it gives greater relief to those who are taxed at a higher bracket. Instead, Mauro advocates a tax *credit* that would give the same benefit to everyone.

Hillary Clinton also champions other education-related ideas, like improving Internet access. At the State University of New York in Oneonta, a man tells her of the problems rural communities have in getting such access. "The government needs to do something to build the trunk line and the infrastructure," the man explains, "something like the Interstate highway system. That's not something the private sector is going to do. We're not going to have a bunch of businesses say, 'Well this is what we need so let's bring it down from Albany and we'll all chip in.'"

"So your analogy would be rural electrification and the Interstate highway system?... That's very interesting to me," Clinton responds, and asks him to send her a memo on the subject—displaying the ability to continue to listen and learn that is part of her appeal. But of course, rural electrification was a New Deal program. And the Interstate highway system was launched by Dwight Eisenhower in a postwar world flush with optimism and wealth and faith in government's ability to solve big problems. It is not clear how the school of smaller steps can tackle such grand ideas.

"It would be good to solve big problems holistically," Weingarten acknowledges. "That's not a Republican or a Democratic idea. Robert Moses solved big problems in a big way. But we may be living in a generation where you can't do it. We have a political situation in our country that is so polarized, you may *have to* solve problems in small steps."

Perhaps, despite the disappointment it may mean for New York's progressive community, Hillary Clinton is the model for the next millennium—someone who has clearly, like her husband, learned to confine her vision to tiny changes that help some of the people, in some ways, some of the time. That may be, for now, all that New York Democrats can expect, or hope for, in a senator. And measured against Rudolph Giuliani, the foot-stomping, welfare-dismantling, police-cheering Mayor of New York City, that may be enough for them.

It's just that once, this seat belonged to Robert Kennedy, who later campaigned for President with the slogan: "Some men see things as they are and ask 'why?' I dream of things that never were and ask 'why not?'" It's hard to imagine those words being part of the 2000 campaign. ♣

The Woman Who Would Be Senator

Michael Tomasky, February 7, 2000

Review of Hillary's Choice *by Gail Sheehy*

As you may have heard once or twice, we have a little Senate race going here in New York. The candidate on the Democratic side, by the middle of January, had subjected herself to many of the self-abasing rituals Democrats seeking statewide office in New York must submit to: The call on Al Sharpton; the obligatory trips upstate to prove that the aspirant is not merely the cat's-paw of urban liberals; the appearance before a power-broking Orthodox Jewish group to pledge fealty to Israel, even though there's no chance in hell that said group's members will vote Democratic. And she has subjected herself to one ritual most candidates don't have to submit to—moving here. The stage furniture, then, is set in place; the next nine months will bring character development, action, climax, coda.

Hillary's Choice, Gail Sheehy's new psychobiography of Hillary Clinton, was evidently intended by its author as an important piece of that stage furniture. It has not, of course, been received in quite so generous a spirit. You've probably read by now some of the sport the media have been making of the inaccuracies found within it. "The Reliable Source," the gossip column in *The Washngton Post*, kept a running tally for a time. The most famous of these errors sits down there on the bottom of page 209, where Sheehy writes that Al Haig sought to reassure America that he was "in charge" not after the attempted assassination of Ronald Reagan, when he actually did it, but after the successful resignation of Nixon.

Before we push ahead, let's note another mistake, one *The Nation*, of all journals, would have done poorly to miss. On May Day 1970, it seems, Yale students—Hillary Rodham would have been in her first year of law school; that much is accurate—held a huge rally on campus in support of the Black Panthers, where "ripe-bosomed coeds" (?) dished up "a soul picnic" (??) for the "incoming Bedouins of the Woodstock nation." (???) Nine Panthers, Bobby Seale among them, were in jail in Connecticut, facing kidnapping charges. Jessica Mitford and husband Robert Truehaft came to town. So did 4,000 reservists from North Carolina, a presence made all the more ominous, Sheehy writes, by the fact that "the country had already witnessed unarmed college students being shot dead by National Guardsmen at Kent State University." Hmmm. Unless those ripe-bosomed nymphs and invading Bedouins moved May Day, not possible. Kent State happened on May 4.

Let's not make more of this error than we should. It symbol-izes nothing and means only that the author doesn't know either when May Day is or when the Kent State shootings occurred and, if ignorant of either or both, didn't bother to look them up. These things happen, presumably even to *The Washngton Post*'s "Reliable Source" column from time to time. (Of course, to Sheehy, *a lot* of them seem to happen.)

I will say this, though: Factual particulars aside, the main arc of Sheehy's story, and much of her conjecture about The Rela-tionship, reads to me as though it's pretty much spot-on. Hillary's decision to move down to Arkansas to be with Bill—the synec-dochic "choice," it turns out, around which HRC's other choices and the book itself are all framed—is described by Sheehy, either explicitly or implicitly, as a function of three things: first, Hillary's ambition, and her belief that Bill would someday be the president of the United States, which she secretly wanted to be herself but knew, as a woman, she would not be; second, a rarely expressed desire on the part of the young-adult Hillary, finally out from under the control of her officious and right-wing father, to shock and dismay and do the unexpected, which she had so rarely had the courage to do; and third—hey, she loved the guy. This actually seemed to be true. And still seems to be.

Much is made, in the book and in reviews, of the possible life that awaited a hot young female Ivy League law school grad such as HRC, which the book's narrative thread virtually forces us to envision: After her Watergate committee work, a job at a white-shoe Manhattan firm. Service on various boards. Groundbreaking legal scholarship of some sort or another. Books. One foot in reform politics. Maybe the city's first female—what, comptroller or something?—with her hardheaded common sense. With any luck, this would happen during the fiscal crisis, when she would have won praise for being the sort of liberal who's not afraid to make "the tough decisions" that the *Times* loves to adulate. And then, who knows, maybe a run for the Senate someday.

But we're getting ahead of ourselves. The "reality" is touchingly described by Sheehy on pages 109-10, where Hillary's Watergate committee chum Sara Ehrman drives her from Washington to Fayetteville, Arkansas, where Bill is teaching at the law school, so Hillary can be with him (but not, alas, live with him; local mores, don't you know).

"He's just a country lawyer," Sheehy says Ehrman said. "Why are you doing this?" Hillary sat mute all the way, staring silently ahead. Finally, Fayetteville. A Saturday. Air filled "with the high-pitched sound of pigs in heat," which "the initiated" recognize as the rallying cry of the Arkansas Razorbacks ("Woo, pig, Suey!"—I happen to know), who were that very day playing archrival Texas. This distillation of the beer-spittled life that awaited her dear friend was a little much for Ehrman, who began to cry. Funny thing, though; when Ehrman and Hillary left Washington, it was a "steamy...August evening" in 1974, just after Nixon's resignation. Nine paragraphs later, two football archrivals are playing each other. That striking me as an autumn ritual, I checked. In 1974 Arkansas played Texas on October 19. Long drive. And oh, yeah— they must have taken a wrong turn somewhere, too, because the game was played at Texas.

I also bought—call me naïve—Sheehy's conjecture about why Bill would do it, in the nonconjugal sense, with Monica. Sheehy describes three episodes—needless to say, she has to gussy them up by calling them three "major personal marker events"—that may have made old Bill feel...well, old. His mother's (i.e., the most important woman in any man's life) death. His tumble, toward the end of the affair, down a flight of stairs at golfer Greg Norman's house and subsequent dependence on the "accoutrements of decay"—cane, wheelchair, "flaccid [hmmm!] muscles." Third, and most crucially, Chelsea's future departure for college. I've never really thought about this before, but it makes sense to me. It's not hard to picture frustrated middle-aged men across America doing the same thing—watching the apple of their eye (daughters) roll pretty far away from the tree and then acquiring a sexual surrogate as a way to keep dealing with the repressed father-daughter sexual tension that's always floating around in the libidinal penumbra somewhere. This isn't the sort of thing we talk about much, and it's certainly not suitable for *Meet the Press*—one can imagine the *New York Post* headline: Shrinks: Bill Wanted Sex With Chelsea!—

but it strikes me as a plausible guess about contributing factors.

So you see, reading *Hillary's Choice* is not a waste of time. You won't find much about politics in it that's interesting, though, if that's your bag. I suppose from a *Nation* reader's (and reviewer's) perspective, the book's aha! moment turns out to be the part where Dick Morris (good old Dick!) tells the author, apropos the early days in Arkansas, that Hillary "was more conservative than Clinton was...she was always pulling him back to the right." (Sheehy leans quite heavily on Morris, who has been using his *New York Post* column to cuff his former client about the ears in every way he can imagine. Ditto Nancy Pietrefesa, the one old friend who's been willing to dish some dirt.) Perspective is added by Don Jones, Hillary's youth minister, the man who opened her eyes to the world beyond the fragrant azaleas and scraped Girl Scout knees of her childhood suburb. He took her to meet Martin Luther King Jr., took her into Chicago's South Side to meet her poor, black coevals, strummed protest songs (inevitably!) on his guitar. Jones: "She definitely has a conservative streak...particularly on abortion, homosexuality, and capital punishment. Surely, she is for gay rights, there's no question about that. But I think both she and Bill still think of heterosexuality as normative." And so on.

This commences a discussion by Sheehy about teacher testing, a cause HRC took up with her usual earnest ardor, which had her reading the curriculums of pretty much every school in the state and which led one school librarian to call her "lower than a snake's belly" (that's how they talk down there in Arkansas, see?). Teacher testing is anathema to liberals. So it was an awkward moment, at Hillary's pre-announcement announcement of her Senate candidacy, which was held in November at the Manhattan offices of the United Federation of Teachers, when someone from the press corps had the bad form to ask her about her old Arkansas enthusiasm for this bane of teachers' unions everywhere. Hillary ducked, muttering something about circumstances being different then. Which of course is true: Then, she didn't need the massive phone-bank operation of one of the most politically influential unions in New York to beat back a popular and well-financed conservative opponent. Now she does!

I don't know what to make of all this. Whom to feel sorry for, which side to take. Hillary's? Ideologically, no; and yet, on the non-political front, I do feel for her. She's been held to standards that the media wouldn't dare hold a man to and, from the right wing especially, has been the target of some unfair, not to say utterly insane, criticism. That's one thing about both Clintons that anyone with an eye for the offbeat has to admire, or at least admit: They send all their opponents into such a lurid state of dementia that no matter how cheesy or corner-cutting they are, they somehow end up looking better than their attackers. And yet, as soon as I write that, I think: Yes, but they've brought so much on themselves.

As has Sheehy. And yet, exactly why the viciousness of the attacks on her? In the immediate wake of the book's publication

Sheehy blamed the White House spin machine. She charged that Hillary's spokespersons, Marsha Berry in the White House and Howard Wolfson on the campaign trail, purposely did not return her calls so that her fact-checkers couldn't verify information, which would then result in inaccuracies that the first lady's henchpersons could blast. This is clever; a line that Rush Limbaugh and the Fox News Channel would gladly parrot and Washington would in general terms accept prima facie.

But I doubt it's true; one mistake Clinton haters have always made is to underestimate the White House's disorganization. I imagine Sheehy's fact-checkers' calls weren't returned because no one worked up the gumption to deal with the questions and Hillary's reputed wrath or, even more simply, because each side thought the other side was taking care of the problem.

But the blame-the-spin-machine defense doesn't account for the merciless reviews of the book virtually everywhere. The literary and political worlds were predetermined to hate *Hillary's Choice* and to judge it harshly. I think, and I hope you'll agree, that we can rule out defense of the Clintons as a motive. The political world surely is no collective defender of the Clintons, and the literary world, though more liberal than the political world, finds them a bit déclassé. Besides, *Hillary's Choice* is not an attack piece. Neither is it a panegyric, but any traffic in psychological explanation tends toward empathy, so the book is more sympathetic than not to its subject. (It was interesting to browse through readers' reviews of the book on Amazon—the favorable reviews mostly came from the pro-Hillary community, while the one-stars were mainly delivered by Hillary haters who seemed to want evidence of outright pelf or the college lesbian affair they are convinced that she and surely all sixties Wellesley girls had.)

I suspect the reaction to the book has little to do with the Clintons and far more to do with what I've found to be one of the most important, and I'd say distressing, or at least confusing, literary—or more precisely, polemical—developments of the Clinton era. In a word: motive. That is to say, we've had intense partisan battles in the recent past over Nixon, over Reagan, over civil rights, what have you. Naturally, in the course of carrying out those arguments we—left and right; society, if you will—have constantly questioned one another's arguments, facts, assumptions and sometimes intentions. But I don't recall people ever questioning others' motives quite the way we do now. If you defend Clinton, you must be hustling invites to the Lincoln Bedroom, trying to wire a gas-pipeline deal for Turkmenistan, seeking soft treatment from the White House or at the very least angling for a regular cable television slot. If you hate Clinton, you're a right-wing nutcase, a left-wing loser who can't stand actually winning elections for a change, lining up a fat book deal or *something*. It's become commonplace, in other words, to pick apart not just a person's position but the motives the person has for taking that position.

What's Sheehy's motive? I don't know. To make money, I guess, for starters. (I'm sure she made quite a lot, though I'm not so sure Random House did: It costs a lot of dough to sign a Gail Sheehy book, and *Hillary's Choice* made the *Times* bestseller list for one week only.) To be kinder, Sheehy may indeed find Hillary one of the most fascinating women of our time. And speaking of motive, we might reasonably inquire about Hillary's. For the Senate race, that is. Sheehy quotes HRC pal Harold Ickes as saying it's about "redemption," a characterization neither new (Ickes has been quoted previously, by me among others, saying the same thing) nor terribly interesting. Nor is it likely to prove terribly useful on the campaign trail. Can redemption get a candidate on a shaky little airplane to go up to Plattsburg on a snowy February Friday to attend a town hall meeting? Beating Rudy Giuliani will require a deeper, not to say more public-spirited, motive than redemption. But I shouldn't play this game, having put myself on record denouncing it. I suppose it's to be expected, in a world in which postmodern irony reigns alongside overwhelming hucksterism, that nothing anybody says can be accepted straightforwardly anymore. This is certainly true in the realms of politics and political commentary, where most people are indeed either lying, speaking on the basis of the wisdom shown them by the latest poll or saying what they believe will get them on television. And—here's another problem with Clinton-era political analysis—it's not just politics. Pundits love to write about the Clintons as if the collapse of public trust is entirely a function of their double talk. Meanwhile, here come Time Warner (where some of those very pundits hold forth) and AOL to tell us how wonderful their merger will be for all of us, which you don't have to have left politics to know is just a screenful of e-shit. This is the proper context, I think, in which to think of *Hillary's Choice*. A book like this is exactly the sort of white noise, like interactive chat rooms and cable talk shows, to which the current Information Age has given birth: It's alternately annoying and engaging; it's, every once in a while, insightful; it's far from all true; it's undemanding; it's of the moment, i.e., synergy-friendly; it's quickly disposable; and it's fundamentally without purpose. And that pretty much describes where we find ourselves these days. ✤

Blond Ambition

KATHA POLLITT, JUNE 30, 2003

illary Clinton's autobiography comes out barely a week after Martha Stewart is indicted for obstruction of justice and fraud related to alleged insider trading, and you still don't believe in God? Two blond middle-aged icons of female pre-eminence, each virtually unique in the testosterone-drenched worlds of politics and business, are ruling the headlines and obsessing the talk shows at exactly the same moment—how likely is that? Obviously this is some kind of harmonic convergence intended to induce mass heart attacks at Fox News. It's not just the sheer excitement—"Hil: Wanted to Wring His Neck"! "Martha's Mug Shots"!—that's raising pulses. It's the fact that despite everything, millions of women insist on adoring them anyway.

I've written many a column criticizing Hillary Clinton for the rightward tilt of her politics—her support for welfare reform, capital punishment, "family values" and so on. I even made a catty remark about her hairband back in 1992, for which I'm truly sorry. Truth, moreover, compels me to admit that *Living History*, her mega-hyped memoir, has that unfortunate, processed-cheese, as-told-to taste. It's the verbal equivalent of her Barbara Walters appearance: one long fixed, glazed smile under the pink lights. But none of that matters. People aren't lining up by the thousands to purchase signed copies because they want to get the real scoop on tax policy or even Travelgate. They want to know if she really believed Bill when he told her there was nothing to the Monica story, how she felt when she finally learned it was true and why she stays with him. The answers to be found in her book are yes; she was really upset; and thanks to prayer and marriage counseling she was eventually able to move on.

Whether this is the whole truth is impossible for a stranger to know. Like Joe Klein, I tend to believe she really loved him—she writes in the book about her first impression of him as a "Viking" and lyrically describes his hands, his boundless energy, his fascinating conversation. I was ready to date him myself! She certainly wouldn't be the first smart, straitlaced woman who fell for a sexy charmer and ended up, as the joke goes, believing what he told her instead of what she saw. Nor, on the other hand, would she be the first wife who decided to live with what she couldn't change rather than throw away a relationship that was also a way of life. Or the first first lady who put up a good front in public while quietly seething at home. I doubt the right-wingers going after Hillary for staying with Bill would have cheered if evidence of George Bush Sr.'s rumored infidelities had come to light and Barbara had abandoned him in his hour of need. Hillary must be the only woman the family-values crowd has ever castigated for sticking with her marriage. Just you try suggesting, though, that Pat Nixon was maybe not the most fulfilled woman in America, or that Laura Bush sometimes looks a little subdued, a little out of focus, and see how fast you get accused of being an East Coast elitist, slut and traitor.

For the right, Hillary's book comes just in time. In the third year of the Bush administration, it was beginning to look like conservatives might finally have to acknowledge that Bill Clinton is not president anymore. Now they can sink into a nostalgic delirium—ah, for the days of Whitewater, Morgan Guaranty, Gennifer Flowers, Paula Jones, Vince Foster and all the other horrors from which the Supreme Court rescued us in December 2000. Hillary's book is handy, too, in helping Bill Kristol and his fellow talking heads brush aside pesky questions about the shifting rationales for invading Iraq, and those missing WMDs. Could Bush have been shading the truth? No, it was Bill Clinton who "lied to the American people." Right, and about something so very important, too! In right-wing mythology, if Hillary knew about Bill's women she is an ambitious schemer; if she didn't, writes Jonathan Alter in *Newsweek*, she's not fit for higher office: "Blinders are understandable in a wife, but could be a concern in a future president." According to Alter, when Bush claimed an "imminent threat" from Iraq or said the "average" tax cut is $1,000 a year, "he is deceiving us, not himself," a pettier crime. So if there's one thing worse than lying to the American people, it's believing your husband is telling the truth.

One hears so much from people who hate Hillary, one forgets that millions think she's great, a self-made working wife and mother who actually managed to turn the routine subordinations—and, in her case, profound humiliations—of political wifehood into real power: from first lady to senator! Martha Stewart offers the same contradictory blend of traditional femininity and modern feminism: She is a brilliant businesswoman, but she sells retro domesticity. Her fans seem to have no trouble integrating these two rather different visions of womanhood or believing that she's been singled out for prosecution as a woman while Ken Lay walks free. Marthatalks.com, a website she set up to mobilize support, has received 7 million hits and features fervent e-mails thanking her for introducing graciousness and beauty into harried and humdrum lives. And why not? Martha never tells women they should quit their jobs in order to make apple pie from their very own organic orchard. She doesn't say they're ruining their kids and ought to work harder at sex. She just tells them a lot of neat stuff about, oh, slipper chairs and how to take the thorns off roses.

Martha's reputation as a first-class bitch (on full view in Cybill Shepherd's portrayal in a recent NBC movie) hasn't put a dent in her cult, and that's only fair. This is a nation that reveres Donald Trump, for heaven's sake, who famously trashed his wife and has devoted his entire life to profiting off gambling and hideous buildings. Donald Trump, icon of manly capitalism, destroyed the beautiful Art Deco frieze on the Bonwit Teller building after promising to preserve it. That's a lot worse than $45,000 worth of insider trading, in my view. True, Trump is a man, and successful men have always been allowed to be mean and worse than mean; only women have to be sweet, kind, gentle, modest, sexually circumspect and scrupulously honest 24/7 no matter what—even in the nasty worlds of politics and business.

Or they did until Hillary and Martha came along. ✤

RACE TO THE BOTTOM

Brand Hillary

GREG SARGENT, JUNE 6, 2005

ot long ago, Senator Hillary Clinton went on a 2006 re-election campaign swing through the North Country, that vast expanse of upstate New York that stretches from Albany to the Canadian border. With its mix of family farms and grubby towns struggling with disappearing manufacturing jobs, the region feels less like the Northeast than like the industrial and agricultural Midwest. In other words, it's not a bad place to gauge how Clinton might play in swing-state America.

It's a question that of late has obsessed the pundits, who frequently, and often quite mindlessly, hold up the most obscure of the senator's utterances or policies—even ones that echo positions she's held for years—as proof that she's readying herself for a 2008 presidential run. The political classes tend to offer us two tidy Hillary narratives to choose from. The first (courtesy of Dick Morris and company) is that Clinton has given herself a moderate makeover designed to mask the fact that she's really a haughty left-wing elitist, in order to appeal to moderate Republicans and culturally conservative, blue-collar Democrats who are deserting their party. The opposing narrative line (courtesy of her supporters) is that Clinton, a devout Methodist, has revealed her true self as a senator; she's always been more moderate than is generally thought, and, as Anna Quindlen wrote recently in *Newsweek*, "people are finally seeing past the stereotypes and fabrications."

Yet if you watch Clinton on one of her upstate swings, as I did earlier this spring, it becomes clear that neither story line gets it right. What's really happening is that Clinton, a surprisingly agile and ideologically complex politician, is slowly crafting a politics that in some ways is new, and above all is uniquely her own.

Clinton's evolving approach—call it Brand Hillary—is sincerely rooted in her not-easily-categorized worldview, but it's also a calculated response to today's political realities. In effect, she's taking her husband's small-issue centrism—its trademark combination of big but often hollow gestures toward the center, pragmatic economic populism and incremental liberal policy gains—and remaking it in her own image, updating it for post-9/11 America with an intense interest in military issues.

At the same time, she's also experimenting with an increasingly national message about smart government and GOP extremism and testing new, unthreatening ways of revisiting her most politically disastrous issue: healthcare. In one setting after another, she offered the same impromptu-seeming refrain: "You may remember that when my husband was president, I tried to do something about healthcare. Well, I still have the scars to show for it. But I haven't given up." That's a line worthy of the man Hillary married—you can picture Bill sitting at the kitchen table in Chappaqua, repeating the line and chuckling, "That's good. That's really good."

Bill Clinton's political success, of course, sometimes came at great cost to liberal Democrats, and Hillary's brand of politics, too, poses a tough dilemma for liberals and progressives. It asks them to swallow their discomfort with her tactically shrewd but sometimes morally questionable maneuvers on big issues like war and abortion. In exchange they get less visible victories for progressivism, as well as the pleasure of seeing the former first lady—the figure most loathed by the right in at least a generation—succeed at a time when Democrats are desperate to figure out how to get that winning feeling again.

For liberals it remains to be seen whether this transaction will prove to be a good deal. Yet for some Democrats the trade is indeed worth it, as you could easily see during one of Clinton's first stops on her upstate swing, a speech to Democrats at a re-election fundraiser north of Albany. The event was closed to the press, and the senator shed her typically demure, bipartisan approach and launched a sharp attack on the GOP. Yet she knew her audience—these were hardly red-meat-craving Democratic activist types. They were rural, moderate Democrats—small-town schoolteachers, librarians, general-store owners. So Clinton's assault was spirited, but even-tempered and larded with patriotic language.

"We're seeing the slow and steady erosion of what made America great in the twentieth century," Clinton told her audience in an even tone. "When I got to the Senate I asked myself, What's going on here? At first I thought the president just wanted to undo everything my husband had done." Clinton waited a beat, then added, "And I did take that personally."

The audience laughed. "But then I thought, Wait a minute. It's not just about turning the clock back on the 1990s…. They want to turn the clock back on most of the twentieth century. They want to turn the clock all the way back beyond Franklin Roosevelt. Back beyond Teddy Roosevelt. That's why they're trying to undo Social Security. Make no mistake about it.

"What I see happening in Washington," Clinton continued, "is a concerted effort by the administration and the leadership in Congress to really create absolute power. They want to control the judiciary so they can have all three branches of government. I really don't care what party you are—that's not in the American tradition…. Right now young men and women are putting their lives on the line in Iraq and Afghanistan, fighting for the America we revere. And that is a country where nobody has all the answers—and nobody should have all the power…. We all need to stand up for what made America great—what created a wonderful set of values that we revere, that we exported and tried to really inculcate in people around the world!"

Wild applause rolled over Clinton now, although it was unclear whether the crowd had appreciated the political subtleties of what they'd witnessed. She had offered a critique of the GOP sharp enough for any progressive—even as she'd given an approving nod to American exceptionalism and a paean to US troops defending our "values" abroad. She'd stoked the partisan passions of her audience—even as she'd sounded an above-partisanship note of concern about the state of the Republic. Indeed, she'd managed to pull off what many Democrats struggle to do these days: She'd woven her criticisms into a larger narrative about America's past and future, criticizing the GOP leadership without sounding as if she wanted America to fail—when she said she was "worried" about America, you believed her.

Not long after that speech, Clinton appeared at a dramatically different event, a speech to a roomful of around 300 farmers. These were hard-bitten people who were fully prepared to believe that the senator from Chappaqua is who her caricaturists say she is. When Clinton strode into that room, she was an entirely different Hillary from the one who'd addressed Democrats only hours earlier. Anyone accustomed to seeing Clinton on TV—where she sometimes seems stiff and insincere—would have been flabbergasted by her sudden transformation. She instantly, and effortlessly, became Homespun Hillary. Her vowels grew flatter, more rural-sounding. "Little" became "li'l." "Get" became "git." Entire pronouns vanished, as in: "Heard there are some places in California selling gas for three dollars a gall'n." She poked fun at city folk. Speaking about how farmers could make money supplying the specialty produce that New York restaurants need, she mimicked a demand made to her by city restaurateurs: "We need all those little funny things you don't know what they are when they put 'em on your plate."

The crowd seemed especially impressed with her command of their pocketbook issues. She talked about fuel prices, protecting farmers from foreign competition, the Senate's neglect of New York agriculture in favor of Western agribusiness. She touted an initiative she'd spearheaded making it easier for local businesspeople to sell products via the Internet: "Fella made fly-fishing rods and lures—all of a sudd'n found there were people in Norway who wanted to buy th'm!"

By the end, you could feel it: Her audience had been won over. Her listeners filed out, murmuring approval of what they'd heard. As Robert Madison, a Republican and owner of a small local dairy farm with his three sons, put it: "Real down-to-earth person. Knows what she wants to do for the farmer."

To Clinton's friends and advisers, scenes like the above—in which she effortlessly wins over people who, we're told, are supposed to hate her—boost their contention that the real Hillary is ideologically complex and surprisingly down-to-earth. They

describe her as genuinely moderate on cultural and national security issues (hence her comfort evoking American values before a
Democratic audience), say she has a voracious appetite for policy
reminiscent of her husband (hence her mastery of farming arcana)
and describe her common-sense economic populism as born of
her Illinois upbringing (hence her ability to speak to the economic
concerns of farmers).

"People have gained a more complete view of Hillary in the
Senate than they had when she was in the White House," says
Mandy Grunwald, a close Hillary adviser. "People are getting past
the cartoon version of her and seeing that she's culturally moderate and sensitive to rural and small-town America. That mix has
always been a part of her."

Of course, to Clinton's critics, particularly on the right, the
same scenes just as easily demonstrate the opposite: that her Senate career has been merely a warm-up exercise for 2008. The
paeans to American values, the small-town banter, the talk of our
troops abroad—it's all a cynical effort to make people forget the
Hillary who proposed a big-government takeover of healthcare
and banned Bill's cigars from the White House. The right's game
plan here is pretty obvious: If she has "moved to the middle," then
she must be, as Dick Morris wrote recently, "a liberal who pretends moderation when she has to."

To critics on the left, however, the real Hillary is far from reli-
ably liberal—and to them, that's the problem. Someone of her stat-

ure might have moved the national dialogue to the left on many fronts. Indeed, many progressives wholeheartedly backed her 2000 Senate run, expecting her to carry the banner for liberal causes in, say, the manner of Massachusetts Senator Ted Kennedy. But they've been disappointed. Clinton has studiously avoided becoming the ideological warrior on big issues many supporters hoped for. "She certainly hasn't been a liberal trumpet like Kennedy, even though she's the senator from New York and has all the freedom she needs," says Robert Borosage, co-director of the Campaign for America's Future. "Kennedy has been a leading opponent of the GOP's militarism. He's called for large investments in education, Medicare for all. Hillary hasn't been out front on any of those issues."

What's more, there's some truth to the claim that various of Clinton's recent public statements and policy positions have come at a real cost to progressivism, much the way her husband's "triangulation" damaged the left in the 1990s. Her justification for voting in support of the Iraq War sounded like a cross between her husband's verbal parsing and John Kerry's maddening rhetorical contortions: "Bipartisan support for this resolution makes success in the United Nations more likely and, therefore, war less likely." The vote seemed to many a huge missed opportunity. A senator from New York, the prime target on September 11, voting against the war might have given a helpful boost to the global antiwar movement, which at the time was mobilizing against America's invasion of Iraq.

More recently, Clinton's flirtation with conservative Senator Rick Santorum—they jointly requested federal funds for research on how electronic media affect children—made liberals uneasy because it stank of pandering to so-called "values" voters. But the Santorum dalliance amounted to more than a mere difference of opinion with traditional liberals. It gave bipartisan cover not just to Hillary but to Santorum as well—legitimizing one of the Senate's ultraconservative standard-bearers. That undercuts broader Democratic efforts to win on various fronts by painting the GOP as captive of the hard right.

Finally, Clinton's January speech seeking "common ground" with pro-lifers on reducing pregnancies seemed intended to distance her from beleaguered pro-choice leaders. She might, for instance, have looked for ways to deliver her message with new NARAL president Nancy Keenan, who's been sounding a similar message. Instead, Clinton's speech enables the right to paint pro-choice groups as pro-abortion.

Yet for all that, there's no denying that Clinton has been extraordinarily successful, at least politically. Her approval rating in New York is nudging 70 percent. Many Republicans are on record as offering high praise. Consider that both Rudy Giuliani and George Pataki have punted on challenging her in 2006, even though dethroning Hillary would provide untold national attention and possibly be a springboard to the presidency in 2008.

What accounts for her success? Partly it can be chalked up to the fact that Hillary Clinton turned out to be a really, really good politician. Yet one could also argue that her success flows from the unique brand of politics that she has been practicing. To describe her approach as "triangulating" or "moving right" misses the point. For all the consternation on the left about Clinton, her approach depends less than her husband's did on using the left as a foil. Instead it relies on two fundamental ingredients: She projects pragmatism on economic issues, and she signals ideological flexibility on social issues. This latter tactic is not, as is often argued, about appeasing the cultural right. It's about appealing to moderates in both parties.

Take the Santorum press conference. You can endlessly debate whether popular entertainment hurts kids, or whether government should fix the problem. Yet if there's one thing most middle-of-the-road parents can agree on, it's that they are worried about how pop culture affects their children. By appearing with a right-wing Republican loathed by liberal Dems, she's essentially telling moderate Republicans, "parenting should transcend ideology, so this Democrat will stand with anyone if it might help kids." Yes, it legitimizes Santorum. But it also helps to defuse an undeniably potent right-wing strategy: the effort to paint Dems as antifamily.

Or take the abortion speech. You could argue that while it might have been discomfiting to -pro-choice groups, it's actually a smart tactical response to the right's increasingly successful strategy of painting pro-choicers as ideological extremists. Polls consistently show that majorities favor legalized abortion. But decades of conservative attacks have fooled voters into believing that pro-choice groups are to the left of public opinion. The speech wasn't really about abortion policy; it was about what to do before conception to reduce pregnancies, and while Clinton stressed teen abstinence, her main focus was on encouraging birth control, a stance objectionable only to the hard right.

The political beauty of this, as NewDonkey.com's Ed Kilgore has observed, is that it makes a subtle play for Republican moderates by forcing right-wing ideologues to reveal themselves as the true extremists, as foes of the common-sense goal of lowering rates of unwanted pregnancies. "When Democrats speak this way about abortion," says one senior Hillary adviser, "it drives a wedge between sensible Republicans, who want to reduce the amount of abortions, and the right-wing crazies, whose main goal is to stop people from having sex."

Her approach on economic issues is, at bottom, quite similar. By all accounts, Clinton has devoted a great deal of energy to dealing with the sluggish upstate economy. But here again it's worth noting the political subtleties of her approach. Her solutions tend to be less about correcting inequalities of wealth or class and more about finding ways that government can make the economy work better for everyone, CEOs and low-level employees alike. This difference is most visible in healthcare. Whereas her 1993 plan called for massive government intervention and pitted employee against employer, today she is careful to talk about the nation's disastrously screwed-up healthcare system as one that's afflicting not just the uninsured but also large employers paying huge premiums. As she likes telling upstate audiences, "GM has become a healthcare company that makes cars." It's not surprising, then, that her onetime nemesis, Newt Gingrich, suddenly finds himself in sympathy with her ideas on healthcare issues.

To the extent that her pragmatic economic approach in turn provides cover for progressive advances, Hillary has torn a page from the Book of Bill. President Clinton recognized that if you could persuade voters that you weren't ideologically rigid, that you were merely interested in government that works, you could get Republican moderates to listen—and getting them to listen is the key—to a Democrat talk about federal spending and fiscal responsibility. The paradox is that the tactic allowed Clinton a freer hand to pursue incremental liberal policy gains. As Joe Klein details in *The Natural*, President Clinton may have sold out on welfare reform and NAFTA, but those decisions gave him elbow room to expand spending on lower-profile liberal programs, from Head Start to Americorps.

To be sure, such advances did little to allay the disappointment many progressives felt when Bill Clinton lurched to the center on economic issues after winning office in 1992 on an aggressively populist platform. Hillary, too, has in some ways followed a similarly cautious approach. She isn't seriously grappling with big-picture economic issues such as growing corporate power and weakening union strength, or articulating a grand economic vision that would help liberalism make a big comeback. And yet, for all the talk about her "moderate makeover," analysts say that Hillary is staking out surprisingly progressive positions on some key economic issues. One example: Hillary voted against the biggest trade bill of the new millennium—the Trade Act of 2002, which many criticized as an effort to dramatically weaken Congress's ability to help craft national trade policy—even though Bill sought a similar version of this "fast track" legislation as president. "Bill Clinton had no genuine long-term progressive economic vision—a lot of it was smoke and mirrors," says Chris Slevin, deputy director of Public Citizen's global trade division. "But now that it's clear that the Clinton free-trade experiment has not delivered on its promises of more jobs in the United States and of progress in Mexico, Hillary has no choice but to take a more thoughtful, progressive approach to trade than her husband ever did."

In other areas too, the "new moderate" Senator Clinton has compiled quite a liberal voting record. If you don't believe it, just ask the liberal group Americans for Democratic Action. In 2004, ADA says, the senator earned a "liberal quotient" of 95 percent (compare that to, say, John Edwards at 60 percent, or the Democratic senators as a whole, at 85 percent).

What about Clinton's biggest lapse—her Iraq vote? For some antiwar progressives, no doubt, it will be a deal-breaker. And, of course, they are unlikely to be comforted by the fact that she really thought she was doing the right thing, as people who are close to her insist she did. Yet to focus on that one vote, again, misses the larger goal of Clinton's politics. As she recognizes, the Democratic Party's problem on national security far transcends the Iraq vote. Decades of assaults on Dems from the right (helped along by international fiascoes presided over by Lyndon Johnson and Jimmy Carter) have succeeded in persuading Americans that Dems are fundamentally uncomfortable with the application of American "hard" power abroad. As Clinton well knows, this is not something that can be corrected by merely donning a pair of plastic hawk's wings. It's a perception problem that will take a long time—and a lot of hard work—to reverse. So she's methodically built up a comfort level—and comfort is the key—with national security issues, joining the Armed Services Committee and spending countless hours mastering military arcana. This approach is far more involved and politically shrewd than just talking tough on the Sunday chat shows. It's not off-putting to the Democratic base, which loathes Joe Lieberman-style militaristic posturing. And it comes across as genuine, because it's rooted in Clinton's strategy of emphasizing smart, pragmatic government over ideology.

Of course, sitting on Armed Services is hardly a substitute for articulating a sweeping foreign policy vision that can compete with

GOP militarism. But it may be a necessary first step. Polls indicate that there's rising disquiet with the direction of Bush's foreign policies. At the same time, Americans appear consistently more comfortable entrusting foreign policy to the GOP. What that suggests is that perhaps the real problem Dems have on national security is not just the quality of their ideas but that moderates simply won't listen to them. That in turn suggests that one key to reversing Democratic decline in the foreign policy arena is to do what Bill Clinton managed to accomplish on various domestic issues: Get moderates to open their ears. Which is, arguably, the larger context of Hillary's Iraq vote. "Putting aside whether her vote was a mistake, which I think it was, she voted what she believed to be right," says John Podesta, head of the Center for American Progress and President Clinton's former chief of staff. "The larger end result may be that the middle of the country sees a senator with a tough nose who is not afraid to use force."

For months Democrats—and some outside the party—have been saying that Hillary can't win in 2008. You've heard the arguments: She starts out with 40 percent against her. She will energize GOP turnout—not to mention fundraising—like nobody else. Sure, Republicans have decided they like the real Hillary. But as Michelle Cottle wrote in *The New Republic*, "the bulk of the electorate, all those folks who won't tune into the race until after Labor Day '08, will be voting on Hillary the icon."

That all may turn out to be true. What's more, the retail politics Clinton has mastered may be lost on the gargantuan stage of a presidential race. And the right's ability to dominate the news cycle these days may guarantee that Hillary's skills remain beside the point—her enduring first lady image could trump her actual politics and persona. "You just have to accept the fact that with any Clinton, the media is going to be difficult," Grunwald says. "You don't ask why. You just deal."

Of course, any speculation about 2008 might take into account the small detail of who her opponent turns out to be, not to mention what the climate of the electorate is three years hence. But whatever the scenario in 2008, she has put together at least the beginnings of a winning political formula right now. Her version of Clinton centrism has been less about doing what Bill needed to do to survive in the White House—pit center against left—and more about doing what she needed to do to survive in the Senate—pit pragmatism and hard work against ideology. In essence, she's triangulating against herself: She's revealing the common-sense-solution-embracing Hillary, in contrast to the left-wing ideologue her caricaturists gave us. It helps that Hillary, while extraordinarily shrewd and calculating, is also really hard-working, hard-headed and culturally moderate. In the end, the irony is that her effort is working not just because it's smart politics but also because it's largely genuine.

It remains to be seen, of course, whether Clinton will be good for progressives or for the party as a whole. In the short term, though, she can certainly help the party—if nothing else, she's at least beginning to develop a Democratic alternative that could constitute one path to political success. "Hillary may not be an iconic liberal, but she fights for the people liberals care about—women, children, veterans, people without healthcare," Podesta says. "Best of all, she's tough, and she knows how to win." ✤

HRC: Can't Get No Respect

KATHA POLLITT, NOVEMBER 20, 2006

If people keep making sexist attacks on Hillary Rodham Clinton, I may just have to vote for her. That means you, Elizabeth Edwards! As tabloid readers know, the wife of John Edwards told guests assembled at a luncheon hosted by *Ladies' Home Journal* that she felt her "choices" had made her "happier" and more "joyful" than HRC. Translation: I've parked my legal career on the shelf to mind the kids, support my husband's political ambitions and tend our wonderful marriage, unlike Hillary, a bitter ambitious career woman with a philandering husband. Well, isn't that special! Isn't she the fulfilled woman of the year! Why are we talking about whether or not a woman senator who, maybe, wants to run for president is less joyful than a (former) senator's wife who, maybe, hopes to be first lady? Nobody would dream of measuring a male presidential hopeful on the happiness scale. If they had, Abraham Lincoln would never have been elected. It is sad to think that Ms. Edwards would play the happy-homemaker card to help her lightweight husband best a woman with about ten times as much political experience. We all know Edwards did such a great job running for vice president—the man was everywhere!—and made such a fantastic impression in his debate with Dick Cheney. Still, I might have gone for him in the 2008 primary, because every now and then he pops up out of nowhere and says poverty is bad. Now I dunno. We bitter ambitious career women have to stick together.

No sooner had Elizabeth Edwards apologized for remarks she claimed were taken totally out of context than John Spencer, HRC's Republican opponent in the Senate race, jumped in. Hillary, he told a reporter, is ugly. "You ever see a picture of her back then? Whew!" He went on, "I don't know why Bill married her." Spencer claimed she had had "millions of dollars" of plastic surgery and now "she looks good." Or maybe not: Photos of HRC looking old and tired are a Drudge Report constant. Well, to hell with you, Mr. Spencer. I've had it with the endless monitoring of women's beauty, age, weight and hotness. You've just given me another reason to vote for her. President Hillary! The anti–Paris Hilton.

Unattractive and not-so-joyful are the least of it, though. How about "cold," "flat" and "unwomanly" (*National Review*'s John Podhoretz); "robotic" (*The Wall Street Journal*'s Peggy Noonan) "angry" (Republican National Committee chair Ken Mehlman); a lesbian who conceived Chelsea after being raped by Bill (biographer Ed Klein); "Nurse Ratched," "a castrating female persona" (*Orlando Sentinel* columnist Kathleen Parker on *The Chris Matthews Show*); "that buck-tooth witch, Satan," "worse" than Osama bin

Laden (Don Imus). Put "Hillary" into a search engine with "Lady Macbeth," "dragon lady," "ice queen," "bitch" or "hag" and up come hundreds of thousands of hits. Oooh, an ambitious woman! A woman who isn't thinking, every minute of every day, about how to make men feel big and strong! I just might vote for her to give these pathetic misogynists what for, and so might the rest of my coven.

Well, actually, they might not, if they're like Code Pink, the women's peace group, which "bird-dogs" HRC around the country because of her support for the Iraq War. When I asked Medea Benjamin, co-founder of the group, why they focused on Clinton, she said it was primarily because the senator is "important and influential" but also because of her sex: "You expect more of a woman." Zillah Eisenstein, whose essay "Hillary's War" is posted on Code Pink's listenhillary.org, wrote me in an e-mail, "Yes, it is because she's female." It's as if Code Pink were some kind of ladies' auxiliary to the antiwar movement.

In her essay Eisenstein argues that HRC is a "female decoy" whose election would harm women because it would put a pink pseudo-feminist gloss on militarism and neoliberalism. There's something in this, but it comes close to holding Senator Clinton's femaleness against her: Logically, a man with the same positions would be less bad, because he couldn't use feminism (or female stereotypes of caring and nurturing) to disguise them. But since anyone with a realistic hope of becoming president will necessarily have made all sorts of unsavory bargains with the status quo, this amounts to saying we'll never have a woman in the White House. We'll continue on as now: "expecting more" of women and tacitly expecting less of men.

Well, count me out. The contemporary women's movement is almost forty years old, and after all that time exactly one woman has managed to reach the point where she can make a credible run for the White House. And I don't see another one around the corner, do you? Polls consistently show the castrating satanic robot way ahead of her potential primary rivals. In general election match-ups she trumps every Republican but Rudy Giuliani and John McCain. Maybe Barack Obama will alter the dynamics, which would be amusing, since I'll bet few of his fans can name even three positions he holds. But right now, if HRC were a man, we wouldn't even be having this conversation. But then, if she were a man, she wouldn't be almost universally perceived as unelectable.

I'm not saying I'd vote for Hillary Clinton in the primary—although by 2008 I expect she'll have come around on the war. I'd like a lefter candidate. But I want respect for women—and power is what gets you that. "It's natural," Medea Benjamin told me, "to want the people who are like you to be especially good." Actually, the history of politics in America demonstrates the opposite: Suppressed ethnicities and communities have put up with everything from drunkenness to corruption to outright criminality in their politicians, as long as those politicians delivered—even just a little—back home. Maybe women should forget about being angels and start being more like Italians, Irish or blacks. Let me put it this way: Any candidate who wants me to vote for him instead of her had better have a whole long list of reasons, beginning with what he will do for women that Hillary Clinton wouldn't do. ❖

Exchange: Wrong About Hillary

ZILLAH EISENSTEIN AND KATHA POLLITT
DECEMBER 4, 2006

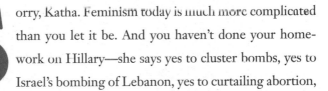orry, Katha. Feminism today is much more complicated than you let it be. And you haven't done your homework on Hillary—she says yes to cluster bombs, yes to Israel's bombing of Lebanon, yes to curtailing abortion, yes to a constitutional amendment against flag-burning, no to gay marriage. She has one of the ten most conservative voting records in the Senate. You need to do your research before you claim Hillary is a good thing for any of us. You rant against Code Pink as though they were the same as the right wing in this country. Shame. And let us take the past forty years of feminisms, as you mention, and realize that your old-fashioned liberal feminism, which claims that a female president will give women power *like* men, is deeply flawed. Most feminists across the globe know better than this.

Just ask the women in Sweden or Liberia or Chile or Germany, for that matter—many with women presidents today. If you follow your own claims, I guess you support Condi Rice as a gain for women and for the world more generally. And she clearly is not that for women here or in Afghanistan or in Iraq.

Last, if you quote me, could you quote the entire sentence? I have said and written elsewhere, "I think Hillary is a dangerous remedy to the present antidemocratic drift in this country, not because she is a female but because her being female allows a cover for her masculinist militarism." You really have this wrong, Katha. You allow the right wing to push you into a corner, and you end up authorizing Hillary the decoy, not a viable progressive or feminist candidate. It would be great if your column precipitates a *Nation* dialogue on the complexities of feminisms for this war-torn moment we all face.

Zillah Eisenstein

My column was a satirical riposte to the sexist insults and gender stereotyping heaped on Senator Clinton, not a serious commitment to vote for her. As I wrote, I would prefer a more left-wing candidate. I just don't like to see a woman knocked, mocked and insulted for being a woman, or held to higher standards than men. I have trouble with Code Pink's focusing on Hillary Clinton when blame for the Iraq War and militarism in general is so widely shared, even among Democrats—despite the title of Eisenstein's essay, the war in Iraq is not "Hillary's War." Unlike Code Pink, I don't expect women to be better than men, and I don't think peace is a women's issue. It's everybody's issue.

Eisenstein is the one who needs to do her research. Small points: Clinton voted *against* a constitutional amendment to ban flag-burning (unfortunately, she supported an anti-flag-burning bill). On gay marriage, she has said she isn't for it, but she wasn't in office to vote on DOMA (1996). She voted no on the federal marriage amendment in 2004 and no on a June resolution that prohibited states from recognizing gay marriage. Big points: She has never—repeat never—voted to "curtail abortion." She has a 100 percent approval rating from NARAL, Planned Parenthood and the National Family Planning and Reproductive Health Association. (If anything, her actions are more pro-choice than her rhetoric: This fall, despite her own past verbal support for parental notification, she campaigned against the California referendum requiring it.) Finally, Hillary Clinton most definitely does not have "one of the ten most conservative voting records in the Senate." According to *National Journal*, which ranks senators numerically, that honor belongs to Orrin Hatch. Clinton is actually the twentieth most liberal senator (Barack Obama, by the way, is sixteenth, not so different).

I don't consider myself a "liberal feminist"—one who believes formal equality is enough. I don't see how anyone could read my columns and put me in that camp. I would never vote for Condoleezza Rice or Germany's Angela Merkel (which doesn't mean I'm not pleased to see American and German men having to deal with a powerful woman—a new experience for too many of them). However, I wonder how Eisenstein knows what "most feminists across the globe" think. That's a lot of people! Surely among them are the women of Liberia and Chile, who worked hard to win the top jobs for Ellen Johnson-Sirleaf and Michelle Bachelet, and the women of Sweden, who have family and work-place benefits, and a level of gender equality, that American wom-en can hardly imagine. I would have thought Eisenstein would applaud these partial but real victories for peace, human rights, women's rights, the rule of law and social progress. Apparently, she would prefer to "bird dog" them all.

Katha Pollitt ❖

Hillary the Hawk

ROBERT SCHEER, MARCH 5, 2007

Let's face it: No matter how much many of us who oppose the war in Iraq would also love to elect a female president, Hillary Clinton is not a peace candidate. She is an unrepentant hawk, à la Joe Lieberman. She believed invading Iraq was a good idea, all available evidence to the contrary, and she has, once again, made it clear that she still does.

"If the most important thing to any of you is choosing someone who did not cast a vote [to authorize the war] or has said his vote was a mistake, then there are others to choose from," she said in New Hampshire last week, confusing contempt for antiwar Americans—now a majority—with the courage of her indefensible conviction that she bears no responsibility for the humanitarian, economic and military disaster our occupation has wrought.

As a candidate for '08, Hillary clearly calculates that her war chest, star power, gender and pro-choice positions will be sufficient for her to triumph in the primaries, while being "tough," pro-military and "supporting our president" will secure her flank in the general election against those who would paint her as that horrible beast, "a liberal."

A winning strategy? That remains to be seen. It certainly does not bode well for the future of the nation, however, should it be. Consider the parallel case of President Lyndon Johnson, who can be heard on tapes of his White House conversations ruminating that he never believed in the Vietnam War and pursued it only to deny Barry Goldwater and the Republicans a winning campaign issue.

In fact, whether out of such callous political calculations or sincere beliefs, mindless militarism has been a bipartisan majority position in Washington for a half-century, and counting. With the end of the cold war, its acolytes went searching for a new enemy to serve as a foil. When one emerged, those with aspirations to the presidency fell in line quite easily.

"Now, I believe the facts that have brought us to this fateful vote are not in doubt," New York Senator Clinton stated in her October 2002 speech when voting to authorize a war the White House had already decided to launch for bogus reasons, and which Clinton dutifully endorsed. "In the four years since the inspectors left, intelligence reports show that Saddam Hussein has worked to rebuild his chemical and biological weapons stock, his missile delivery capability and his nuclear program. He has also given aid, comfort and sanctuary to terrorists, including Al Qaeda members."

That none of this was true is now airily dismissed by Clinton as the result of her being mislead by "false intelligence." Yet Clinton had to be aware that the case for Saddam's WMD and ties to Al Qaeda was weak, when not obviously misrepresented. Surely she was in contact with the intelligence and diplomatic sources from her husband's administration who were telling anyone who would listen that the Bush team was obsessed with invading Iraq.

Leaving aside the absurdity that Democratic senators such as Clinton and '04 presidential candidate John Kerry didn't have the access and means to do the same basic fact-checking of Bush administration claims that independent journalists, intelligence analysts and published skeptics such as ex-arms inspector Scott Ritter undertook, how is it that they could have ignored the historical evidence that occupying Iraq with the vague goal of "fostering democracy" was a phenomenally dangerous endeavor? Had Clinton caught the "fever" for invading Iraq that Secretary of State Colin Powell attributed to Vice President Dick Cheney?

If not, Clinton certainly forgot her role as a senator to balance the power of the president, instead blindly following his lead: "I will take the president at his word that he will try hard to pass a UN resolution and will seek to avoid war, if at all possible," she said. Yet, when the president clearly broke his word five months later, blindsiding the UN inspectors on the ground in Iraq who had found no evidence of WMD, Clinton simply cheered him on.

No, Congress failed to take seriously the obligation built into its constitutionally mandated exclusive power to declare war, and Senator Clinton's refusal to admit that is not a minor issue. This paired with her strident support, ever since the invasion of Iraq, for a huge increase in the standing army to fight other wars, including a possible confrontation with Iran, shows a fondness in Clinton for war and bullying adventurism that vastly overshadows her sensible stances on many domestic issues. As Barry Goldwater supporters stated in kicking off the Republican revolution, what we need is a choice, not an echo. ❖

Senator Inevitable

WILLIAM GREIDER, MARCH 26, 2007

Considering the formidable advantages Hillary Clinton has assembled for 2008, why should anyone feel sorry for her? Because the senator is in a trap, and many of her assets have swiftly turned into liabilities. This predicament is largely of her own making but also of changed circumstances she did not foresee. Front-runners have often fared poorly in Democratic nominating contests during the last thirty years, especially when establishment insiders promoted an aura of inevitability for them. Hillary is a candidate for the same fate.

Inevitability actually is (or was) her core strategy. For six years, talented ranks of Clintonistas have assiduously worked Washington and Wall Street to create that expectation for her. They promoted romantic yearnings for a Clinton restoration in the age of George W. Bush. They amassed awesome advantages to scare off less famous opponents or, if need be, to crush them. Senator Inevitable has all the money and brains and influential connections.

Plus, she has a rock-star-popular husband, the ex-president, who's a brilliant strategist and performer.

What could go wrong? Well, things changed—dramatically—and the front-runner now finds herself scrambling to catch up with the zeitgeist. The watershed election of 2006 confirmed that Bush and the conservative order are in collapse. That inspires Democrats to embrace a far more ambitious sense of what's possible. Senator Clinton, the brainy policy wonk conscientiously calculating her next move, suddenly seems miscast for an era when Democrats are on offense and bolder ideas are back in play.

Clinton's great vulnerability was captured brilliantly by Barack Obama in a single sentence, without a mention of her name. "It's time to turn the page." People are looking forward, not back, he declares. People long for a promising new generation in politics. Let's not turn back to old fights, the acrimony of decades past.

Nothing personal. But Hillary Clinton is the past.

When she cites the family accomplishments—his and hers—or reminds audiences that "Bill and I" stood up to the vicious right-wing assaults, it sounds almost as though she is offering a co-presidency. If anyone misses the connection, the former president seems to be everywhere, touting his own thoughts on how to govern the country (presumably cleared with her, but who knows?).

This is the central tension in Senator Clinton's campaign. It's what makes her sound conflicted. Does she intend to emulate the risk-averse, center-right juggling act by which her husband governed? Or, as she sometimes suggests, will Clinton II be more aggressively progressive, less beholden to business and financial interests, more loyal to the struggles of working people? Senator Clinton tries to have it both ways: running on her husband's record and popularity, yet hinting she will not be like Bill.

That sounds like a tough sell. Some Democrats love him forever, others still loathe him for what he did or failed to do in office. The senator seems to be betting that nostalgia will prevail among party faithful, perhaps accompanied by amnesia. In any case, this contradiction undermines her aura as a forceful leader. Bill Clinton had the persuasive skills to get away with this, charming even those he had betrayed. Hillary Clinton may lack the insincerity to pull it off.

Senator Clinton's struggles are visible in her repeated efforts to recalibrate her positions on major issues—adding a little muscle each time but always a step or two behind public opinion. A year ago, she was still straddling the gut question of withdrawing from Iraq. Now she wants action in ninety days. She is molting a little, but still sounds more comfortable as a hawk.

The demands for an apology on her original go-to-war vote is not the point. It reflects a deeper suspicion that Hillary is as cynical as Bill on the fundamental matter of warmaking. One recalls Bill Clinton's scolding advice to Democrats after they lost the 2002 Congressional elections. People, he said, would "rather have someone who is strong and wrong rather than somebody who is weak and right."

Globalization and trade—another deeply divisive issue for the party—has produced a similar dilemma for Senator Clinton. She keeps ratcheting up her position, step by step, even voting against CAFTA in 2005. But she cannot embrace fundamental reforms (and mean it) without colliding with her husband's championing of free trade and with Robert Rubin, whose Wall Street money-raising machine will be a major factor in financing her campaign. If she did divorce herself from the Clinton-Rubin doctrine, that would create other problems for her.

The senator has one more problem, and his name is Bill. She and the Clintonistas probably regard the former president as their greatest asset, but he has the personal potential to become a fatal liability. I do not refer to the scandalous behavior that over the years has occasionally humiliated his wife (though that risk provides constant grist for insider gossip). I mean the threat that Bill Clinton simply won't get off the stage. He loves to talk and collect popular adulation, and people love to hear him. Last fall, he held a glamorous sixtieth birthday party in New York that lasted three days. He has the capacity—unconsciously or otherwise—to steal his wife's show just by being himself.

One thing we know from the past is that Bill can't help himself. Self-control has never been his strong point. But, as we also know from experience, Hillary Clinton and her campaign staff can't control him either. His egotism poses a real and present danger to her ambitions.

I am mischievously reminded of Lurleen Wallace, another political wife, who stood in for her husband when George Wallace was ineligible for another term as governor of Alabama. But that seems unfair. Hillary Clinton is accomplished in her own right and she has twice been elected as a senator from New York.

A more poignant comparison is with Senator Edward Kennedy, another inheritor of the family mantle. After his older brothers were killed, Teddy Kennedy was propelled by legendary expectations that he would someday run for president and restore the Kennedy name to the White House. When he finally did run but lost his party's nomination Kennedy, ironically, was freed to fulfill his real talent as a legislator and become the courageous and savvy liberal lawmaker of lasting fame. If Hillary should lose in '08, perhaps she will be liberated too. ❖

Hillary, Inc.

ARI BERMAN, JUNE 4, 2007

In a packed ballroom in midtown Manhattan, Hillary Clinton is addressing hundreds of civil rights activists and labor leaders convened by the Rev. Al Sharpton for his annual National Action Network conference. The junior senator from New York starts slowly but picks up steam when she hits on the economic anxiety many in the room feel. "We're not making progress," she says, her sharp Midwestern monotone accented with a bit of Southern twang. "Wages are flat." Nods of agreement. "This economy is not working!" Applause. She's not quite the rhetorical populist her husband was on the campaign trail, but she can still feel your pain. "Everything has been skewed," Clinton says, jabbing her index finger for emphasis, "to help the privileged and the powerful at the expense of everybody else!"

It's a rousing speech, though ultimately not very convincing. If Clinton really wanted to curtail the influence of the powerful, she might start with the advisers to her own campaign, who represent some of the weightiest interests in corporate America. Her chief strategist, Mark Penn, not only polls for America's biggest companies but also runs one of the world's premier PR agencies. A bevy of current and former Hillary advisers, including her communications guru, Howard Wolfson, are linked to a prominent lobbying and PR firm—the Glover Park Group—that has cozied up to the pharmaceutical industry and Rupert Murdoch. Her fundraiser in chief, Terry McAuliffe, has the priciest Rolodex in Washington, luring high-rolling contributors to Clinton's campaign. Her husband, since leaving the presidency, has made millions giving speeches and counsel to investment banks like Goldman Sachs and Citigroup. They house, in addition to other Wall Street firms, the Clintons' closest economic advisers, such as Bob Rubin and Roger Altman, whose DC brain trust, the Hamilton Project, is Clinton's economic team in waiting. Even the liberal in her camp, former deputy chief of staff Harold Ickes, has lobbied for the telecom and healthcare industries, including a for-profit nursing home association indicted in Texas for improperly funneling money to disgraced former House majority leader Tom DeLay. "She's got a deeper bench of big money and corporate supporters than her competitors," says Eli Attie, a former speechwriter to Vice President Al Gore. Not only is Hillary more reliant on large donations and corporate money than her Democratic rivals, but advisers in her inner circle are closely affiliated with unionbusters, GOP operatives, conservative media and other Democratic Party antagonists.

It's not exactly an advertisement for the working-class hero, or a picture her campaign freely displays. Her lengthy support for the Iraq War is Clinton's biggest liability in Democratic primary circles. But her ties to corporate America say as much, if not more, about what she values and cast doubt on her ability and willingness to fight for the progressive policies she claims to champion. She is "running to help and restore the great middle class in our country," Wolfson says. So was Bill in 1992. He was for "putting people first." Then he entered the White House and pushed for NAFTA, signed welfare reform, consolidated the airwaves through the Telecommunications Act of 1996 (leading to Clear Channel's takeover) and cleared the mergers of mega-banks. Would the first lady do any different? Ever since the defeat of healthcare reform, Hillary has been a committed incrementalist, describing herself as a creature of the "moderate, sensible center" whom business admires and rewards. During her six years in the Senate, she's rarely been out front on difficult economic issues. Given her proximity to money and power, it's not hard to figure out why she keeps controversial figures close to her—even if their work becomes a liability for her campaign.

Polling Czar

After the 1994 election, Democrats had just lost both houses of Congress, and President Clinton was floundering in the polls. At the urging of his wife, he turned to Dick Morris, a friend from their time in Arkansas. Morris brought in two pollsters from New York, Doug Schoen and his partner, Mark Penn, a portly, combative workaholic. Morris decided what to poll and Penn polled it. They immediately pushed Clinton to the right, enacting the now-infamous strategy of "triangulation," which co-opted Republican policies like welfare reform and tax cuts and emphasized small-bore issues that supposedly cut across the ideological divide. "They were the ones who said, 'Make the '96 election about nothing except V-chips and school uniforms,'" says a former adviser to Bill. When Morris got caught with a call girl, Penn became the most important adviser in Clinton's second term. "In a White House where polling is virtually a religion," *The Washington Post* reported in 1996, "Penn is the high priest."

Penn, who had previously worked in the business world for companies like Texaco and Eli Lilly, brought his corporate ideology to the White House. After moving to Washington he aggressively expanded his polling firm, Penn, Schoen & Berland (PSB). It was said that Penn was the only person who could get Bill Clinton and Bill Gates on the same line. Penn's largest client was Microsoft, and he saw no contradiction between working for both the plaintiff and the defense in what was at the time the country's largest antitrust case. A variety of controversial clients enlisted PSB. The firm defended Procter & Gamble's Olestra from charges that the food additive caused anal leakage, blamed Texaco's bankruptcy on greedy jurors and market-tested genetically modified foods for

Monsanto. PSB introduced to consulting the concept of "inocula-tion": shielding corporations from scandal through clever adver-tising and marketing.

In 2000 Penn became the chief architect of Hillary's Senate victory in New York, persuading her, in a rerun of '96, to eschew big themes and relentlessly focus on poll-tested pothole politics, such as suburban transit lines and dairy farming upstate. Follow-ing that election, Penn became a very rich man—and an even more valued commodity in the business world (Hillary paid him $1 million for her re-election campaign in '06 and $277,000 in the first quarter of this year). The massive PR empire WPP Group acquired Penn's polling firm for an undisclosed sum in 2001 and four years later named him worldwide CEO of one of its most prized properties, the PR firm Burson-Marsteller (B-M). A key player in the decision to hire Penn was Howard Paster, President Clinton's chief lobbyist to Capitol Hill and an influential pres-ence inside WPP. "Clients of stature come to Mark constantly for counsel," says Paster, who informally advises Hillary, explaining the hire. The press release announcing Penn's promotion not-ed his work "developing and implementing deregulation infor-mational programs for the electric utilities industry and in the financial services sector." The release blithely ignored how utility deregulation contributed to the California electricity crisis manip-ulated by Enron and the blackout of 2003, which darkened much of the Northeast and upper Midwest.

Burson-Marsteller is hardly a natural fit for a prominent Democrat. The firm has represented everyone from the Argentine military junta to Union Carbide after the 1984 Bhopal disaster in India, in which thousands were killed when toxic fumes were released by one of its plants, to Royal Dutch Shell, which has been accused of colluding with the Nigerian government in committing major human rights violations. B-M pioneered the use of pseudo-grass-roots front groups, known as "astroturfing," to wage stealth corporate attacks against environmental and consumer groups. It set up the National Smokers Alliance on behalf of Philip Morris to fight tobacco regulation in the early 1990s. Its current clients include major players in the finance, pharmaceutical and energy industries. In 2006, with Penn at the helm, the company gave 57 percent of its campaign contributions to Republican candidates.

A host of prominent Republicans fall under Penn's purview. B-M's Washington lobbying arm, BKSH & Associates, is run by Charlie Black, a leading GOP operative who maintains close ties to the White House, including Karl Rove, and was a partner with Lee Atwater, the consultant who crafted the Willie Horton smear campaign for George H.W. Bush in 1988. In recent years Black's clients have included the likes of Iraq's Ahmad Chalabi, the darling of the neocon right in the run-up to the war; Lockheed Martin; and Occidental Petroleum. In 2005 he landed a contract with the Lincoln Group, the disgraced PR firm that covertly placed US military propaganda in Iraqi news outlets.

Black is only one cannon in B-M's Republican arsenal. Its "grassroots" lobbying branch, Direct Impact—which specializes in corporate-funded astroturfing—is run by Dennis Whitfield, a former Reagan cabinet official, and Dave DenHerder, the political director of the Bush/Cheney '04 campaign in Ohio. That's not all. B-M recently partnered with lobbyist Ed Gillespie, the former head of the Republican National Committee, in creating the new ad firm 360Advantage, run by two admen for the Bush/Cheney campaigns. Its first project was a campaign against "liberal bias" in the media for the neoconservative *Weekly Standard* magazine.

As expected with such a lineup, B-M has a highly confrontational relationship with organized labor. "Companies cannot be caught unprepared by Organized Labor's coordinated campaigns," read the "Labor Relations" section of its website, describing that branch of the company (the section was altered after *The American Prospect* quoted it in March).

Back in 2003, two large unions, UNITE (which later merged with the hotel and restaurant union HERE) and the Teamsters, launched a major drive to organize 32,000 garment workers and truck drivers at Cintas, the country's largest and most profitable uniform and laundry supply company (it posted $3.4 billion in sales and $327 million in profits last year). Its longtime CEO, Richard Farmer, was a mega-fundraising "Pioneer" for George W. Bush. Cintas was sued for overcharging consumers and denying workers overtime pay—it settled both cases out of court—and was ordered by a California superior court to give employees $1.4 million for not paying them a living wage. It has also maintained unsafe working conditions (an employee in Tulsa died recently when caught in a 300-degree dryer) and, according to union officials, has used any means necessary to block the organizing drive. According to worker complaints documented by the unions, management fired employees on false grounds, vowed to close plants and screened anti-union videos. A plant manager in Vista, California, threatened to "kick driver-employees with his steel-toed boots," according to a complaint UNITE HERE filed with the National Labor Relations Board (NLRB). To put a soft face on its harsh tactics, Cintas hired Wade Gates, a top employee in B-M's Dallas office, as its chief spokesman. Gates coined Cintas's shrewd response to labor: "the right to say yes, the freedom to say no," which has been repeated endlessly in the press. In a speech at USC Law School last year, he outlined Cintas's strategy, calling for an "aggressive defense against union tactics." Says Ahmer Qadeer, an organizer for UNITE HERE, "It's the Burson influence that's made Cintas much, much slicker than they were." The unions have won two NLRB rulings against Cintas, but for four years the company has continued to resist the organizing campaign. Penn disclaimed any responsibility for B-M's activities before his arrival at the firm, and he told *The Nation* he has "never personally participated in any anti-union activity," even though B-M's anti-labor arm is still operating under his tenure. (Penn added a personal note: "My father was for many years a union organizer in the poultry workers union.")

In 2004 Hillary Clinton asked for an investigation into whether Cintas had received preferential regulatory treatment from the Environmental Protection Agency in return for giving large political donations to President Bush. Union officials say she's been supportive of their organizing drive. She's a co-sponsor of the Employee Free Choice Act, which would let workers form unions if a majority sign cards authorizing representation, thus avoiding coercion and intimidation during union election campaigns (Cintas bitterly opposes the EFCA). She told the International Association of Firefighters recently, "I believe that it is absolutely essential to the way America works that people be given the right to organize and bargain collectively."

Hillary apparently sees no contradiction between her advocacy and the anti-union work of her chief strategist's company. "Clearly not," says spokesman Wolfson. "I don't think it reflects on her at all. Mark's work away from the campaign is Mark's work, and his campaign work is separate from that."

Penn recently told *The Washington Post*, in a largely flattering profile, that he'd been "cleared of all client responsibilities, except for Microsoft, for the duration of the campaign." Microsoft is a strange exception, given that it was the corporate entity the Clinton administration challenged most directly. Moreover, Penn has no plans to take a formal leave from B-M. (Because B-M is a subsidiary of the WPP Group, a British company, it doesn't have to report its CEO's salary or ownership stake in the company.) George W. Bush forced Karl Rove to sell his direct-mail business in 1999, but don't expect a similar move from Hillary. Her campaign pays Penn's polling firm, which is part of B-M. "Senator Clinton is no different, frankly, from Mark's other clients," Howard Paster says. "Burson-Marsteller is a lot bigger firm than Senator Clinton. There's a whole 'nother life we live."

Yet occasionally the work of Penn's company spills onto Hillary's political terrain. Penn's polling firm has worked with the Clean and Safe Energy Coalition—a PR front group for the nuclear power industry—which purports to show "strong support among Americans for nuclear energy." Coincidentally, one of B-M's big projects is the Indian Point nuclear power plant, twenty-four miles north of Manhattan, dubbed by environmentalists "Chernobyl on the Hudson." The plant received the lowest safety rating from the Nuclear Regulatory Commission in 2000, and after 9/11 there were widespread calls from environmentalists, consumer groups and elected officials to shut it down. It has had nine unplanned shutdowns since 2005.

With the help of B-M, Indian Point's owner, Entergy Corporation, struck back with a multipronged ad campaign. Its post-9/11 slogan, "Safe, secure, vital," emphasized security, warning that if Indian Point were closed New York could face a Califor-

nia-style energy crisis. In 2003, after Westchester County legis-
lators passed resolutions condemning Indian Point, B-M set up
a classic astroturf group on Entergy's behalf, the Campaign for
Affordable Energy, Environmental and Economic Justice, which
targeted Democratic incumbents in low-income sections of Westchester who supported closing the plant. If Indian Point were
shuttered, the bilingual campaign informed residents, electricity bills would increase, power to public transportation would be
jeopardized and dirty power plants would go up in low-income
and minority neighborhoods. At the same time, B-M unveiled
another organization also bankrolled by Entergy that promoted
Indian Point. Following the '06 elections, Entergy unveiled a new
slogan, "Right for New York," citing Indian Point as an asset in
the fight against global warming. Hillary has called for an "independent safety assessment" but has declined to join Governor
Eliot Spitzer and twelve members of Congress in urging that the
plant be shut down. Entergy, founded in Arkansas, was a major
supporter of Bill Clinton in the 1990s and contributed generously
to Hillary in 2000 and 2006.

It's difficult to tell where Penn's corporate life ends and his
political one begins. Most Democratic consultants do some business work—it's the easiest way to pay the bills. Yet nobody wears
as many hats—and advises as many corporations—as Penn. "Penn
and Schoen have displayed a thirst for corporate work, often in

conflict with the policy agendas of their political clients, that has long set the bar among Democratic pollsters," wrote Democratic pollster Mark Blumenthal on his blog recently. Furthermore, few Democratic consultants so consistently and publicly advocate an ideology that perfectly complements their corporate clients. Every election cycle Penn discovers a new group of swing voters—"soccer moms," "wired workers," "office park dads"—who happen to be the key to the election and believe the same thing: "Outdated appeals to class grievances and attacks upon corporate perfidy only alienate new constituencies and ring increasingly hollow," Penn has written. Through his longtime association with the Democratic Leadership Council, Penn has been pushing pro-corporate centrism for years. Many of the same companies that underwrite the DLC, such as Eli Lilly, AT&T, Texaco and Microsoft, also happen to be clients of Penn's.

Penn's views often clash with the work of other Democratic pollsters. Half a dozen former PSB staffers say Penn has stretched to get the answers he wanted, including manipulating data, phrasing misleading questions and shifting the demographics of those polled, whether it was for the Clinton campaign in 1996 or a corporate client like Procter & Gamble. For example, Penn was insistent that Clinton's poll numbers in '96 match his poll numbers in '92, say two staffers who worked at PSB during the campaign. If Clinton was underperforming, Penn would artificially add more Democratic-aligned groups to the survey sample to make Bill look better. "He was a great showman, and he'd paint you a nice picture," says one former staffer who worked with Penn in the late '90s. "But the way he got you the data—it was cooked." Staffers who left started a PSB survivors message board documenting what they perceived as personally abusive and unethical behavior in the workplace.

When presented with these allegations, Penn said, "Polling in '96 was 100 percent accurate, to the point," adding, "no staffer you could have talked to ever attended any meeting with any of the clients." He insists that "all weightings and question wording turned out to be accurate." Former partner Doug Schoen adds, "No data was ever manipulated…. There was never any discussion of the polling from 1992 during 1996." In response to the complaints on the message board, Penn dismissed "a nearly decade-old anonymous site with inaccurate material from an unhappy few."

Clients have usually been uninterested in Penn's methodology because they liked his results. But not always. Al Gore fired Penn as his pollster before the 2000 Democratic primaries, in part because he wanted to move in a more populist direction and in part because he didn't trust him. Penn "would write polls to get the result he felt was important," Tony Coelho, Gore's campaign chair, told *Rolling Stone*. Recently two poll interviewees accused the Denver-based field office of Penn's firm, PSA Interviewing, of conducting misleading telephone polls in California and New Hampshire. The interviewers read to respondents statements like

"John Edwards chose not to run for another Senate term because he didn't think he could win, abandoning the fight in Congress against the administration," and "Barack Obama failed to vote in favor of abortion rights nine times as a state senator." Hillary, by contrast, is presented as someone who "was born into a middle-class home where she learned the value of hard work and frugality." At the end of the script the poll asks, "Based on what you've heard, who would you choose as the Democratic candidate for president: Hillary Clinton, John Edwards or Barack Obama?" In response to these accusations, Penn said the charges were false and that "this firm conducts standard political and market research polls...and does not do push polling." He would not confirm or deny that the questions above came from PSA.

These days Penn's few political clients lean to the right. He worked on Joe Lieberman's ill-fated presidential run and the Venezuelan recall referendum in 2004 and Italian billionaire Silvio Berlusconi's unsuccessful re-election campaign last year.

Yet despite his outsized role in the corporate world, his company's close ties to GOP operatives and questions about his polling techniques, Penn remains a leading figure in Hillary's campaign, pitching the inevitability of her nomination to donors and party bigwigs. According to *The New York Times*, "[Hillary] Clinton responds to Penn's points with exclamations like, Oh, Mark, what a smart thing to say!" His presence means that triangulation is alive and well inside the campaign and that despite her populist forays, Hillary won't stray far from the center or think too big. "Penn has a lot of influence on her, no doubt about it," says New York political consultant Hank Sheinkopf, who worked with Penn in '96. "He's not going to let her drift too far left."

White House in Exile

Penn's not the only major player in Hillary's corporate orbit. There's also the Glover Park Group, a fast-rising lobbying and PR firm known as the "White House in Exile" because it's packed with former Clintonites. Its roster includes former Clinton press secretary Joe Lockhart and deputy chief of staff Joel Johnson. From Hillary's orbit come Peter Kauffman, her former press secretary, and Gigi Georges, her New York director. Campaign manager Patti Solis Doyle used to work there, and until recently so did Howard Wolfson.

Wolfson, a pugnacious operative who's said he admires Karl Rove's skills, took a leave of absence in March (unlike Penn), though he still has a stake in the firm. Partners at Glover Park downplay connections to Hill and Bill, but the association—along with the Democratic takeover of Congress—has been good for business. Glover Park was Washington's fastest growing private company in 2005. The day before the 2006 election it got a huge infusion of private-equity cash from a firm in Chicago, Svoboda, Collins. Business has doubled since then. No one at Glover Park is now officially part of the Clinton campaign, yet there are plenty of unofficial relationships. Johnson, for example, is giving to and raising money for Hillary. The firm still lobbies her office, as it presumably would a Clinton II White House.

Glover Park's clients have included standard liberal groups like the United Federation of Teachers and the ACLU. Yet the Clinton ties have also helped the firm make an alliance with Rupert Murdoch. Hillary started cozying up to Murdoch after her 2000 Senate victory, in a calculated attempt to defang his conservative media empire, News Corp. In 2004 the billionaire required a favor of his own: Nielsen was preparing to change the way it measured viewership in US TV markets, a plan that Murdoch's Fox network feared would cost it millions in ad revenue. So Murdoch called on Glover Park. Wolfson secured a $200,000 contract and unveiled a PR blitz under the guise of a supposedly independent minority front group called Don't Count Us Out. The group played on fears of voter disenfranchisement, arguing that minorities would be undercounted in the new system. Don't Count Us Out ran more than 100 ads in two days, and Nielsen was deluged with hate mail. Letters of support came in from politicians, including Senator Clinton, who warned, "Nielsen would be remiss in pushing forward with its rollout plan." The campaign eventually fizzled when influential supporters, including Jesse Jackson, realized that Glover Park's claims were bogus and viewers were simply moving from broadcast channels like Fox to cable. Yet Murdoch kept Glover Park on retainer and held a $60,000 fundraiser for

Clinton last July. News Corp. executive Peter Chernin is hosting a top-dollar shindig for her in LA in late May. Asked what she thought of Murdoch, Clinton spokesman Phillippe Reines told *The New Yorker*, "Senator Clinton respects him and thinks he's smart and effective."

News Corp wasn't an exception for Glover Park. It's used similar tactics on behalf of another frequent Democratic bête noire—the pharmaceutical industry. As with Penn, it's been difficult to tell where business ends and politics begins. In the run-up to passage of the Medicare Modernization Act in 2003, Johnson (who partnered with disgraced former Tom DeLay staffers and associates of Jack Abramoff at his previous lobbying job) lobbied for the industry's chief arm, the Pharmaceutical Research and Manufacturers of America (PhRMA). Last summer, as the law came under scrutiny from both liberals and conservatives, he wrote a memo to Hill staffers arguing that "early polls call into question the political value in strongly attacking the weakness in the Medicare prescription drug plan." Johnson failed to note that he was on the industry's payroll, as were other firms whose work he cited. After the election Glover Park inked deals with drugmakers Amgen and Pfizer to block a proposal to lower drug prices under Medicare and help the latter slash 10,000 workers this year and close five manufacturing sites.

Glover Park has also been trying to get liberals to support a program called Medicare Advantage. According to the federally run Medicare Payment Advisory Commission, this privately run plan overcharges the government by 12 percent compared with traditional Medicare. And it paves the way for privatization. As a result, Congressmen like Pete Stark and Charlie Rangel want to redirect some of the money toward children's healthcare. That proposal has drawn fierce resistance from America's Health Insurance Plans (AHIP), which has recruited Glover Park and another Democratic firm, the Dewey Square Group, to argue that cutting benefits to Medicare Advantage would disproportionately hurt low-income and minority enrollees (note a pattern?), a claim the Center on Budget and Policy Priorities calls "distorted" and "based on misleading use of data." Nevertheless, former Hillary spokesman Peter Kauffman has asked community groups in New York to join a Medicare Advantage minority advisory committee, which now includes former big-city mayors and the NAACP. And Glover Park put out polling, in conjunction with a GOP firm and AHIP, that shows "record high satisfaction" among enrollees, according to Johnson. Hillary was supportive of the Medicare Advantage program during the debate over Medicare but voted against the final bill. She hasn't commented on whether she favors preserving the current system.

Murdoch and PhRMA aren't the only odd couples to enlist the Clintonites. There's also the government of Dubai, which has paid Bill handsomely for speeches and strategic advice. Around the time of the furor over the proposed management of US ports by Dubai Ports World, Glover Park launched a lobbying drive to broker the sale of two US military plants to the government-owned Dubai International Capital. The two New York senators led opposition to the ports deal but didn't raise objections to the plant takeover. According to *Newsday*, the $100,000 contract was routed through the LA law firm of Raj Tanden, brother of Hillary's top domestic policy adviser, Neera Tanden.

Glover Park has also fronted for Verizon to kill "net neutrality" and allow telecom companies to charge more for certain Internet content, for the insurance industry on asbestos claims, for Ernst & Young on immunity from shareholder lawsuits and for the Swift banking coalition's collaboration with the Bush administration on "antiterror" financial records.

Partners at Glover Park say business is business—if their work puts them at odds with fellow Democrats, so be it. "On some days you're working on the other side of an issue from a Democratic Congressman," says Johnson. "The next day you're helping them raise money." It's a world Hillary knows well.

The Compromised Candidate

It's hard to see how her advisers' corporate work doesn't reflect poorly on Clinton's progressive claims or create a liability for her with Democratic voters. There's no evidence that she has taken a position specifically to benefit one of her advisers' clients or a top supporter. More likely, the ties to corporate

America, along with the bruises of past defeats, have limited what she believes is possible and will fight to achieve. "If you surround yourself by people who live off of big corporations, that's going to affect the advice they give you and your own worldview," says a former Clinton adviser.

Clinton has a consistently liberal Senate voting record, earning near-perfect scores from Americans for Democratic Action. She's fought to get New York its fair share of federal money after 9/11 and has advocated for long-neglected, though politically safe, issues like children's health and veterans care. Yet voting records capture only so much. Since the healthcare reform disaster of 1993-94, she has rarely stuck her neck out on contentious issues. "She votes the issues that come up, rather than take the leadership role," says Joan Claybrook, president of Public Citizen. "We tried to do too much, too fast twelve years ago," Clinton told the Federation of American Hospitals last year, "and I still have the scars to show for it." She's now the number-one Congressional recipient of donations from the healthcare industry.

Clinton's rarely been the threat to the business community that many on the right typically allege. She's often partnered with Republicans like Newt Gingrich and Bill Frist. In 2002 she backed a harsh position on welfare reform reauthorization that put her at odds even with conservative Republicans like Orrin Hatch. She persuaded her husband to veto the bankruptcy bill in 1997, voted for a similar version in 2001 and missed the vote in 2005, when Bill was in the hospital. She advocated weakening the McCain-Feingold campaign finance reform law, telling Feingold to "live in the real world." Unlike Edwards and Obama, she accepts campaign contributions from lobbyists and corporate PACs. "Ask *them* why they don't take money from lobbyists," Wolfson retorts. "We're proud of our support."

The conservative caricature that Hillary is to the left of her husband is a myth. She, like Bill, talks a good game. She's aggressively courted organized labor and distanced herself from policies like NAFTA. She privately tells public-interest groups and liberal commentators that she's on their side. At the same time, she's premised her presidential campaign on a restoration of the Clinton era, frequently invoking "Bill and I" on the stump as a way of claiming credit for the perceived successes of the 1990s. She's expressed no qualms about her closest advisers' forays into the corporate world. Courting elements of the Democratic base while signaling to the corporate right that she won't shake up the system is a tricky juggling act. Even the first lady of triangulation may not be able to pull it off. ❖

What Women See When They See Hillary

LAKSHMI CHAUDHRY, JULY 2, 2007

"I love [Hillary Clinton] so completely that, honestly, she would have to burn down the White House before I would say anything bad about her!" exclaimed Nora Ephron in a 1993 *Newsday* interview. Three years later, she told the Wellesley class of 1996, "Understand: Every attack on Hillary Clinton for not knowing her place is an attack on you." Come late 2006, however, Ephron was the one on the attack as a self-described "Hillary resister"—those who believe that "she will do anything to win, who believe she doesn't really take a position unless it's completely safe," as she wrote on her Huffington Post blog, "who believe she has taken the concept of triangulation and pushed it to a geometric level never achieved by anyone including her own husband, who can't stand her position on the war, who don't trust her as far as you can spit."

This rather dramatic change of heart encapsulates one of the great ironies of Hillary Clinton's bid for the presidency. Many of the very same feminists who were her most ardent supporters as first lady are now fiercely opposed to her historic bid to become the first female president of the United States. The woman once described by Susan Faludi as a symbol of "the joy of female independence" now evokes ambivalence, disdain and, sometimes, outright vitriol. The right wing's favorite "femi-nazi" now has to contend with Jane Fonda comparing her to "a ventriloquist for the patriarchy with a skirt and a vagina."[5]

So what's up with the Hillary-bashing? "Women don't trust Hillary. They see her as an opportunist; many feel betrayed by her," wrote Susan Douglas in a May *In These Times* article titled "Why Women Hate Hillary." A month later, in her *Newsweek* column, Anna Quindlen declared, "The truth is that Senator Clinton has a woman problem."

Not exactly true, as it turns out. Hillary Clinton was the number-one choice of 42 percent of likely Democratic primary women voters in a recent Zogby survey, compared with 19 percent for Barack Obama and 15 percent for John Edwards. And her favorable rating among independent women is a whopping twenty-one points higher than among independent men.

Let's be clear: Hillary has a "feminist problem," and more so with those who lean left.

---

5. Fonda had said in an interview with *LA Weekly*: "It may be that a feminist, progressive man would do better in the White House than a ventriloquist for the patriarchy with a skirt and a vagina." Fonda denied that her comment had been directed specifically at Clinton, and *The Nation* ran a correction regretting the confusion.

At first glance, the fault line dividing feminists in their view of Hillary Clinton is merely a matter of ideology. On one side are the mainstream moderate women's organizations such as NOW and EMILY's List, facing off against more radical progressive feminists, especially those opposed to the Iraq War. Some of her supporters claim that much of the anger is inspired by her now-infamous 2002 Congressional vote. "It's about this one vote, which was not to invade Iraq but to authorize the president to wage war. I can't understand how this can be held up against a lifetime of important political work," says NOW president Kim Gandy.

Antiwar sentiments run high indeed, but when it comes to feminism and feminists, the "Hillary divide" also mirrors a deeper debate over the relationship between gender and political power. The ambivalence over Hillary's candidacy has just as much to do with increasing skepticism about the value of making it to the top.

"Having a woman in the White House won't necessarily do a damn thing for progressive feminism," writes *Bitch* magazine founder Lisa Jervis in *LiP* magazine. "Though the dearth of women in electoral politics is so dire as to make supporting a woman—any woman—an attractive proposition, even if it's just so she can serve as a role model for others who'll do the job better eventually, it's ultimately a trap. Women who do nothing to enact feminist policies will be elected and backlash will flourish. I can hear the refrain now: 'They've finally gotten a woman in the White House, so why are feminists still whining about equal pay?'"

Jervis's views were echoed by her peers on the blog Feministing, where Jen Moseley wrote, "As women sign up to work with
anyone but Senator Clinton, of course, they're being asked why.
That's the bad news. The good news is they're all giving the same
answer. Being a woman does not get you the automatic support of
women. There's no vagina litmus test, people."

Simply breaking the glass ceiling, once a cherished goal of
all feminists, has lost much of its appeal, especially after seven
years of the Bush administration. Over the course of his presidency, George W. Bush has appointed women to some of the most
prominent positions in his administration—all the while working
to undermine women's rights across the board. So it is that we
witnessed a fierce assault on women's reproductive rights even as
Condoleezza Rice became the first African-American woman to
make secretary of state.

Opting for Edwards or Obama—who are often perceived as
more liberal—becomes an attractive proposition for feminists who
believe "gender is not the only thing, not even the most important
thing in feminism," as Center For New Words program director Jaclyn Friedman puts it. "Hillary's not my friend. She's not
actually progressive. The fact that she's a woman is an unfortunate red herring." Feminist principles may be better served, she
claims, by electing a truly liberal candidate who will move us
further toward a more progressive and therefore more equitable
future—an imperative that feels all the more urgent after eight

years of Bush. "Things are so bad in this country, and the person we elect is going to be so important," she says. "The whole put-a-woman-in-the-White-House seems too abstract and theoretical, a middle-class luxury."

To be fair, the women and the organizations supporting Hillary are hardly advocating a "vagina litmus test." As Gandy points out, NOW has supported male candidates in the past and is now backing Clinton because of "a demonstrated history" of her commitment to feminist ideals. Even Laura Liswood, co-founder of the White House Project, which is dedicated to putting women in office, fully embraces the idea that women should vote their politics rather than their gender, "if the choice is between a woman who doesn't represent you at all and a man who does."

But Liswood cautions against undervaluing what she calls "the power of the mirror, of knowing who it is we can be by who it is that we see." By becoming the first female president of the United States, Liswood says, Hillary would "change the whole memory scan of young people, in terms of...what leaders look like." Even Condoleezza Rice, reviled as she may be for her conservative views, has done her bit for gender equality simply by virtue of the position she occupies. "It's an important social progression. You can't write these women off just because we highly disagree with them," says former Planned Parenthood president Faye Wattleton, who now heads the Center for the Advancement of Women.

"It moves us toward a time when we can attack someone like her because of what she stands for and not because she is black or a woman, because we already know that the country won't go up in smoke because we had an African-American woman from Alabama as secretary of state."

Clinton's supporters also argue that women candidates are unfairly subjected to higher standards, especially by women themselves. It's why antiwar feminist organizations like CodePink are less likely to give her a pass for her Iraq vote than they would, say, John Edwards. Explaining the reasoning behind their "bird-dog Hillary" campaign to *The Nation*, founder Medea Benjamin wore her double standard on her sleeve: "You expect more of a woman."

When it comes to presidential politics, this double standard also works in subtler ways. "There's not one man of either party who is at the top of the race right now who, if he were a woman, would be taken seriously," says White House Project's Marie Wilson. "We wouldn't tolerate the lack of experience or the marital history [of Rudy Giuliani]. If Obama were a woman, and I don't care how articulate or wonderful, we'd be telling her that she didn't have enough experience." Or, as Susan Estrich wrote in her 2005 book, *The Case for Hillary Clinton*: "Imagine if Hillary weren't a woman. She'd simply be the best-qualified candidate, with absolutely everything going for her.... If she were a he—Harry Rodham, let's say—the Democratic Party would be thrilled." Of course, come 2007, the party establishment is suitably enthused about Clinton. And for their part, progressive feminists would say that their problem with Hillary Clinton is not that she is a woman but that she has turned out to be no better than Harry Rodham.

Still, there's no question that Clinton bears an extra burden, not least because her victory would represent such a historic breakthrough. "The fantasy was that the first woman president would be someone who would turn the whole lousy system inside out and upside down. Instead the first significant woman contender is someone who seems to have the system down to a fine art," wrote Quindlen in her column.

Yet most feminists recognize that the chance of a true-blue lefty becoming the first female president is about as likely as that proverbial snowball's. Much as we like to bemoan our nation's backward ways in matters of female leadership, the kind of women who actually make it to the top in other parts of the world—leaving aside Chile's Michelle Bachelet—are cut from the same cloth as their male counterparts. Susan Douglas may accuse her of epitomizing "the Genghis Khan principle of American politics," but Hillary Clinton is not a patch on dear old Maggie Thatcher or Indira Gandhi, and she's definitely left of Germany's Angela Merkel.

At least part of the problem with Hillary is Hillary, as in her outsized and often caricatured public persona, which makes it hard to figure out just who she is. Is she a misunderstood moderate, accused of selling out positions she never held? Ruth Mandel, director of the Eagleton Institute of Politics at Rutgers University, certainly thinks so: "She is a centrist. She is a political pragmatist in the most solid American tradition."

Or is she a much-maligned liberal, whose Senate voting record on critical issues places her even with Obama and solidly to the left of progressive favorite John Edwards? So say the ratings of Americans for Democratic Action. Then there are those who label her the ultimate political operator, ever eager to trade principle for poll numbers. Her many critics certainly have no shortage of evidence to muster toward their cause. Claims made on either side of the "Hillary divide" are varied, confusing, often contradictory and sometimes compelling—perhaps because the debate over Hillary is very often not about Hillary at all.

In a 1993 *Time* magazine cover story, Margaret Carlson described the then–first lady as "the medium through which the remaining anxieties over feminism are being played out." In 2007, however, Hillary Clinton's presidential bid is becoming a lightning rod for a debate *within* feminism, and over its goals. What do we liberated women want: to join the clubhouse or burn it down?

Forty years after the launch of the modern women's movement, there are still no easy answers to that question. And it is why, once you get past the rhetoric, the emotion Hillary Clinton most often evokes is painful ambivalence, even among her harshest feminist critics. "Women are especially hard on Hillary because she's such a Rorschach and we all want her to be exactly like us, whoever we are," said Ephron in a recent *Salon* article. But feminists will also just as readily acknowledge the high price of playing with the big boys, even when they don't like her one bit. "She tried to be something different [as a first lady], and she was ultimately beaten into submission—by the media, the voters, the politicos," says Friedman. "I don't know what I would expect her to do. I couldn't expect myself to do better in the same place. I really don't."

For all her skepticism about the value of electing minorities to high office and her personal affinity for Edwards, Jervis says she balks at the idea of voting for a white male in the Democratic primary when she has the historic opportunity to choose otherwise. "I'm not sure what will happen when I actually step into the voting booth and have to pull that lever," she says. But she has no doubt that if Hillary Clinton does make it past the primaries, "I know I'll have an emotional reaction to a Hillary candidacy. It is going to be meaningful to me."

Whether or not Hillary wins the nomination, makes it to the big white house or falls by the wayside, her admirers and critics alike understand that she has done far more than any of her predecessors for women in national politics simply by running. She is the first woman to be the front-runner for her party's presidential nomination—with the blessing of the old boys' club, i.e., the Democratic Leadership Council, no less.

But equally important, as Faye Wattleton points out, whatever her failings, Hillary Clinton is no Pat Schroeder, whose

1988 presidential bid ended early and ignominiously in a flood of tears. "This is not a candidate who is going to dissolve in the enormous heat of presidential politics," she says. Over the past fifteen years, every aspect of Hillary's life has been subjected to the kind of scrutiny—and many times abuse—that would make male politicians cry. As the latest crop of biographies demonstrate, the media's appetite for Hillary "exposés" shows no signs of waning. Carl Bernstein's *A Woman in Charge*, and *Her Way: The Hopes and Ambitions of Hillary Rodham Clinton*, by Jeff Gerth and Don Van Natta Jr., spend 1,000-plus pages between them re-examining every personal, political, romantic and sartorial decision she's ever made, often with unflattering results. And there will be plenty more of the same over the next year. "Someone who can conduct herself with credibility under that kind of scrutiny and hold up to it is definitely opening the door for a future woman in the White House. She must be given credit for that," says Wattleton.

Hillary Clinton is the first female candidate—love her or hate her—who is impossible to dismiss simply because she is a woman, even by Republican strategists like Frank Luntz, who offered this caution: "Put gender aside. Just treat her like you would any other candidate." It's not exactly the end of patriarchy, but it's surely reason enough for all feminists—left, right or center—to cheer. ❖

Who Is Hillary Clinton?

BARBARA EHRENREICH, JULY 9, 2007

ne theory, which functions as a kind of cargo cult among some American liberals, is that behind the bland, smiling, exterior and the thick gauze of platitudes, crouches a fiery liberal feminist, ready, when she has finally amassed enough power—say in her second term as president—to spring forth and save the world.

If Carl Bernstein's exhausting 600-page biography, *A Woman in Charge: The Life of Hillary Rodham Clinton*, accomplishes anything, it should be to euthanize this touching hope. Hillary Rodham Clinton was always a moderate, given to technocratic centrism. In her lifetime, she has glided effortlessly from one side to another on key issues—the death penalty, for example, or entitlements for poor women and children—all the while maintaining the self-righteousness granted, supposedly, by her Methodist God.

In Bernstein's account the mystery of Hillary is largely explained by her fraught relationship with Bill. She was pretty

enough, but an awkward, wonky, young woman; he was a brilliant, ambitious, sexually magnetic stud; and in following him to
Arkansas she seemed to have thrown her future as, say, a high-profile Washington public interest lawyer. "My friends and family
thought I had lost my mind," Bernstein quotes her as saying. He
insists that theirs is, or sometimes was, a deep connection—sexual,
intellectual and committed to their joint political "journey."

But it was a relationship irreparably twisted by Bill's compulsive priapism, which seems to have put the young Hillary into a
permanent rage, but, perversely, also bound them ever more tight-
ly together. In the unstable molecule we used to call "Billary," he
was the id and she was the super-ego, a role she clearly relished
even as it poisoned her with resentment. As Bernstein argues, Bill's
dalliances only increased her power in the relationship, since, as
a rising political star, he needed a smart, loyal wife to fend off
the press and publicly stand by her man. When they entered the
White House in 1993 on the heels of the Gennifer Flowers scandal, the outwardly forgiving Hillary was at the height of her power, eager to assume the "co-presidency."

In Bernstein's account, which strives nobly for fairness, Hillary's early behavior as first lady was stunningly arrogant. She dis-
dained the press, alienated the White House staff, turned on her
close friend Vince Foster (who responded by committing suicide)
and appalled Al Gore by trying to claim the West Wing office
suite traditionally reserved for the vice president. She demanded a

cabinet position, and when that was overruled, insisted on leading Clinton's efforts at healthcare reform, despite the objections of Health and Human Services secretary Donna Shalala, who was no less a feminist than Hillary.

Hillary's attempt to create a national health insurance system—which she will have to undertake a second time as a presidential candidate—was a disaster in every way. Procedurally, she screwed up by conducting the planning under conditions of extreme secrecy, not even bothering to reach out to potentially supportive members of Congress, never mind the usual populist trimming of few televised town meetings. What Bernstein omits is her out-of-hand dismissal of the kind of single-payer system the Canadians have, which led to a tortured, 1,300-page piece of legislation that almost no one could comprehend. The bottom line, unnoted by Bernstein, is that, despite the right's charges of "socialized medicine," her plan would have maintained the nation's largest private insurance companies' death grip on American healthcare.

Now it was Hillary's turn to be the liability, rather than the super-ego, in the Billary team. Revelations about her involvement in an obscure land deal in Arkansas suggested a conflict of interest between her prior role as both first lady of that state and an attorney at Little Rock's Rose law firm. The real scandal is that she had worked for Rose at all, which represented the notorious anti-labor firms Tyson Poultry and Walmart, but Bernstein makes nothing of that.

Soon Hillary, facing the possibility of a criminal indictment, was undertaking to recreate herself in a softer, cuddlier, mode. She wrote a book called *It Takes a Village*, on the importance of children, notable only for its sappiness and the spurious claim that her own family of origin had been idyllic. She wore pink for a defensive press conference held in the White House's Pink Library, where Bernstein politely describes her as "preternaturally calm," though the impression—with her eyelids drooping and her voice slowed, was of over-medication.

Having failed with her own hard-won health portfolio, and besieged now by the press for her sleazy deals in Arkansas, Hillary began to flail—reaching out for help from New Age healer Marianne Williamson. Compared to the Bush-era White House scandals, the Whitewater land deal was microscopic—no one died or was tortured—and surely the "vast right-wing conspiracy" played a role in keeping it alive. But as Bernstein writes, what magnified it out of proportion was Hillary's own pattern of "Jesuitical lying, evasion, and…stonewalling." She was not in the habit of being wrong—that was Bill's job—and admitting to wrong-doing was simply not in her repertoire.

It took Monica Lewinsky to restore Hillary's upper hand within her marriage and, with it, her self-confidence. Apparently believing her husband's protestations of innocence, she took over the management of his defense within the White House, and, disconcertingly, started exploring the possibility of running for the Senate from New York State at the very same moment the already-elected Senate was voting on Bill's impeachment. But even in this time of extreme crisis—for her marriage as well as the presidency—she could not resist asserting to a family adviser that "my husband may have his faults, but he has never lied to me." Bernstein, ever the gentleman, comments only that "that statement speaks for itself."

Most of the lies Bernstein documents along the way are, in the great scheme of things, inconsequential and well in the past. But Bernstein breaks off his biography somewhat abruptly after Hillary's election to the Senate, where she distinguished herself by helping push through a statute forbidding flag-burning. For a current and far more disturbing bit of mendacity, we have to turn to another new Hillary book, *Her Way: The Hopes and Ambitions of Hillary Rodham Clinton*, by Jeff Gerth and Don Van Natta Jr. As a presidential candidate, Hillary has repeatedly and confusingly claimed that she did not vote to authorize the war in Iraq, only to give Bush the authority to pursue a war if he should decide to. What she doesn't mention is that she voted against an amendment to the war resolution, proposed by Senator Carl Levin, that would have required the president to return to Congress for a war authorization if diplomatic efforts failed.

Worse, she has dodged the question of whether she ever actually read the full text of the 2002 National Intelligence Estimate, which was offered as a *casus belli* despite its equivocations on the subject of Saddam Hussein's purported WMDs. "If she did not bother to read the complete intelligence reports," Gerth and Van Natta observe, "then she did not do enough homework on the decision she has called the most important of her life. If she did read them, she chose to make statements to justify her vote for war that were not supported by the available intelligence." Since the start of her candidacy, antiwar Democrats have implored her to admit that she made a mistake on Iraq, which she stubbornly, even childishly, refuses to do.

In the end, the question of who Hillary is seems almost a bit anthropomorphic. Surely she has loved, laughed and suffered in the usual human ways, but what we are left with is a sleek, well-funded, power-seeking machine encased in a gleaming carapace of self-righteousness. She's already enjoyed considerable power, both as a senator and a "co-president," and in the ways that counted, she blew it. What Americans need most, after fifteen years of presidential crimes high and low, is to wash their hands of all the sleaze, blood, and other bodily fluids, and find themselves a president who is neither a Clinton nor a Bush. ❖

A Progressive Who Can Win—And Govern

ELLEN CHESLER, NOVEMBER 26, 2007

This piece appeared as part of a forum in which Nation *writers explained their support for particular Democratic presidential candidates. Other contributors included John Nichols on Joseph Biden, Bruce Shapiro on Christopher Dodd, Katherine S. Newman on John Edwards, Richard Kim on Mike Gravel, Gore Vidal on Dennis Kucinich, Rocky Anderson on Bill Richardson and Michael Eric Dyson on Barack Obama.*

The stakes could not be higher. The treacherous reign of Bush/Cheney has seriously weakened our democracy. To the "war on terror" we have been asked to sacrifice fundamental human rights and civil liberties. Meanwhile, a newly conservative Supreme Court majority ruthlessly guts longstanding state obligations to protect equal rights and expand opportunity. Abroad, the good will America briefly enjoyed after 9/11 has been squandered by Bush's cowboy diplomacy.

Democrats must win in 2008. We must take back the White House with a candidate who adheres to core progressive principles but is also able to build coalitions and sustain majorities across ideological and partisan divides—first to win and then to govern successfully.

Hillary Clinton is that candidate. She is intelligent, energetic and disciplined. She has shown herself to be warm and likable. She has turned an interminable campaign into an asset through effective campaigning and six stellar debate performances. She stumbled momentarily in the seventh round under withering personal attack by six angry men. Next time out, she will definitely need those flashy boxing gloves her AFSCME endorsers provided afterward.

But she will prevail, just as she did in her Senate races, the second of which she won with an astonishing 67 percent of the vote, taking thirty-seven of the forty-one "red" counties in New York that George W. Bush carried two years earlier. Indeed, she may be the most electable of the Democrats—and not because she "stands for nothing," as the chattering classes often allege. Rather, Clinton wonkishly acknowledges the complexity of issues and modestly admits to not having all the answers. She has learned to respect people with whom she disagrees and to succeed within a system that requires compromise. She works hard and exudes competence and integrity. Ordinary voters, and especially independent women whose swing votes will determine the outcome of this election, find this a relief. They are tired of overweening ego and bluster in politics. These women, along with disenchanted Republicans and many others who have never voted before but are registering in large numbers this time, will provide the margin of her victory.

But what of Clinton's core convictions? A common canard, often repeated in these pages, is that she's not a true progressive. But actions speak louder than words. Her voting record measures up well on scorecards compiled by the major labor unions, the ACLU, Americans for Democratic Action, Planned Parenthood and other progressive organizations.

Indeed, Clinton has been an outspoken advocate for raising the minimum wage. Though a longtime supporter of free trade, she endorses policies that enforce stronger labor and environmental standards abroad, and she voted against the Central American Free Trade Agreement. Her green energy agenda, partially financed by taking away tax breaks for oil companies, will create thousands of jobs. With nearly half the labor force now women, she is leading efforts to achieve pay equity. Influential as first lady in passing the Family and Medical Leave Act, she now proposes paid leave and greater workplace flexibility. She supports universal preschool education. Pushing tax fairness, she announced early on that she would crack down on loopholes for Wall Street fund managers.

Universal healthcare is, of course, her signature issue. Her plan ends Bush-era tax breaks to the very rich in order to expand Congress's own healthcare plan to cover the country's nearly 50 million uninsured, while leaving in place private options for those content with what they already have. Her proposal builds in important regulations on private insurers—capping administrative costs and prohibiting cherry-picking on the basis of pre-existing conditions, genetic testing or other forms of discrimination. As first lady, she lobbied intensely for S-CHIP, which provides health coverage to children in poor working families. As a member of the Senate Armed Services Committee, she fashioned a bipartisan consensus to expand health coverage to uninsured veterans and their families.

Understandably sensitive to concerns about security, Clinton argues nonetheless that we can be safe and free. She led Democrats in the fight to restore habeas corpus rights to Guantánamo detainees held under the Military Commissions Act of 2006. Cajoling votes on both sides of the aisle, she came within several votes of beating back last year's legislation, winning praise from the Center for Constitutional Rights.

Clinton deserves special praise for her impassioned opposition to Supreme Court nominees John Roberts and Samuel Alito and to attorney general nominee Michael Mukasey. She's inventively exposed the Bush administration's assault on scientific integrity in evaluating stem cells, abstinence-only sex education, emergency contraception and abortion. By placing a hold on confirmation of the president's FDA appointee, she was able to gain over-the-counter access for the morning-after pill.

Some progressives cannot forgive her Iraq War vote, no matter how forcefully she now condemns the futility of the American effort and calls for a responsible withdrawal of our troops. Today we need to concentrate on how to exit Iraq and engage the UN in restoring order to the country. We need to address the Herculean task of returning professionalism and integrity to our own battered diplomatic and intelligence agencies and to our military. Clinton has the experience and stature to lead in the diplomatic talks she endorses with states like Iran and North Korea. She will restore our once-proud leadership in global efforts to alleviate poverty, promote health and sustain the environment. Recent clamor over a nonbinding resolution on Iran—which most Democrats supported and Barack Obama did not even vote on—should be understood as little more than disingenuous political theater.

And one more thing. I am supporting Hillary Clinton because I think she is the best candidate for this job, but I shamelessly want her to win because she is a woman. Obama tells me to get over my baby boomer fixations, but I look at the Supreme Court today, and I say not yet. I came of age in the 1960s and have spent a lifetime advancing women's rights and opportunities. Nothing will give me more confidence that those efforts are secure than to have Hillary Clinton choose my next Justice. ♣

The Weepy Witch and the Secret Muslim

KATHA POLLITT, FEBRUARY 4, 2008

The media are hopelessly sexist and relentlessly trivial. So much we've learned from the mass hysteria over Hillary Clinton's "emotional moment" in New Hampshire. (*Seattle Post-Intelligencer* columnist Robert L. Jamieson: "She morphed into a 'compassion brand'—like, irony of ironies, Kleenex"; *New York Times* columnist Maureen Dowd: "Can Hillary Cry Her Way Back to the White House?") Even Southern charmer John Edwards couldn't resist observing that a commander in chief needed "strength and resolve"—a view echoed by Fox commentator Dick Morris ("There could well come a time when there is such a serious threat to the United States that she breaks down") and given full misogynous display by nationally syndicated cartoonist Pat Oliphant's "Madam President Meets the Bad Guys," portraying a dumpy, tearful Hillary surrounded by Osama, Kim Jong Il and similar. All this fuss over a welling of the eyes so brief that if you blinked your

own you'd miss it. I have moments like that every day! This was
the Dean Scream all over again: a nano-nothing whipped into a
self-congratulatory media typhoon.

In the 24/7 chat room, reality never dawns: the narrative is
tweaked, not junked. Thus, when Hillary dared to win the New
Hampshire primary although pundits had already gleefully hus-
tled her off the stage, the script was quickly rewritten from Tears
Sink Woman to Tears Save Woman: 46 percent of women voters,
the silly dears, supported a "humanized" Hillary, according to exit
polls. (Bill Maher: "They wanted to see the robot cry.") But maybe
women supported Hillary this one time to protest cable blowhards
like Chris Matthews, who capped his long career of insane Hillary hatred with this zinger: "The reason she's a front-runner is
because her husband messed around." Or perhaps, as Susan Faludi
and Gail Collins suggested, middle-aged women see in Hillary a
calm and competent multi-tasker like themselves. Lost in the ker-
fuffle: Hillary won not only among women but also among voters
over 40 and those without a college degree.

I've written many times about sexist attacks on Hillary Clinton
as an old, ugly, castrating witch-and-what-rhymes-with-it, but Gloria Steinem's *New York Times* op-ed in defense of her, "Women Are
Never the Front-Runners," was not helpful, to put it mildly. "Gender is probably the most restricting force in American life," Steinem
wrote. "Black men were given the vote a half-century before wom-
en of any race were allowed to mark a ballot, and generally have

ascended to positions of power, from the military to the boardroom, before any women (with the possible exception of obedient family members in the latter)." Yes, black men got the vote first, although they could be lynched for using it. Shirley Chisholm, the black congresswoman who ran for president in 1972, did famously write, "Of my two handicaps, being female put many more obstacles in my path than being black." But Barack Obama is only the third black senator in the modern era; Deval Patrick is only the second black governor. It may be true, as Steinem suggests, that "the sex barrier [is] not taken as seriously as the racial one." But that doesn't mean the racial barrier really is less serious. It just means that the public expression of racism is beyond the pale in a way that the public expression of misogyny is not.

True, nobody's likely to compare Obama to Kleenex; there will be no cartoons involving watermelon and fried chicken. Instead, as his campaign becomes more of a threat, opponents will try to remove his "postracial" mantle. Already, e-mails circulate claiming he's a secret Muslim who took the oath of office on a Koran—indeed these rumors are so widespread MSNBC's Brian Williams asked Obama about them in the Nevada debate. Hillary's campaign strategist Mark Penn, and Hillary supporters black billionaire Robert Johnson and Representative Charles Rangel, have reminded the world of Obama's self-confessed teenage drug experiences. (The Clinton campaign claimed that when Johnson referred to Obama "doing something in the neighborhood—I won't say what he was doing, but he said it in the book," he merely meant community organizing. Yeah, right.) Most recently, *Washing Post* columnist Richard Cohen, mainstreaming attacks that have been bubbling for weeks in the right-wing blogosphere, floated the question of anti-Semitism because Obama belongs to a black megachurch run by the Rev. Jeremiah Wright Jr., whose house magazine last year honored Louis Farrakhan. "It's important to state right off that nothing in Obama's record suggests he harbors anti-Semitic views," Cohen writes, before going on to suggest exactly that. "I don't for a moment think that Obama shares Wright's views on Farrakhan. But the rap on Obama is that he is a fog of a man. We know little about him, and, for all my admiration of him, I wonder about his mettle." (In fact, Obama has denounced anti-Semitism many times and has said of Wright, "We don't agree on everything.") Meanwhile, Mitt Romney practices Mormonism, which until a 1978 "revelation" explicitly preached black inferiority and is still explicitly sexist in about a thousand ways. Mike Huckabee gets a free pass from the media for being a Southern Baptist minister who in 1998 went on record supporting the denomination's new doctrine of wifely submission.

Barring an Edwards upset, the Democratic Party is going to nominate either a white woman or a black man as its presidential candidate. This is indeed a testament to how far we have come. Still, it wouldn't take much innuendo and truth-twisting to turn Barack Obama into the Muslim Al Sharpton—surely no more than it's taken to turn Hillary Clinton into the lesbian Lady Macbeth. That's why it's crucial not to get into an oppression sweepstakes. If the campaign becomes a competition between race and gender—Frederick Douglass versus Elizabeth Cady Stanton, as one *New York Times* graphic put it—the winner on election day will be whichever white man the Republican Party nominates. ❖

Racial Politics, Clinton Style

ARI BERMAN, FEBRUARY 4, 2008

In the escalating battle between his campaign and Hillary Clinton's over civil rights history and racial politics, Barack Obama launched a pre-emptive strike of civility earlier this week. "I don't want the campaign at this stage to degenerate to so much tit-for-tat, back-and-forth, that we lose sight of why we are doing this," Obama said Monday while campaigning in Nevada. "Bill Clinton and Hillary Clinton have historically been on the right side of civil rights issues." Clinton responded by saying that "when it comes to civil rights and our commitment to diversity, when it comes to our heroes—President John F. Kennedy and Dr. King—Senator Obama and I are on the same side." A truce was declared by the national media.

It didn't last. On Tuesday, the Clinton campaign released "talking points" to reporters that kept the issue alive. "Over the last few days, the Obama campaign has distributed recent comments from Senator Clinton and President Clinton to suggest that they were diminishing Senator Obama's candidacy and casting aspersions on the legacy of

Martin Luther King," the talking points stated. "There are media reports that the Obama campaign is distributing a memo in an effort to sensationalize and drive this story. This is unfortunate, especially coming from a campaign that says it is about bringing people together." The release went on to declare that "Nobody wants to see the injection of race or gender into this campaign."

It's a little late for that. No matter who injected race or gender into this campaign, it's not going away. Obama and Clinton had nothing but nice things to say about the other's civil rights record at Tuesday's debate in Nevada. But at the same time, the subject of race could rear its ugly head at any time. After all, race has always been used as a wedge issue in campaigns, including by the Clintons, dating back to Bill's run for the presidency in 1992.

During his famed "Sister Souljah" moment in June 1992, Bill Clinton went before Jesse Jackson's Rainbow Coalition and condemned the black rapper for seeming to justify the Los Angeles riots and advocate the killing of whites. "Her comments before and after Los Angeles were filled with the kind of hatred that you do not honor," Clinton said. His remarks were cheered by establishment pundits, but they stirred controversy and resentment among prominent black political figures. "Clinton's speech was arrogant, and it was cheap," longtime civil rights activist Roger Wilkins told *The New York Times*. "He came there to show suburban whites that he can stand up to blacks. It was contrived." The Rev. Jesse Jackson accused Clinton of staging "a very well-planned sneak attack, without the courage to confront but with a calculation to embarrass," intended "purely to appeal to conservative whites." Harlem Congressman Charles Rangel, now a top supporter of Hillary Clinton, labeled Bill's behavior "insulting."

During the campaign, Clinton angered African-Americans in other ways, too. He went back to Arkansas to preside over the execution of a mentally ill black man, Rickey Ray Rector, who'd been convicted of shooting a white cop; he played golf on numerous occasions at a segregated country club in Little Rock; he was photographed at a Georgia prison in front of an all-black chain gang.

These moments are now mostly forgotten, and today Clinton is widely regarded as the "first black president," in Toni Morrison's immortal words. As the junior senator from New York, Hillary Clinton forged close ties with New York's black community. President Clinton chose to base his foundation's operations in Harlem. No right-thinking person would accuse the Clintons of being insufficiently committed to racial equality or civil rights.

Yet as Hillary Clinton fell in the polls last winter, her campaign and its supporters, whether intentionally or not, began floating racially coded attacks against Obama. They started with Obama's admitted use of marijuana and "maybe a little blow when you could afford it" as a high schooler in Hawaii, described briefly with refreshing candor in his 1995 memoir, *Dreams From My Father.* On December 12, Clinton's New Hampshire co-chair Bill Shaheen insinuated that if Obama were the Democratic nominee, "one of the things [Republicans] certainly are going to jump on is his drug use," asking questions like, "'When was the last time? Did you ever give drugs to anyone? Did you sell them to anyone?'" The Clinton campaign quickly disassociated themselves from Shaheen's tasteless remarks.

There is evidence that the Clinton campaign itself was pushing similar tactics. A day before Shaheen's remarks, veteran reporter Thomas B. Edsall wrote a column on the Huffington Post titled "As Iowa Nears, Clinton Allies Quietly Raise Obama's Cocaine Use." Edsall didn't name the "allies" but reported that Democratic activists had received e-mails from Clinton partisans with a link to an *Iowa Independent* story headlined "The Politics of Obama's Past Cocaine Use." Members of Clinton's campaign urged reporters to dig deeper into this matter.

On December 13, Clinton's top strategist, Mark Penn, appeared on MSNBC's *Hardball* and kept repeating the word "cocaine," drawing a strong rebuke from Edwards strategist Joe Trippi and supporters of Obama. The topic of drugs died down but other smears took its place, namely the right-wing e-mail lie that Obama is a Muslim. Two Clinton county chairs in Iowa were caught forwarding an e-mail claiming that Obama attended a madrassa as a child in Indonesia, where he lived from the age of 6 until 10. Bob Kerrey, a former Nebraska senator and prominent Clinton supporter, referred to the Illinois senator as "Barack Hussein Obama" on national TV and then declared that there was nothing wrong with

Obama's having attended a "secular madrassa."

Clinton supporters also raised the issue of race in terms of electability. "We've got to keep an eye on electability," said a Clinton precinct captain in Cherokee, Iowa. "Is America ready for a black president?" Obama supporters never asked whether America was ready for a woman president.

After Clinton's loss in Iowa, some of her supporters adopted a harder edge, trying to paint Obama as a radical black man; another unelectable Sharpton or Jackson. "He is the candidate of the 'identity left,'" one Clinton supporter told the Huffington Post. According to Tom Edsall, Clinton aides pointed to Obama's "alliances with 'left-wing' intellectuals in Chicago's Hyde Park community," on the city's South Side and "his liberal voting record on criminal defendants' rights," such as opposition to mandatory minimum sentences for federal crimes, raising the age-old fear of black politicians being soft on crime. One Clinton adviser told *The Guardian*: "If you have a social need, you're with Hillary. If you want Obama to be your imaginary hip black friend and you're young and you have no social needs, then he's cool." Following New Hampshire, New York Attorney General Andrew Cuomo, a Clinton supporter, said in response to a question about retail campaigning in Iowa and New Hampshire: "You can't shuck and jive at a press conference. All those moves you can make with the press don't work when you're in someone's living room." This was interpreted by some in the media to be a racial slur against Obama, but there was no mention of Obama in the question or the answer.

There was also an attempt by Clinton partisans to create a rift between Obama's African-American supporters and Latinos, who play an increasing role in states like Nevada and California. "The Hispanic voter—and I want to say this very carefully—has not shown a lot of willingness or affinity to support black candidates," Clinton pollster Sergio Bendixen told *The New Yorker*. A Democratic operative called this the "Do the Right Thing factor," after Spike Lee's famous film about tensions between blacks and Italians in Brooklyn.

It's difficult to know whether or not the Clinton campaign orchestrated or encouraged such statements as part of a larger strategy, or whether surrogates, supporters and even campaign aides were just acting on their own. Either way, the comments about race created a disturbing pattern.

The increasingly nasty simmer came to a boil in New Hampshire and after, when Clinton appeared to give President Lyndon Johnson more credit than Martin Luther King Jr. for the signing of the Voting Rights Act, a crowning achievement of the civil rights movement. Clinton claimed that her words were twisted out of context; she meant that it took a sympathetic president to sign the act into law. Yet some prominent black politicians, like South Carolina Congressman James Clyburn, argued that if not for the blood, sweat and tears of the civil rights movement, LBJ would never have had the political space to sign the law—a fact Hillary later acknowledged—and a fierce war of words broke out between the two campaigns and their supporters.

The discussion grew even more heated when Robert Johnson, the founder of Black Entertainment Television, said the following while introducing Senator Clinton at a campaign stop in South Carolina: "As an African-American, I am frankly insulted that the Obama campaign would imply that we are so stupid that we would think Hillary and Bill Clinton, who have been deeply and emotionally involved in black issues—when Barack Obama was doing something in the neighborhood; I won't say what he was doing, but he said it in his book." After not so subtly injecting the subject of Obama's teenage drug use back into the campaign, Johnson continued, "that kind of campaign behavior does not resonate with me, or a guy that says, 'I want to be a reasonable, likable Sidney Poitier [in] *Guess Who's Coming to Dinner.*" In a matter of minutes, Johnson, himself a controversial figure in the black community, managed to hurl a handful of racial stereotypes, front and center, into the campaign.

Washington Post columnist Eugene Robinson wrote that "it's surprising that the Clinton campaign has been so aggressive in keeping the race issue alive." He postulated a few theories. "The charitable explanation would be that the Clintons are, in terms of their political position, simply disoriented," Robinson wrote. "They are accustomed to Bill Clinton's campaigns, in which African-

American support was pretty much assumed." There were two less charitable theories. "It could be that the idea is to engage Obama in so much tit-for-tat combat that his image as a new kind of post-partisan politician is tarnished." Then Robinson came to the Sister Souljah proposition. "Is it possible that accusing Obama and his campaign of playing the race card might create doubt in the minds of the moderate, independent white voters who now seem so enamored of the young black senator?"

Indeed, after flinging mud at Obama for weeks, the Clintons turned the tables and claimed to be the victims of racially tinged attacks—coming from Obama! Bill alleged that the Obama campaign had called Hillary "a racist." Congressman John Lewis, a civil rights pioneer and Clinton supporter, cited "a deliberate, systematic attempt on the part of some people in the Obama camp to really fan the flame of race and really try to distort what Senator Clinton said." Added Charles Rangel: "How race got into this thing is because Obama said 'race.'" (Rangel also accused Obama of writing about his adolescent drug experimentation in order to "sell books.")

The confrontation seemed to be helping neither candidate, which is likely why Obama called a truce and Clinton accepted. The hope is that from now on, as evidenced by the surprisingly civil debate in Nevada, the Democratic campaign will stay above the fray. But don't count on it. Hillary hasn't had a "Sister Souljah" moment, but she also might not need one. Courting African-American voters, in South Carolina and elsewhere, and accusing the Obama campaign of playing the race card while employing racial arguments against Obama—by her campaign and by unscripted surrogates—could be seen as a textbook example of Clinton-style triangulation. ❖

Race to the Bottom

BETSY REED, MAY 19, 2008

In the course of Hillary Clinton's historic run for the White House—in which she became the first woman ever to prevail in a state-level presidential primary contest—she has been likened to Lorena Bobbitt (by Tucker Carlson); a "hellish housewife" (Leon Wieseltier); and described as "witchy," a "she-devil," "anti-male" and "a stripteaser" (Chris Matthews). Her loud and hearty laugh has been labeled "the cackle," her voice compared to "fingernails on a blackboard" and her posture said to look "like everyone's first wife standing outside a probate court." As one Fox News commentator put it, "When Hillary Clinton speaks, men hear, Take out the garbage." Rush Limbaugh, who has no qualms about subjecting audiences to the spectacle of his own bloated physique, asked his listeners, "Will this country want to actually watch a woman get older before their eyes on a daily basis?" Perhaps most damaging of all to her electoral prospects, very early on Clinton was deemed "unlikable." Although other factors also account for that dislike, much of the venom she elicits ("Iron my shirt," "How do we beat the bitch?") is clearly gender-specific.

Watching the brass ring of the presidency slip out of Clinton's grasp as she is buffeted by this torrent of misogyny, women—white women, that is, and mainstream feminists especially—have rallied to her defense. On January 8, after Barack Obama beat Clinton in the Iowa caucuses, Gloria Steinem published a *New York Times* op-ed titled "Women Are Never Front-Runners." "Gender is probably the most restricting force in American life, whether the question is who must be in the kitchen or who could be in the White House," Steinem wrote. Next came Clinton's famous "misting-over moment" in New Hampshire in response to a question from a woman about the stress of modern campaigning. For that display of emotion, Clinton was derided, on the one hand, as calculating and chameleonlike—"It could be that big girls don't cry...but it could be that if they do they win," said Chris Matthews—and, on the other, as lacking "strength and resolve," as her Democratic rival John Edwards put it, in a jab at the perennial Achilles' heel of women candidates. Riding a wave of female sympathy, Clinton won New Hampshire in what was dubbed an "anti–Chris Matthews vote."

Thus, feminist opposition to the sexist treatment of Hillary Clinton has morphed into support for the candidate herself. In February Robin Morgan published a reprise of her famous 1970 essay "Goodbye to All That," exhorting women to embrace Clinton as a protest against "sociopathic woman-hating." In the *Los*

Angeles Times, Leslie Bennetts, author of *The Feminine Mistake*, wrote of older female voters fed up with the media's dismissive treatment of Clinton: "There are signs the slumbering beast may be waking up—and she's not in a happy mood." A recent *New York* magazine article titled "The Feminist Reawakening: Hillary Clinton and the Fourth Wave" described how "it isn't just the 'hot flash cohort'...that broke for Clinton. Women in their thirties and forties—at once discomfited and galvanized by the sexist tenor of the media coverage, by the nastiness of the watercooler talk in the office, by the realization that the once-foregone conclusion of Clinton-as-president might never come to be—did too."

The sexist attacks on Clinton are outrageous and deplorable, but there's reason to be concerned about her becoming the vehicle for a feminist reawakening. For one thing, feminist sympathy for her has begotten an "oppression sweepstakes" in which a number of her prominent supporters, dismayed at her upstaging by Obama, have declared a contest between racial and gender bias and named sexism the greater scourge. This maneuver is not only unhelpful for coalition-building but obstructs understanding of how sexism and racism have played out in this election in different (and interrelated) ways.

Yet what is most troubling—and what has the most serious implications for the feminist movement—is that the Clinton campaign has used her rival's race against him. In the name of demonstrating her superior "electability," she and her surrogates have invoked the racist and sexist playbook of the right—in which swaggering macho cowboys are entrusted to defend the country—seeking to define Obama as too black, too foreign, too different to be president at a moment of high anxiety about national security. This subtly but distinctly racialized political strategy did not create the media feeding frenzy around the Rev. Jeremiah Wright that is now weighing Obama down, but it has positioned Clinton to take advantage of the opportunities the controversy has presented. And the Clinton campaign's use of this strategy has many nonwhite and nonmainstream feminists crying foul.

While 2008 was never going to be a "postracial" campaign, the early racially tinged skirmishes between the Clinton and Obama camps seemed containable. There were references by Clinton campaign officials to Obama's admission of past drug use; the tit-for-tat over Clinton's tone-deaf but historically accurate statement that Martin Luther King needed Lyndon Johnson for his civil rights dreams to be realized; and insinuations that Obama is a token, unqualified, overreaching—that he's all pretty words, "fairy tales" and no action.

From the point of view of Obama's supporters, the edge was taken off some of these conflicts by the mere fact of his stunning electoral success, built as it was on significant white support. Melissa Harris-Perry, a professor of politics and African-American studies at Princeton and an Obama volunteer, recalls that for black Americans "Iowa was an astonishing moment— watching Barack win the caucus felt like Reconstruction. There was something powerful about feeling as though you were a full citizen." In democracy, Harris-Lacewell explains, "the ruled and rulers are supposed to be the same people. The idea that black folks could be engaged in the process of being rulers over not just black folks but over the nation as a whole struck me as very powerful."

Soon enough, however, that powerful idea came under attack.

"More than any single thing, that moment with Bill Clinton in South Carolina represents the rupture that was coming," says Harris-Lacewell. The moment occurred in late January, when the former president compared Obama's landslide win, in which he received a major boost from African-American voters, to Jesse Jackson's victories there in 1984 and 1988. Because the former president offered the comparison unprompted, in response to a question that had nothing to do with Jackson or race, the statement was widely read as chalking up Obama's win to his blackness alone and thus attempting to marginalize him as a doomed minority candidate with limited appeal. Obama was now "the black candidate," in the words of one Clinton strategist quoted by the AP.

By March, multiple videos of Wright, Obama's former pastor, had popped up on YouTube and had begun to play on an endless loop in the right-wing media. "God damn America for treating your citizens as less than human," Wright inveighed, reciting a litany of racial complaints. And he said in his sermon immediately following 9/11, "America's chickens are coming home to roost."

According to Smith College professor Paula Giddings, author of a new biography of Ida B. Wells, *Ida: A Sword Among Lions and the Campaign Against Lynching*, Wright's angry invocation of race and nation tapped into a reservoir of doubt about the very American-ness of African-Americans. "American citizenship has always been racialized as white. Who is a true American? Are African-Americans true Americans? That has been the question," she says.

In Obama's case—given his mixed-race lineage, his Kenyan father, his experiences growing up in Indonesia, his middle name (Hussein)—questions about his devotion to America carry a special potency, as xenophobia mingles with racism to create a poisonous brew. The toxicity is further heightened in this post-9/11 atmosphere, in which an image of Obama in Somali dress is understood as a slur and e-mails claiming that he is a "secret Muslim" schooled in a madrassa spread virally, along with rumors that he took the oath of office on a Koran. The madrassa and Koran canards have been thoroughly debunked, but still they persist—and few have been willing to stand up and say, So what if he is a Muslim? For her part, Clinton, asked on *60 Minutes* whether Obama was a Muslim, said, "There is nothing to base that on, as far as I know."

Giddings calls the Wright association a "litmus test" that Obama must pass, saying, "It will be interesting to see if a man of color, a man who's cosmopolitan, can be the quintessential symbol of America" as its president.

Obama initially responded to that challenge with his speech in Philadelphia on March 18. While condemning Wright's words, he placed them in a historical context of racial oppression and said, "I can no more disown him than I can disown the black community." (More recently, of course, Obama did renounce him.) But in the Philadelphia speech, called "A More Perfect Union," Obama also outlined a racially universal definition of American citizenship and affirmed his commitment to represent all Americans as president. "I chose to run for the presidency at this moment in history because I believe deeply that we cannot solve the challenges of our time unless we solve them together—unless we perfect our union by understanding that we have different stories, but we hold common hopes; that we may not look the same and we may not have come from the same place, but we all want to move in the same direction."

A mere three days after Obama spoke those words, Bill Clinton made this statement in North Carolina about a potential Clinton-McCain general election matchup: "I think it'd be a great thing if we had an election year where you had two people who loved this country and were devoted to the interest of this country. And people could actually ask themselves who is right on these issues, instead of all this other stuff that always seems to intrude itself on our politics." Whether or not this statement constituted McCarthyism, as one Obama surrogate alleged and as Clinton supporters vigorously denied, the timing of the remark made its meaning quite clear: controversies relating to Obama's race render him less fit than either Hillary or McCain to run for president as a patriotic American. A couple of weeks later, *Washington Post* columnist Richard Cohen went so far as to call on Obama to make another speech, modeled after John F. Kennedy's declaration in 1960 that, despite his Catholicism, he would respect the separation of church and state as president—as though Obama's blackness were a sign of allegiance to some entity, like the Vatican, other than the United States of America.

In the Democratic debates, enabled by the moderators, Hillary Clinton has increasingly deployed issues of race and patriotism as a wedge strategy against her opponent. First, in the debate in Cleveland on February 26, she pressed Obama not only to denounce but to reject Louis Farrakhan—to whom he was spuriously linked through Reverend Wright, who had taken a trip with the black nationalist leader in the 1980s. In style as well as content, that attack was a harbinger of things to come. In the most recent debate, ABC's George Stephanopolous and Charles Gibson peppered Obama with questions such as, "Do you believe [Wright] is as patriotic as you are?" and, regarding former Weatherman Bill Ayers, a Chicago neighbor and Obama supporter, "Can you explain that relationship for the voters and explain to Democrats why it won't be a problem?" Time after time, Clinton picked up the line and ran with it. "You know, these are problems, and they raise questions in people's minds. And so this is a legitimate area...

for people to be exploring and trying to find answers," she said, seeming to abandon her argument that these issues are fair game now only because they will be raised by Republicans later and thus are relevant to an evaluation of Obama's electability.

The Wright, Farrakhan and Ayers controversies have been fueled by a craven media, and ABC's performance in the debate has rightly been condemned. But given that Clinton is the one who is running for president and who purports to represent liberal ideals, her complicity in such attempts to establish guilt by association is far more troubling. While she has dealt gingerly with the matter of Wright in the wake of his recent appearance at the National Press Club—accusing Republicans of politicizing the issue—she also took pains to remind reporters that she "would not have stayed in that church under those circumstances."

It's disappointing, to say the least, to see the first viable female contender for the presidency participate in attacks on her black opponent's patriotism, which exploit an anxious climate around national security that gives white men an edge both over women and people of color—who tend to be viewed, respectively, as weak and potentially traitorous. Says Paula Giddings, "This idea of nationalism and patriotism pulling at everyone has demanded hypermasculine men, more like McCain than the feline Obama, and demanded women whose role is to be maternal more than anything else."

For Hillary Clinton, the gendered terrain of post-9/11 national security politics has been treacherous indeed. As Elizabeth Drew observed in *The New York Review of Books*, Clinton took steps in the Senate, like joining the Armed Services Committee, "to protect herself from the sexist notion that a woman might be soft on national security." As a 2002 study by the White House Project, a women's leadership group, found, "Women candidates start out with a serious disadvantage—voters tend to view women as less effective and tough. Recent events of war, terrorism, and recession have only... increased the salience of these dimensions." Clinton has been quite successful in allaying these concerns, although she faces a Catch-22: her reputed toughness and ruthlessness have helped ratchet up her high negatives. The White House Project study found that a woman candidate faces a unique tension between the need to show herself "in a light that is personally appealing, while also showing that she has the kind of strength needed for the job she is seeking."

Of course, Clinton's decision to play the hawk may have had other motivations. Perhaps she really believed that voting to authorize the war in Iraq was the right thing to do (which is, arguably, even more worrying). But her posture in this campaign— threatening to "totally obliterate" Iran after being asked how she would respond in the highly improbable event of an Iranian nuclear strike against Israel, for example—has at least something to do with a desire to compete on a macho foreign policy playing field. It's the woman in this Democratic primary race who has the cowboy swagger: the nationalist and militaristic rhetoric, the whiskey-swilling photo-ops, the gotcha attacks for perceived insults to a

working-class electorate (as in "Bittergate") that is usually depicted as white and male.

Clinton has, to be sure, faced a raw misogyny that has been
more out in the open than the racial attacks on Obama have been.
But while sexism may be more casually accepted, racism, which is
often coded, is more insidious and trickier to confront. Clinton's
response to "Iron my shirt" was immediate and straightforward:
"Oh, the remnants of sexism, alive and well." Says Kimberlé Crenshaw, law professor at Columbia and UCLA and executive director of the African American Policy Forum, "While sexism can be
denounced more directly, that doesn't mean it's worse. Things that
are racist have yet to be labeled and understood as such."

While on occasion Obama's campaign has complained of
racial slights, Obama himself has avoided raising the charge
directly. Even so, Clinton supporters make the twisted claim that
it is Obama who has racialized the campaign. "While promoting
Obama as a 'post-racial' figure, his campaign has purposefully pol-
luted the contest with a new strain of what historically has been
the most toxic poison in American politics," wrote Sean Wilentz
in *The New Republic* in an article titled "Race Man." Bill Clinton
recently groused that the Obama camp, in the controversy over his
Jackson remark, "played the race card on me."

As for the way the Clinton campaign has dealt with race,
Crenshaw says, "It started with a small drumbeat, but as the campaign has proceeded, as Hillary has taken part in things, more peo-

ple are really seeing this as a 'line in the sand' kind of moment."

Among the black feminists interviewed for this article, reactions to the declarations of sexism's greater toll by Clinton supporters—and their demand that all women back their candidate out of gender solidarity, regardless of the broader politics of the campaign—ran the gamut from astonishment to dismay to fury. Patricia Hill Collins, a sociology professor at the University of Maryland and author of *Black Feminist Thought*, recalls how, before they were reduced to their race or gender, the candidates were not seen solely through the prism of identity, and many Democrats were thrilled with the choices before them. But of the present, she says, "It is such a distressing, ugly period. Clinton has manipulated ideas about race, but Obama has not manipulated similar ideas about gender." This has exacerbated longstanding racial tensions within the women's movement, Collins notes, and is likely to alienate young black women who might otherwise have been receptive to feminism. "We had made progress in getting younger black women to see that gender does matter in their lives. Now they are going to ask, What kind of white woman is Hillary Clinton?"

The sense of progress unraveling is profound. "What happened to the perspective that the failures of feminism lay in pandering to racism, to everyone nodding that these were fatal mistakes—how is it that all that could be jettisoned?" asks Crenshaw, who co-wrote a piece with Eve Ensler on the Huffington Post called "Feminist Ultimatums: Not in Our Name." Crenshaw says that, appalled as she is by the sexism toward Clinton, she found herself stunned by some of the arguments pro-Hillary feminists were making. "There is a myopic focus on the aspiration of having a woman in the White House—perhaps not *any* woman, but it seems to be pretty much enough that she be a Democratic woman." This stance, says Crenshaw, "is really a betrayal."

Frances Kissling, the former president of Catholics for a Free Choice, attributes this go-for-broke attitude to the mindset of corporate feminism. "There's a way in which feminists who have been seriously engaged in electoral politics for a long time, the institutional DC feminist leadership, they are just with Hillary Clinton come hell or high water. I think they have accepted, as she has accepted, a similar career trajectory. They are not uncomfortable with what has gone on in the campaign, because they see electoral campaigns as mere instruments for getting elected. This is just the way it is. We have to get elected."

The implications of all this for the future of feminism depend significantly on the outcome of the primary, says Kissling. "If Clinton wins, the older-line women's movement will continue; it will be a continuation of power for them. If she doesn't win, it will be a death knell for those people. And that may be a good thing— that a younger generation will start to take over."

Many younger women, indeed, have responded to the admonishments of their pro-Hillary second-wave elders by articulating a sophisticated political orientation that includes feminism but is not confined to it. They may support Obama, but they still abhor the sexism Clinton has faced. And they detect—and reject—a tinge of sexism among male peers who have developed man-crushes on the dashing senator from Illinois. "Even while they voice dismay over the retro tone of the pro-Clinton feminist whine, a growing number of young women are struggling to describe a gut conviction that there is something dark and funky, and probably not so female-friendly, running below the frantic fanaticism of their Obama-loving compatriots," wrote Rebecca Traister in *Salon*.

It's not just young feminists who have taken such a nuanced view. Calling themselves Feminists for Peace and Obama, 1,500 prominent progressive feminists—including Kissling, Barbara Ehrenreich and this magazine's Katha Pollitt—signed on to a statement endorsing him and disavowing Clinton's militaristic politics. "Issues of war and peace are also part of a feminist agenda," they declared.

In some sense, this is a clarifying moment as well as a wrenching one. For so many years, feminists have been engaged in a pushback against the right that has obscured some of the real and important differences among them. "Today you see things you might not have seen. It's clearer now about where the lines are between corporate feminism and more grassroots, global feminism," says Crenshaw. Women who identify with the latter movement are saying, as she puts it, "'Wait a minute, that's not the banner we are marching under!'"

Feminist Obama supporters of all ages and hues, meanwhile, are hoping that he comes out of this bruising primary with his style of politics intact. While he calls it "a new kind of politics," Clinton and Obama are actually very similar in their records and agendas (which is perhaps why this contest has fixated so obsessively on their gender and race). But in his rhetoric and his stance toward the world outside our borders, Obama does appear to offer a way out of the testosterone-addled GOP framework. As he said after losing Pennsylvania, "We can be a party that thinks the only way to look tough on national security is to talk, and act, and vote like George Bush and John McCain. We can use fear as a tactic and the threat of terrorism to scare up votes. Or we can decide that real strength is asking the tough questions before we send our troops to fight."

As comedian Chris Rock quipped, Bush "fucked up so bad that he's made it hard for a white man to run for president." Rock spoke too soon: many are hungry for a shift, but the country needs the right push to get there. Unfortunately, from Hillary Clinton, it's getting a shove in the wrong direction. ❧

Hillary's Gift to Women

BARBARA EHRENREICH, MAY 26, 2008

In Friday's *New York Times*, Susan Faludi rejoiced over Hillary Clinton's destruction of the myth of female prissiness and innate moral superiority, hailing Clinton's "no-holds-barred pugnacity" and her media reputation as "nasty" and "ruthless." Future female presidential candidates will owe a lot to the race of 2008, Faludi wrote, "when Hillary Clinton broke through the glass floor and got down with the boys."

I share Faludi's glee—up to a point. Surely no one will ever dare argue that women lack the temperament for political combat. But by running a racially tinged campaign, lying about her foreign policy experience and repeatedly seeming to favor McCain over her Democratic opponent, Clinton didn't just break through the "glass floor," she set a new low for floors in general, and would, if she could have gotten within arm's reach, have rubbed the broken glass into Obama's face.

A mere decade ago Francis Fukuyama fretted in *Foreign Affairs* that the world was too dangerous for the West to be entrusted to graying female leaders, whose aversion to violence was, as he established with numerous examples from chimpanzee society, "rooted in biology." The counter-example of Margaret Thatcher, perhaps the first head of state to start a war for the sole purpose of pumping up her approval ratings, led him to concede that "biology is not destiny." But it was still a good reason to vote for a prehistoric-style club-wielding male.

Not to worry though, Francis. Far from being the stereotypical feminist-pacifist of your imagination, the woman to get closest to the Oval Office has promised to "obliterate" the toddlers of Tehran—along, of course, with the bomb-builders and Hezbollah supporters. Earlier on, Clinton forswore even talking to presumptive bad guys, although women are supposed to be the talk addicts of the species. Watch out—was her distinctly unladylike message to Hugo Chávez, Kim Jong-Il and the rest of them—or I'll rip you a new one.

There's a reason it's been so easy for men to overlook women's capacity for aggression. As every student of Women's Studies 101 knows, what's called aggression in men is usually trivialized as "bitchiness" in women: men get angry; women suffer from bouts of inexplicable, hormone-driven, hostility. So give Clinton credit for defying the belittling stereotype: She's been visibly angry for months, if not decades, and it can't all have been PMS.

But did we really need another lesson in the female capacity for ruthless aggression? Any illusions I had about the innate moral superiority of women ended four years ago with Abu Ghraib. Recall that three out of the five prison guards prosecuted for the torture and sexual humiliation of prisoners were women. The prison was directed by a woman, Gen. Janis Karpinski, and the top US intelligence officer in Iraq, who also was responsible for reviewing the status of detainees before their release, was Major Gen. Barbara Fast. Not to mention that the US official ultimately responsible for managing the occupation of Iraq at the time was Condoleezza Rice. Whatever violent and evil things men can do, women can do too, and if the capacity for cruelty is a criterion for leadership, as Fukuyama suggested, then Lynndie England should consider following up her stint in the brig with a run for the Senate.

It's important—even kind of exhilarating—for women to embrace their inner bitch, but the point should be to expand our sense of human possibility, not to enshrine aggression as a virtue. Women can behave like the warrior queen Boadicea, credited with slaughtering 70,000, many of them civilians, or like Margaret Thatcher, who attempted to dismantle the British welfare state. Men, for their part, are free to take as their role models the pacifist leaders Martin Luther King and Mahatma Gandhi. Biology conditions us in all kinds of ways we might not even be aware of yet. But virtue is always a choice.

Hillary Clinton smashed the myth of innate female moral superiority in the worst possible way—by demonstrating female moral inferiority. We didn't really need her racial innuendos and free-floating bellicosity to establish that women aren't wimps. As a generation of young feminists realizes, the values once thought to be uniquely and genetically female—such as compassion and an aversion to violence—can be found in either sex, and sometimes it's a man who best upholds them. ❖

Hillary's
Feminist Moment

CHRISTOPHER HAYES, JUNE 30, 2008

Five months ago, in what now feels like a different epoch, Hillary Clinton was addressing a packed auditorium in New Hampshire when two men suddenly began shouting, "Iron my shirt!" The air went out of the room, but as soon as the miscreants had been tossed out, Clinton shot back with relish: "Ah, the remnants of sexism—alive and well." The crowd went wild. As I sat in the auditorium it struck me that it was the most rhetorically alive I'd seen her during the entire campaign.

Fast-forward to Saturday, June 7, when Clinton officially suspended her campaign and endorsed Barack Obama. The speech has been praised as the best of her campaign (if not her career). "I am a woman," she said. "Like millions of women, I know there are still barriers and biases out there, often unconscious, and I want to build an America that respects and embraces the potential of every last one of us."

Clinton's campaign did not emphasize her gender for most of the seventeen months she was running. "When I was asked what it means to be a woman running for president, I always gave the same answer," she told the crowd at the National Building Museum, "that I was proud to be running as a woman but I was running because I thought I'd be the best president." It's hard to second-guess this tactical choice, since the path of a serious woman presidential contender is an uncharted one. Many of Clinton's supporters have noted, rightly, that she was operating under gendered constraints, like making voters believe a woman could be commander in chief, to name the most obvious. All of that said, the campaign began to embrace a kind of feminist core as the race went on, and it culminated in Clinton's final speech, which was, without a doubt, the most unabashed feminist address in the history of presidential politics.

Running for president can be a radicalizing experience. Al Gore ran as a safe centrist, and in the wake of his illegitimate defeat he became an outspoken and full-throated progressive voice. Howard Dean began as a DLC governor and ended up an antiwar icon and the man who has reinvested the DNC with grassroots energy. Clinton laid out her mission going forward in strong terms: "We must make sure that women and men alike understand the struggles of their grandmothers and their mothers, and that women enjoy equal opportunities, equal pay and equal respect.... Let us resolve and work toward achieving very simple propositions: there are no acceptable limits, and there are no acceptable prejudices in the twenty-first century in our country." That may not have been the raison d'être of her campaign, but recent history proves that sometimes the most ambitious goals can be sought only outside the confines of presidential politics. ♣

Hillary Does the Right Thing

KATHA POLLITT, SEPTEMBER 15, 2008

Hillary Clinton gave a great speech last night, full of fire and feeling. She talked about all those "left out and left behind" by the Bush administration—working people struggling to stay afloat, veterans, single mothers, people without healthcare. She talked about the need to end the war in Iraq, about education, renewable energy and the need to defend civil rights, labor rights, women's rights, gay rights. She spoke movingly of the seventy-two-year struggle for women's suffrage, a cause handed down the generations (August 26 was Women's Equality Day, the anniversary of the Nineteenth Amendment). Often criticized as stiff and starchy, to say nothing of sartorially challenged, she even poked gentle fun at herself and her staff—"my sisterhood of the traveling pantsuits." (Last night's was a vivid orange, which the glaring lights of the Pepsi Center gave a pinkish cream-of-tomato-soup tinge.)

As I said, it was a great speech—and she not only gave it everything she had, she looked energized, confident and happy doing so. But the most important thing about it was that she called herself "a proud supporter of Barack Obama." In the very first sentence. These were the words people needed to hear—the crowd went wild, perhaps with relief. (I was pretty nervous myself about whether she would convey real enthusiasm.) Just to make sure everyone got the point, she made it again and again. She praised Obama for building his campaign "on a fundamental belief that change in this country must start from the ground up, not the top down." In an inspired piece of oratory bound to resonate with the many black women in the audience, she evoked Harriet Tubman's fearless determination ("If you hear the dogs, keep going, if you see the torches in the woods, keep going…keep going…don't ever stop") and segued to the need to "get going by electing Barack Obama." She asked her followers, a little plaintively, "Were you in this campaign just for me?"

That is the question.

The Hillary die-hards have been the uncrowned stars of the convention, avidly sought out for interviews and photo ops. It's as if the media cannot let go of their obsession with her, and with the Clinton-Obama rivalry narrative that was such a draw for them. We've heard about the die-hards' anger, their disappointment, their sorrow, their grievance, their need to mourn and find "closure," their fears of women's progress stalled forever. Susan Faludi just wrote one such piece for *The New York Times*. The paranoid fantasies of a small subset of these women have gotten respectful,

if bemused, attention: the DNC sabotaged Hillary. The media—
for which Howard Dean and Nancy Pelosi are responsible—sabotaged Hillary. The primary rules sabotaged Hillary—after all,
if the primary rules had been different, Hillary might have won,
so actually she did win. Besides, the point of the process was to
choose the most electable candidate, and clearly that was... Hillary! As I write, the wrangling is still going on about the roll call—
will Hillary delegates be allowed to cast a first ballot for her?

Can Clinton bring her base to Obama? "Well," said the white
woman sitting next to me, who had waved her Hillary sign through-
out the speech, "I may actually vote for him now, and I wouldn't
before." "Oh, it was a wonderful speech," said a 70-something
woman festooned with Hillary-themed jewelry and sporting a Hillary hat. "Yes, it will bring the party together. Yes, I'm voting for
Obama. She's a great woman, and I trust her judgment." I ran into
Donna Edwards, the newly elected progressive Congresswoman
from Maryland and longtime Obama supporter, being interviewed
by GRIT TV's Laura Flanders. Laura was skeptical of the speech—
she thought Clinton should have praised Obama more as a person.
Edwards thought the speech was fine. "She humanized why Democrats need to make this change. She struck those chords."

On the other hand, a Clinton supporter from Asheville, North
Carolina, wearing a T-shirt that read Love Fun Inspiration was
more equivocal. A John Edwards supporter who moved to Clinton "because of Chris Matthews," she told me that her 72-year-

old mother and her mother's best friend were voting for McCain "because they're mad at the media and the DNC." She herself is on the fence—the roll call vote is a biggie for her. "We'll see what the next two months bring. I'll either not vote or vote for Obama."

I was an Obama supporter in the primary, but I can relate to the disappointment many feel at Clinton's defeat, including women who are friends of mine. You would never know it from reading *The Nation*, but Clinton was and is beloved by many progressive women—women in the labor movement, for example. It is sad to come so close and still lose. But it is sadder when a whole social movement is reduced to one single thing and when not winning that one thing makes you walk away, or even trash the larger cause. A woman president would be an important symbol, but more important is the substance it would represent: the unstoppable progress of women toward full equality. That progress can continue under President Obama, too—in fact, it can become richer and more complex by strengthening ties to the young women and women of color who are in his base. Under a President McCain the momentum will shift into reverse—with a Supreme Court already stacked with Bush conservatives poised to turn hard right and set women back for decades.

Sisters, I am humbly reaching out. I am feeling your pain. But sometimes, as my grandmother used to say, you have to rise above. The stakes are too high to let disappointment and, yes, I'll say it, pride, carry the day. Because if you do that, McCain will win. If you believe in women and women's rights—to reproductive freedom, healthcare, decent jobs, education and all the other things we need so we can flourish—you will listen to Hillary and work as hard for Obama as you would have done for her. You made her your leader. It's time to follow her lead. ❖

HAWK OR HUMANITARIAN?

Hillary Clinton at the State Department

Barbara Crossette
and Bob Dreyfuss, June 5, 2012

The following debate was published at TheNation.com.

Barbara Crosette

n early 2008, when Hillary Clinton still had high hopes of emerging as the Democratic nominee for president, she projected herself as an experienced foreign policy player with better credentials on national security than Barack Obama. Recall her TV ad in which a telephone rings at 3 AM in the White House and viewers are asked, "Who do you want answering the phone?"

Four years later, as she prepares to leave the State Department, Secretary of State Clinton's legacy promises a markedly different tone from that fearmongering image.

A natural diplomat skilled at public diplomacy, Clinton has done more than any other Obama administration official to chip away at the image of the United States left behind by George W. Bush. She has established strong working relationships with numerous countries that will ease the way for future American diplomats and State Department officials.

In that alone, she has served Barack Obama and the country well. While Obama lurched through an inadequate response to the unending economic crisis and paralyzing missteps trying to build bipartisanship at home, Clinton grabbed international attention in new ways, meeting with a wide range of people—from the bottom up—including those in trouble with the governments whose policies the White House hoped to influence. On a recent tour of Asia, Clinton displayed her talent for navigating potentially explosive situations that could damage US relations with important countries, as in the case of the Chinese dissident Chen Guangcheng, who had taken refuge in the American Embassy in Beijing on the eve of her arrival in China. Forget for the moment the mainstream media's attempts to make this a "who won, who lost, who got humiliated" story. There were large policy issues at stake, and both sides worked from that base.

The long-planned talks in Beijing, in which Treasury Secretary Timothy Geithner also took part, were billed as a broad review of strategic and economic questions of global concern to these two powerful permanent members of the United Nations Security Council. On the American agenda were devising common policies on Iran's nuclear program, North Korea's potential for troublemaking in East Asia, the lingering crisis in Syria and China's role in Sudan and South Sudan.

Coincidental to the talks was the presence of Chen in the US Embassy, and the negotiations in which American diplomats and Chinese officials were deeply engaged to find a way to end the incident satisfactorily for both sides, and for Chen himself. He left the embassy with American assurances that he would be protected, and later was given Chinese promises that he could leave the country for the United States—after he had given conflicting signals about what he wanted to do. For the time being at least, a full-blown dispute was averted, and Chen arrived here with his family over the weekend.

While in Beijing, Clinton talked publicly in general terms about human rights in China, but was not inflammatory, and obviously did not care about the reaction of congressional Republicans, who demand more open criticism. Clinton may have angered those who wanted tougher statements on human rights in China, and on the Chen case in particular, but she weighed that against the need for some practical successes in discussions on pressing global issues with the Chinese, and struck a productive balance.

After China, Clinton went on to Bangladesh, where she stood beside the Nobel Peace Prize–winner Muhammad Yunus, who has been forced out of the Grameen Bank he founded, a much-praised lending institution for the poor. Yunus could also lose control of other parts of the Grameen network to the government of Prime Minister Sheikh Hasina; his "crime" was to consider entering politics, now controlled by two dysfunctional, antagonistic parties.

The Indian government has been a strong supporter of Hasina and her treatment of Yunus. His critics, including Prime Minister Manmohan Singh, chided him publicly after the Grameen founder derided Indian microcredit as being commercialized and not true to its anti-poverty mission and vision. Clinton's gesture would not have been lost on Indians, and news reports in India made a point of calling her a "close friend" of Yunus.

In India, Clinton sought out Mamata Banerjee, now the sharpest thorn in the side of the ruling national coalition government. Banerjee, chief minister of West Bengal, is one of the few women in South Asia to reach the heights of politics on her own, not because of a dynastic succession. Clinton noted Banerjee's accomplishment approvingly, sparking tough criticism from Indians, who accused the secretary of interfering in Indian politics. (She had also come to ask the Indian government to cut back its purchases of oil from Iran.) A blogger in the *Hindustan Times* online, Dr. Amit K. Maitra, took a longer view. Clinton, he wrote, is "a force to be reckoned with."

Frances Zwenig, a progressive trade expert at the US-ASEAN Business Council in Washington, is trying to bring Myanmar (which the United States still calls Burma) out of sanctions and into the global economy. She has watched Clinton maneuver between the Burmese military leadership and Aung San Suu Kyi, the democracy leader with whom the secretary of state has built a personal relationship.

"She's in her element and she's going to be missed," Zwenig said of Clinton.

Clinton's visit to Myanmar early last December was the first by a high-ranking American official in more than half a century. After talks with the country's president, Thein Sein, Clinton announced that she planned to upgrade the US diplomatic representation to ambassador level and would consider other measures if the government stuck to its reform agenda. Since then, Myanmar has released prisoners, Aung San Suu Kyi has been elected to Parliament and Clinton has announced other measures, including a relaxing of sanctions. Underlying these US actions, of course, is the hope that China's overwhelming presence in Myanmar can be tempered by an end to its isolation from the West. It is all part of the Obama strategy of restoring a larger American presence in East Asia and the Pacific.

Since taking office, Clinton has traveled nearly 780,000 miles to ninety-six countries. She has held more than fifty "town hall" events, some with women in places as diverse as Kyrgyzstan, Georgia, Kosovo, Nigeria and Oman, where she was asked to talk to Arab women about how she balances her public and family lives.

At the State Department, she created the position of ambassador-at-large for women's global issues. Clinton also held the department's first conference bringing together heads of US diplomatic missions around the world to share ideas.

Paradoxically, Clinton's effusive demeanor on the campaign trail in 2008—those contrived expressions of undiluted delight at meeting yet another crowd or voter, which rang false—works very well in international diplomacy, where niceties still count. Now she is reaching out with that same eager smile and firm handshake to some odious interlocutors. In town halls in Pakistan, for example, she has put down combative comments from media with frank retorts.

In July 2010, Clinton was criticized in Islamabad for the "negative connotations" of US aid in Pakistan. "I'm aware of the fact that in some parts of Pakistan, US aid is not appreciated," she said, "and that bothers me a lot because you've got to understand that from an American perspective, especially during the economic crisis that we all have encountered and a higher than usual unemployment rate in the United States, the idea to, say, an unemployed autoworker or a laid-off secretary somewhere in the United States that the aid we provide to a country may not be appreciated, raises the question in their minds, Well, why are you sending money to a country that doesn't want it?"

A year later, she was asked why Pakistan is demonized in the

American media. "I would respectfully say, I think that there's been press articles on both sides that have been wildly inaccurate and wildly accusatory, to the detriment of the seriousness of what we are trying to do together," she said, adding that the media in Pakistan can be dangerously off base a lot of the time. "When I became secretary of state, I was told by our embassy in Islamabad that they had just given up trying to respond to all the wild stories."

"Look," she said, "I'm here in part because I don't think that's useful."

BOB DREYFUSS

L et's start with a backhanded compliment: Secretary of State Hillary Clinton isn't a neoconservative. But if you like the job she's doing at Foggy Bottom, then you probably liked Dean Rusk, Secretary of State under Kennedy and Johnson, and Bill Clinton's Secretary of State Madeleine Albright, too. Here's the book on Hillary: hawkish and pro-military, skilled at using human rights as a cudgel against regimes she doesn't like while glossing over human rights abuses by allies, a liberal interventionist who's on the wrong side of the administration's internal debates on Afghanistan, China, Libya and Syria.

Let's hope that Clinton's next war isn't Syria, where the United States is coordinating weapons delivery to rebels, including Islamist militants.

Though she isn't a neocon—if "neocon" means someone addicted to the unilateral use of hard power to impose the American will overseas, regardless of the views of America's allies, the United Nations, and international law—Clinton isn't averse to hiring one as her spokeswoman. That would be Victoria Nuland, a polyglot diplomat who previously served most prominently as Vice President Dick Cheney's national security adviser from 2003 to 2005, during the peak moment of neoconservative influence in the administration of George W. Bush, before becoming the US ambassador to NATO. She was appointed as Clinton's spokeswoman in 2011.

Little remembered now, three years ago Clinton shocked some supporters of Barack Obama by hiring Dennis Ross, a neocon-linked official from the Washington Institute for Near East Policy—itself founded in the 1980s by a former research director at the American Israel Public Affairs Committee (AIPAC)—for in a vaguely defined role as special adviser on something called "the Gulf and Southwest Asia," meaning Israel and Iran. (Ross later moved to the White House, where he led a confrontational phalanx of Obama advisers on the tangled issue of Iran's nuclear program.)

With Ross handling Iran, Clinton then managed to slough off the other two biggest foreign policy issues to so-called special envoys: Richard Holbrooke on Afghanistan and Pakistan and

George Mitchell on the Middle East. But her hawkish views on issues such as Afghanistan and Libya, expressed frequently inside the White House, often pushed Obama to the right.

It's impossible, of course, to precisely define Clinton's role as distinct from Obama's own views. As secretary of state, Clinton carries out whatever emerges as America's chosen foreign policy, and what happens inside the administration's national security debates is hard to unravel. One day, perhaps, we'll know whether Clinton and Obama agreed on everything, on most everything, or hardly anything at all. But Clinton's history as a hawk, including her obsequious deference to the Israel Lobby as senator from New York, allows us to make some judgments, and here and there enough has leaked out that it's crystal clear that Clinton is rarely, if ever, on the side of the doves.

On Afghanistan, thanks to Bob Woodward's *Obama's Wars* and other reported accounts, it's widely known that Clinton twice pushed Obama to escalate that bungled adventure. In March 2009, when Obama ordered more than 20,000 additional troops to Afghanistan, Clinton opposed Vice President Joe Biden and other doves who argued, presciently, that more troops wouldn't solve the problem. The exact same alignment in late 2009 had Clinton siding with the generals once again in pressing Obama to add 30,000 more US forces, once again overriding Biden's objections. Perhaps influencing Clinton's resolute hawkishness on Afghanistan is her self-styled role as advocate for Afghanistan's women. Again and again, her advocacy for the women of that war-scarred nation has seemingly steeled her against the necessary and inevitable reconciliation with the Taliban-led insurgency, even though some Afghan women themselves argue that women are suffering intensely from a war without end. To her credit, though, when the Obama administration decided to wind down the war in 2011, it was Clinton who delivered an important speech signaling a major softening of US preconditions for talks with the Taliban.

Her views on Afghanistan, and many other issues, so dovetailed with those of former Defense Secretary Robert Gates, a centrist Republican appointed by President Bush and retained by Obama, that Clinton and Gates were something of a tag team during the Obama administration's first three years. Especially on Afghanistan, Clinton and Gates joined Gen. David Petraeus and other uniformed officers to demand a tough line on the war.

But her alliance with Gates also draws a distinct line between Clinton and the neoconservatives. Like Gates—and like Obama himself—Clinton is a fierce advocate for multilateralism. She is a strong partisan of NATO, of the US alliance with Israel, of building UN and international consensus to support American military action. As senator, and then as secretary, she strongly backed an expansion of the army and the marines, and she supported Defense Secretary Leon Panetta's opposition to cuts in the bloated Pentagon budget. However, Clinton doesn't favor go-it-alone actions, à la Cheney. She does, however, often see human rights as a handy way to create a rationale for war. (Obama's ambassador to the UN, Susan Rice, agrees. Not long ago, before taking office, Rice called for airstrikes of or a naval blockade of Sudan over the ongoing civil strife in the western region of Darfur.)

Case in point: Libya. In that case, one of the few on which she differed from Secretary Gates, Clinton (along with Rice) was a strong advocate for the use of American military power against the government of Muammar el-Qaddafi (Gates later supported intervention). And Clinton went far beyond the UN's support for limited action, using US-coordinated air power backed by France and Britain to support ground actions by anti-Qaddafi rebels. President Obama's rationale for the action—namely, that the city of Benghazi was about to be slaughtered by the Qaddafi forces, which now appears to have been exaggerated—was a clear instance of supposedly humanitarian justification for a war in support of American interests.

On Syria, too, Clinton has backed the UN and former UN Secretary General Kofi Annan's diplomatic mission to find a peaceful solution through talks between the government of President Bashar Assad and Syrian rebels, but has warned that if Syria does not cooperate, it will face increasing pressure and isolation. Clinton has denounced Assad and lent her support to anti-regime dissidents. And now, alongside Saudi Arabia and Qatar—two oil rich kleptocracies that gleefully suppress human rights—the United States is reportedly coordinating the delivery of weaponry to anti-Assad fighters, including hard-core Islamists inspired by the Saudi regime.

Clinton has hardly distinguished herself during the so-called Arab Spring. First, in deference to Saudi Arabia and Israel, Clinton backed the regime of Hosni Mubarak in Egypt. Shortly before it was toppled, she called for "real democracy," but has joined Gates and the Pentagon in working with Egypt's military to preserve what's left of the Mubarak era. A footnote to her close relationship with the king of Saudi Arabia is her utter lack of support for the rebels in Bahrain, a strategic linchpin in the Persian Gulf that was invaded by Saudi troops in 2011 to protect its thievery-minded Sunni monarchy. Apparently, to Clinton, the human rights of Bahrainis are far, far less important than those of, say, Syria or Libya. Perhaps the US naval base in Bahrain, the ongoing US confrontation with Iran, and the intemperate desires of the Saudi king have something to do with her preferences. Recently, Clinton met with visiting senior officials from Bahrain to announce the resumption of US arms sales to the island kingdom.

On China, too, Clinton has a mixed record at best. In 2009, during her first visit there, she seemed to back away from an aggressive, pro–human rights stance in favor of a sensible view that US-China ties were far too complex and important for the United States to meddle in internal Chinese affairs.

But she's recently moved away from that more "realist" view. And the saga of the blind Chinese dissident and lawyer Chen Guangcheng raises concern that Clinton is now willing to anger China on this volatile front, even if it means provoking China's own militant, anti-American contingent in the Communist Party there. Why, exactly, was Chen given asylum in the US embassy in Beijing days before crucial US-China talks? And did President Obama know about the decision to shield Chen? According to *The New York Times*, Obama was informed only after Chen was in the embassy.

Clinton has meddled, too, in China's relations with various neighbors, bluntly supporting several countries that challenge China in disputed areas of the South China Sea. She's backed military aid to a controversial, human rights–violating Indonesian paramilitary group, and she's generally supported a stepped up US military presence around China, backing the Philippines and Vietnam against Beijing and supporting the deployment of US forces in Australia. If this isn't designed to "contain" China, it's hard to see what it is.

Clinton isn't afraid to play hardball. She believes that the United States can assert its primacy through military means. Her supporters call that using "smart power," but the conventional definition of smart power really means combining soft power (such as economic might and diplomacy) with hard power, i.e., guns, battleships, aircraft carries and drones. Not smart, in my opinion.

BARBARA CROSETTE

An American secretary of state, the highest-ranking member of a president's cabinet, has two basic roles. One is defined as the president's chief foreign affairs adviser. That one is the inside-the-Beltway part.

The other role is to carry abroad the policy priorities and decisions of the United States, and explain and enforce them to this country's best advantage. That is the image of Hillary Clinton the world sees, and through which a large number of civil society leaders she meets at public forums take stock of American intentions, as much as they may loathe or fear specific American policies or actions.

The job has limitations. In Washington, the days of all-powerful secretaries of state are over. Think of Thomas Jefferson, who before becoming president established an American geopolitical presence in Europe after the Revolution; John Quincy Adams, who with President James Monroe (a former secretary of state) devised the controversial Monroe Doctrine; or George C. Marshall and the Marshall Plan. Henry Kissinger, who engineered a US opening to China (beginning as national security adviser in 1971) and James Baker, whose diplomacy made the first American war against Saddam Hussein a true international response to the occupation of

Kuwait, but then kept the scope of that war well defined and under control. Like them or not, they are universally remembered.

Secretaries of state have many more competitors for power in Washington today. The inroads of strong national security advisers, a few offices away from the president and not a mile away, have not only created a second and at times much more important center of foreign policy decisions but have also proved again and again to be fierce competitors for attention. Defense secretaries and military commanders have expanded foreign policy roles, as Dana Priest of *The Washington Post* so brilliantly demonstrated in her series of articles titled "The Proconsuls: A Four-Star Foreign Policy?"

Supporting the president can be humiliating and embarrassing. Madeleine Albright had to join other high-ranking women in Bill Clinton's administration to cheerlead publicly for him during the Monica Lewinsky affair in 1998. (I was in the Iraqi government press center when CNN broadcast the event; the Iraqis were bug-eyed at the spectacle.) Colin Powell regrets his performance at the UN Security Council in February 2003. Before the invasion of Iraq, he held up a little vial of white powder and said that "less than a teaspoon of dry anthrax, a little bit, about this amount" had been enough to shut down the US Senate in the fall of 2001, and said that UN inspectors estimated that Iraq may have produced 25,000 liters of the stuff.

Then there are the special envoys, a global phenomenon. The United Nations has dozens of them. The United States has many running all over the State Department's turf, in Sudan, Somalia, the Middle East and, of course, Afghanistan, among other places. Like Richard Holbrooke, a number of the envoys demand a direct line to the White House, not the State Department, which they apparently do not consider the center of policy.

Envoys serve a purpose, however, no matter to whom they report. When crises are multiple, no secretary of state can concentrate much time on any one of them, while arid debates go on over stalemated issues with uncooperative governments, even when they are allies. Unless some measure of success seems possible, Kissinger-style shuttle diplomacy is a waste of time.

There is a big world out there to deal with. Clinton has spent considerable time in Asia and the Pacific beyond Pakistan. It is a region she and the president apparently consider neglected, and one where the rise of a more expansionist China is a concern to regional governments from India to Australia. For India, a nuclear power that began the South Asia nuclear arms race, China is an obsession and the excuse for testing nuclear-capable missiles and running up a huge defense budget.

Clinton, trying to bring India "on side" on a number of international issues, has like her boss, gone easy on the country's dark human rights record. There have been politically inspired killings of thousands of Sikhs and Muslims in recent decades and costly corrupt behavior in international institutions such as the World Bank. Women's rights are not respected or enforced.

In Washington, the State Department's current human rights report is explicit on these issues. Moreover, the chief minister of the economically go-go Indian state of Gujarat, Narendra Modi, continues to be denied an American visa because of evidence of his support for a deadly anti-Muslim pogrom in 2002. On the diplomatic road to Delhi, this gets toned down. It isn't just Middle Eastern princes who are handled with kid gloves for self-interested US reasons.

The ambassador-at-large for women's issues, an innovation of the Obama administration, is Melanne Verveer, formerly the chair and co-CEO of the international nongovernmental organization Vital Voices and before that Hillary Clinton's chief of staff during the presidency of Bill Clinton. Verveer and Hillary Clinton worked closely together on women's issues at the UN in the 1990s, where they were widely recognized as strong advocates for girls and women worldwide. The office of global women's issues at the State Department now continues to promote a broad range of programs—from environmental issues, education, health and economic empowerment to gender violence to assist women and women's organizations in scores of countries, including Pakistan, Afghanistan and the Democratic Republic of the Congo. The new emphasis on women's issues has grown simultaneously with Obama administration efforts to expand diplomatic action on lesbian, gay, bisexual and transgender rights, which US embassies around the world have been told to raise with governments that discriminate or persecute people because of their sexual preferences. These social issues have never figured so prominently in US foreign policy.

BOB DREYFUSS

I t's hard to think of a recent secretary of state who's been worse than Hillary Clinton. On the plus side, it's hard to think of one who's been more irrelevant.

Perhaps Barbara Crossette focuses so heavily on Clinton's work on secondary and tertiary issues—such as Bangladesh, Myanmar, and women's rights in the Congo—because as secretary of state Hillary Clinton has been stripped of nearly all the important portfolios. Since its start, the administration of Barack Obama has aggregated the making of foreign policy to a small group inside the White House. Maybe that's because Obama didn't trust either Clinton or Bob Gates, a Republican appointed by George W. Bush: Clinton because during the campaign she attacked Obama from the right on foreign policy, and Gates because of his GOP ties and shady past as a manipulator of intelligence at the CIA in the 1980s. In any case, it's nearly universally accepted that when it comes to foreign policy, the White House runs the show. By and large—except for her hawkish advice, often in tandem with the secretary of defense and the military—irrelevant. On the big issues—Iraq, Afghanistan, Iran, Israel—Clinton is an afterthought.

On Iran, for instance, where war and peace looms in the balance in talks over Iran's nuclear program, Clinton has hardly been a factor. Following the conclusion of the May 23 Baghdad talks between Iran and the P5+1, I asked Aaron David Miller, a longtime diplomat and Middle East expert, who was in charge in Washington on Iran, and he said that the policy is "made, controlled, and micromanaged by the White House." That, he noted, is true of most important areas of work. Clinton, he said, "doesn't own any issues."

On Iraq, the administration's point man for policy was Vice President Joe Biden. On Afghanistan and Pakistan, it was Richard Holbrooke and his successor, Marc Grossman, along with a team of exceedingly independent-minded ambassadors who owed little or nothing to Clinton. Cameron Munter, the outgoing U.S ambassador to Pakistan, "was an ally of Richard Holbrooke, Obama's larger-than-life envoy to the region before he died in 2010." And while Obama relied too heavily, especially in 2009, on tendentious advice from the generals on Afghanistan, if Clinton played any role at all it was to echo the military brass.

It's hard to think of a single major accomplishment of Clinton since she took office. To the extent that America's image in the world has improved since 2009, it's almost entirely because allies and adversaries alike saw Obama as a breath of fresh air after the heavy-handed, bungling warmongers of the previous administration. Crossette says that Clinton "has done more than any other Obama administration official to chip away at the image of the United States left behind by George W. Bush." But that's faint praise. All the softening up was done when Bush packed his suit-cases, and—at least at the beginning—Obama had most of the world's leaders at hello.

Crossette asks us to think about Thomas Jefferson and John Quincy Adams, but I've forgotten whatever I once knew about ancient history to understand why she mentions them. As far as more recent secretaries of state, I find myself going all the way back to Al Haig (1981-1982) to come up with one worse than Clinton. Condi Rice, for all her faults (and there are many), pre-sided over the exile of the neoconservatives from the Bush admin-istration. Colin Powell, who disastrously served as White House mouthpiece in the run-up to war in Iraq, at least argued internally against that reckless fiasco. Madeleine Albright, perhaps as hawk-ish as Clinton, didn't succeed in drawing Bill Clinton into major wars outside the Balkans mess. And the array of white men who preceded them—Warren Christopher, Larry Eagleburger, James Baker and George Shultz—were Cold War hawks but mostly realists who understood that the United States is limited by bal-ance-of-power politics abroad. If Clinton is not worse than any of them, she's certainly no better.

Crossette cheers Clinton's role in promoting "the office of global women's issues at the State Department" as well as her efforts to "expand diplomatic action on lesbian, gay, bisexual and transgender rights." All to the good—but hardly the big-think issues that a secretary of state ought to focus on. If, in extricating the United States from the Afghan quagmire, the United States has to finesse its commitment to the rights of women in that exceedingly male-dominated, tribal society, will Clinton be the grease under the wheels on the exit ramp or the anchor that entangles us further?

Meanwhile if Obama lurches dangerously toward a containment policy vis-à-vis China, will Clinton suggest a softer course? Not likely. So far, by her own rhetoric, she's waving the flags of various Southeast Asian nations against what some of their leaders see as Chinese hegemony.

Going forward, if Obama does indeed see more "flexibility" in his second term on foreign policy, as he suggested to then President Medvedev of Russia in the famous live-mic moment, he ought to usher Clinton quietly into her retirement after the election. We can hope that successor will be someone who brings a more dovish, and humble, counsel when he or she sits down with Obama. ❖

Hillary Clinton, State Feminist?

TARA MCKELVEY, MARCH 4, 2013

Hillary Clinton stood at a podium at the Council on Foreign Relations in Washington and began her speech, one of the last she would make as secretary of state. Wearing rectangular-framed glasses, pale pink lipstick and tapered heels, she looked out on a crowd of foreign-policy wonks, lawyers and journalists. She directed some of her remarks to members of the media—"the pundits," as she calls them, who see women's issues as "a bit soft"—and wondered aloud, imitating those selfsame pundits, "What about the hard stuff?"

"Well, that is a false choice," she continued, explaining the need for an American foreign policy that encompasses so-called soft issues, like the advancement of women, economic development and energy diplomacy, as well as the usual "hard power" concerns. At various times during her speech, she held her right hand aloft and lightly touched her index finger and thumb together, as if to illustrate the concept of something that was both delicate and precisely calibrated. Her approach to the job of secretary of state—a four-year effort to balance military might, women's issues and diplomacy—as well as her overall investment in a career that spans more than two decades in Washington, have also been exercises in patience, balance and fine-tuning.

On this day, at least, she got things right. Her speech was a virtuoso performance, a thirty-three-minute discourse on "American leadership," done without notes, in which she riffed on "smart power" and name-checked Frank Gehry (foreign policy needs a new architecture, "highly intentional and sophisticated"), as well as Osama bin Laden and current joint chiefs of staff chair Gen. Martin Dempsey. Then she sat down and waited for questions. Richard Haass, president of the Council on Foreign Relations, later told the audience that Clinton's successor at the State Department, John Kerry, had "some fairly large Manolo Blahniks to fill." (In fact, Clinton told me later, her shoes were designed by Miuccia Prada.)

Despite the inescapable fixation on Clinton's brand of femininity (right down to the designer of her shoes), as well as her claims concerning her women-oriented policy priorities, the balance of her work as secretary of state has actually favored muscle over soft power. Clinton pressed to send additional troops to Afghanistan, lobbied for military intervention in Libya and supported a more aggressive targeted-killing program.

Still, many see in Clinton a secretary of state who was attuned to the needs of women. "Having a female secretary of state is sometimes a game changer in itself," says Shelby Quast, a senior policy adviser at Equality Now. Perhaps more than her predecessors (some of whom were, of course, female), and certainly more than Obama, Clinton has been able to charm political leaders, both men and women, because of her warmth, her deep knowledge of the issues people are facing, and a curiosity about the world and the people around her. Sherry Rehman, Pakistan's ambassador to the United States, told me at a breakfast in Washington that Clinton has reached out to women in Pakistan, leaving behind "a legacy that will endure."

During her first five months as secretary, Clinton mentioned women 450 times in the speeches she gave, according to columnist Madeleine Bunting in *The Guardian*. Later, in a *Newsweek* interview, Clinton said, "I have been working hard to integrate women's rights as a cornerstone of our foreign policy. Women are key to the success of the Obama administration's major development and economic-growth initiatives.

"They are often discriminated against, even brutally enslaved, or simply not able to contribute to society or realize their potential," Clinton added. "We have an obligation to stand up for their rights." And she has worked hard to create programs that will help create gender equality, promoting women's right to education and addressing problems like the high rate of female fetuses aborted in China.

One of Clinton's most important achievements was to shine a spotlight on the dangers women face in war-torn countries. She went to the Democratic Republic of Congo during her first year as secretary, for instance, and met with women who had endured sexual violence. She also pushed for United Nations Security Council resolutions that "have put real teeth into tackling the issue," Bunting wrote, including the appointment of a special representative on sexual violence in conflict, and the creation of a team of experts responsible for tracking down its perpetrators.

But some view Clinton's impact in a different light. "There were moments with Hillary Clinton when I felt like we were getting too close to a rescue narrative: 'Here's Hillary Clinton and here's the United States. We are going to save the women of the world,'" says Mallika Dutt, the president of Breakthrough, a human rights organization.

As Dutt points out, the situation for Clinton is complicated. "There are aspects of US foreign policy that have created that situation in these countries. We supported the *mujahedeen*" and helped to create the conditions that led to the Taliban. "We've supported Saudi Arabia for decades," she says. "Here we are, strong advocates for women's rights, and we're going to rescue women in the global South, while we are creating circumstances that allow these things to occur."

During Clinton's tenure, for example, expanded US counterterrorism operations have made parts of the countries where she was attempting to help women, such as Pakistan's Federally Administered Tribal Areas, more volatile. Pakistani Ambassador Rehman is a fan of Clinton's, but she has denounced the US drone program, which is "creating an entire community of future recruits and radicalizing people who were standing up against militancy and terrorists." Rehman refuses to talk about the role Clinton has played in expanding the drone program, but those efforts have been well documented.

"One of the first things I did as secretary was to elevate the Office of Global Women's Issues under the first ambassador at large, Melanne Verveer," Clinton said during her speech at the Council on Foreign Relations. Verveer was sitting in the audience, and so was the office's deputy, Jennifer Klein, who told me earlier that helping women and girls around the world was "not only the morally right thing to do, but also the smart thing to do."

At the Office of Global Women's Issues, Verveer and her staffers have assisted women in countries around the world who are fighting sexual violence and other crimes. In July, for instance, officials announced that the United States would contribute $5 million to a public-private partnership, Together for Girls, that works to reduce sexual violence in Kenya, Haiti and other countries.

The office also funds workshops through the Small Grants Initiative, such as the one-day conference for the Female Lawyers Association in Gambia in August 2011, and helped lead the China-US Women's Leadership Exchange and Dialogue program, which brought together female leaders from both countries.

As secretary of state, Clinton has "mainstreamed" women's issues, just as President Jimmy Carter once did with human rights, says Alan Henrikson, a director of diplomatic studies at the Fletcher School of Law and Diplomacy at Tufts University. The State Department's annual human rights report now includes information on the legal age of marriage in every country, showing the places where girls are routinely forced into early marriage. In Yemen, for instance, there is no minimum age, and girls as young as 8 can be forced to marry.

Aside from helping draw attention to the plight of women and girls in Congo, Clinton has led a widely publicized cookstove initiative to raise awareness of the dangers of primitive stoves in the developing world. Cookstoves, which cause diseases and illnesses such as pneumonia, kill 2 million people a year. These stoves also produce black carbon, one of the biggest causes of global warming. In 2010, Clinton said that the United States would commit $50 million to the Global Alliance for Clean Cookstoves, an organization that aims to convince people in 100 million households around the world to switch to cleaner stoves. Since then, that figure has increased to $105 million, with yet more funding to come.

"She was genuine about the stoves, as it turned out," says New York University's Richard Gowan, an expert in international cooperation. Critics argue, however, that the new stoves don't make a difference: in fact, some of the new models cause more pollution than the old ones. In addition, as one study by Harvard and

MIT researchers showed, families who received the new stoves did not use them properly, or stopped using them altogether after a few months. In that study, they essentially gave the stove away and did not find great results. "I'm like, 'Big surprise,' says the State Department's Jacob Moss, director of the US Cookstoves Initiative. He explained that the study showed that technology alone, or simply giving away better stoves, is not enough. Instead, experts have to look at the problem holistically, which, he says, is what he and others at the State Department are doing.

Others who appreciate Clinton's dynamic leadership on women's issues question whether she has always followed through with commensurate resources. "She was good at making statements and getting policies in place," says Equality Now's Quast, "but they didn't necessarily come with the money."

Françoise Girard, president of the International Women's Health Coalition, recalls how she and Nobel laureate Desmond Tutu, former Anglican archbishop of Cape Town, South Africa, and other activists waited in an anteroom on the seventh floor of the State Department to meet with Clinton in October 2012. "The doors swung out," she recalls, and Clinton, dressed in a gown of reddish-pink African cloth, stepped to greet them. "She's very charismatic," says Girard. "There's a lot of wattage." Tutu bowed toward Clinton and said, "Oh, I am so honored."

Girard, Tutu and the other activists in the room were hoping that Clinton would support their efforts to fight child marriage by creating a coordinated approach to the problem—and also by investing $100 million in US funds in a public-private partnership. They all sat together in a meeting room. Tutu "was really pressing for a commitment," Girard says. "Instead, we got a couple of programs," such as the ones in Bangladesh and Congo that were designed to help girls stay in school and avoid early marriage. "Some commitments," Girard allows, "but not at the level we'd hoped for."

Girard and her colleagues have also attempted to help HIV-positive women in developing countries have access to contraceptives, which would reduce unwanted pregnancies and minimize the risk of mother-to-child infections. US government officials could approve money for contraceptives at HIV clinics.

"The secretary of state could sit down and take a look at this and say, 'It would be a lot more convenient for women in Gambia, when they go to an HIV clinic, to also get access to family planning,'" Girard says. "We got no action on that."

In addition, Clinton could have allowed funds to be used for abortions for women in serious need overseas. The 1973 Helms amendment states that foreign-aid money may not be used for abortions, but it provides exceptions for when a woman's life is in danger and in cases of rape or incest. "That's something Hillary Clinton could consider doing," Girard says, but she did not. "We expect more from our friends."

Still, many experts believe that Clinton has done a great deal for women. "She's made the issues for women much more central," says Anju Malhotra, principal adviser on gender and rights with UNICEF. "Those things are no longer these little dinky side projects." Still, it's hard to measure her achievements in this area, since even with her ample support of women's issues, progress is slow. "You can't turn around things that are very embedded and that are wrong for women in four years," Malhotra says. "Global rates on things take ten years to change."

Data on child marriage, which is measured by the percentage of 20- to 24-year-old women who were married by age 18 in a particular country, show how long it takes to improve the lives of women and girls. In Nicaragua, for example, the decline in child marriage over a five-year period from 2001 to 2006 was just three percentage points, from 43 to 40 percent, according to Malhotra. The next review of trends will not be released by UNICEF until 2014; at that point, the impact of Clinton's efforts to fight child marriage will be easier to measure.

Meanwhile, some changes in the world have made the situation harder for women. "US foreign policy creates conditions for enormous amounts of violence against women," says Breakthrough's Mallika Dutt. "It is ironic—I don't think [Clinton] would have been able to get much traction on women's issues if she hadn't been seen as being tough in these other spaces." Many believe that Clinton has struck the right balance overall as secretary, achieving enough good in the world for women and girls to offset the harm America is inflicting. But it may be years before her real legacy becomes known, as the fate of people in Libya, Pakistan and other countries makes it clear whether she managed to help women and girls and also promote US interests through her brand of realpolitik, or whether the US interventions set the whole society back.

Today, one thing is certain: Clinton has commanded the global spotlight. During the Bush administration, people were barely aware of America's top diplomat. At the time, Donald Rumsfeld and other defense officials took center stage. That dynamic has changed, says the Brookings Institution's Thomas Wright, adding: "I don't think anyone's overshadowed Hillary."

"We felt as if there was no daylight between Obama, [Defense] Secretary Panetta, Admiral Mullen [of the joint chiefs of staff] and Secretary Clinton," says Ellen Tauscher, who served as under secretary of state for arms control and international security during Obama's first term. "When they sat in the Situation Room and made decisions, they listened respectfully. And that sense of cooperation projected to the rest of the two buildings, State and Defense."

Not everyone is sold on Clinton's approach, though. "There is no question that the close relationship between State and the Defense Department has been good for Hillary Clinton," says Gordon Adams, a former Office of Management and Budget associate director who is now a professor at American University. "The question is whether it has empowered State—and the jury is still out."

For Clinton, the emphasis on hard power was strategic. Colin Powell floundered in his dealings with Rumsfeld and soon found himself marginalized. In contrast, Clinton cultivated friendships with defense secretaries and became one of Obama's most trusted advisers. I ask Ellen Tauscher if she thinks there might be a downside to the current close relationship between State and Defense. She laughs loudly. "No," she says. "There can't be anything bad to having a secretary have such an important voice. She brought enormous credibility to the mission and helped to project the power of the State Department."

With boundless enthusiasm, Clinton has shaken things up in Washington, at least stylistically. And she certainly put her listeners at the Council on Foreign Relations in a good mood. After her speech, she made her way through the room, gossiping with old friends and shaking hands with other people. Smiling and waving, she looked like someone on the campaign trail. ❖

WHO'S READY?

Why I'm Voting for Her

JESSICA VALENTI, MAY 15, 2013

In 2008, I was one of the young feminist whippersnappers who voted for Barack Obama over Hillary Clinton in the Democratic primaries—or as many of my older counterparts called me at the time, a traitor. I didn't believe there was (as Jen Moseley, my then-colleague at Feministing, put it) a "vagina litmus test." I wanted to vote for the most feminist candidate, regardless of gender.

Next time around, though, I'm voting for a woman. Not because I believe that the female Democratic candidate (and I think we all have a good idea who *that* will be) is guaranteed to be the most feminist, but because I'm just too fed up to do anything else. I've made a full transition from youthful idealism to jaded orneriness, and my vote will be just as angry as I am.

EMILY's List has just launched a more optimistic appeal: "Madam President," a campaign to put the first woman in the White House. Stephanie Schriock, the president of EMILY's List, said in a statement that enthusiasm for women's leadership is at historically high levels: "It is clear that this is our time."

"Americans are not only ready for a woman president, but—this is the best part—they see women's leadership as a positive," Schriock told me. "We are in a new time, and I can feel this bubbling everywhere. We're seeing more women step up and run for office. And we've quintupled our size in two years."

The organization's polling tells the same story: 90 percent of voters in battleground states would vote for a qualified woman candidate from their party, and 86 percent believe that America is ready to elect a female president. At least some of that sentiment has to come from a place of frustration with the all-male status quo—not just the presidency, but so many places of power. The popular "100 Percent Men" Tumblr, for example, shines a light on those "corners of the world where women have yet to tread"—from the list of the top twenty highest-paid American CEOs to the all-male leadership at companies like T-Mobile. And if the firestorm surrounding Sheryl Sandberg's bestseller *Lean In* is any indication, women aren't just ready to see more of their gender in power—they're champing at the bit.

Voting for a woman with the sole purpose of breaking the most important political glass ceiling in the country—possibly the world—does give me pause. The belief that a female politician is inherently more woman-friendly is the same misguided notion that allowed even Sarah Palin—who, as mayor of Wasilla, made women pay for their own rape kits and, as governor of Alaska,

cut funding for a shelter for teen moms—to call herself a feminist. And the insistence on putting gender above all other identi-
ties often means that white women take the lead. I'll never forget
being told by a representative of a mainstream women's organization that they were looking for a panelist for an election-related
event who "wouldn't trump race over gender." I still believe that
my 2008 vote was the right one, and that expecting women to vote
for a female politician simply because they share the same gender
is cynical and short-sighted.

But I'm also absolutely exhausted. Why?

Because campus rapists are being "punished" by research
papers, not prison. Because the man in charge of curbing sexual
assault in the Air Force was himself charged with sexual battery.
Because the leading cause of death for pregnant women is murder
by a partner. Because the Obama administration would rather play
politics than make emergency contraception available to all wom-
en. Because "legitimate rape."

It's not that these intractable problems would magically disappear if we had a woman president. But it just might make the relentless sexism easier to bear. Maybe, despite the seemingly endless
misogyny and the daily offenses, a female president would be a hopeful reminder of progress made. Because right now, I don't see any.

It's no exaggeration to say that feminists have been stuck in
the same defensive crouch for decades. We've been so busy trying
to hold on to the ground already won that imagining a feminist

future has been a luxury we haven't had the time, money or energy for. Maybe the way to kick the movement into forward motion is with a bang: the presidency. Schriock believes that having a female president would cause reverberations around the world, and that when it comes to the power of role models, "sometimes you have to see it to understand."

"Will it end sexism as we know it?" she adds. "No, but it starts changing the conversation rapidly."

I don't have any illusions about women's "innate goodness" or think that a woman president would transform the United States into a feminist utopia. (Birkenstocks for everyone!) Like most politicians, a woman president could be just another disappointment. So why not a female disappointment? Equal representation of jerks is still equality.

But there is something to be said for the power of figure-heads. After Hillary Clinton became secretary of state, a record number of countries posted female ambassadors to the United States—some of whom have dubbed this "the Hillary effect." In 2010, Mozambique's ambassador to the United States, Amélia Matos Sumbana, told *The Washington Post*: "Hillary Clinton is so visible. She makes it easier for presidents to pick a woman for Washington." In the same way, seeing a woman serve as president of the United States could be the proverbial game-changer.

I don't know that my course of action is the one I'd recommend for others—in many ways, it's a marker of my dying idealism. But I do know that seeing a woman hold the nation's highest office would bring me great joy, and that if there's anything American women need right now, it's a win.❖

The Feminist Case Against a Woman President

Amy Schiller, May 22, 2013

eminism is dead. Long live politics as usual. At least, that's the suggestion of Jessica Valenti's latest column, "Why I'm Voting for Her," in which she announces, by turns sheepish and defiant, that she intends to vote for a woman for president in 2016. In that case, it seems obvious that she'll be supporting Hillary Clinton, whose speculative 2016 candidacy is already casting the (rather familiar) pall of inevitability.

It's not Valenti's choice of candidate that's disappointing so much as her rationale. After years of distinguishing between representation and substance as measures of feminist progress and cheering online activism and campus organizing for drawing more attention to rape culture and sexual assault, Valenti now views the feminist situation as so dismal that the likeliest available consolation is the symbolic victory of electing a moderate Democratic female president.

After resisting the siren song of identity politics for one entire election cycle, namely 2008, where Valenti rejected the "vagina litmus test" when choosing Barack Obama over Hillary Clinton, Valenti is prepared to vote for a woman "not because I believe the female Democratic candidate…is guaranteed to be the most feminist, but because I'm just too fed up to do anything else."

The trap of valorizing any woman, and particularly Clinton, as an icon and losing sight of her as a politician was foreshadowed by the "Texts From Hillary" phenomenon and her social media renaissance. There are arguments to be made for and against Clinton as a candidate, but the problem is less about her than about a voter's self-indulgent investiture of the nation's highest office with redemptive powers. Our focus as movement-builders should be supporting day-to-day organizing. Feminism is not any single person or outcome, it's a practice, and a far more active one than Valenti gives credit for.

Consider one of the controversies that has Valenti so fed up, the "legitimate rape" controversy, starting with former representative Todd Akin's whiplash-inducing remarks that women who are raped are far less likely to get pregnant, as a result of "the body… shutting that whole thing down." According to Valenti, evidence of feminism's retreat can be found in the persistence of Akinesque worldviews and gender politics—and the remedy is to "kick the movement…into forward motion…with a bang: the presidency."

Reframe the question: Didn't the "legitimate rape" controversy result in exactly the kind of feminist victory that Valenti wants? Once Akin made his remarks, Democrats and Republicans alike condemned his remarks, including President Obama's "rape is rape" statement. Akin's loss of a Senate race where he had previously been the front-runner was directly attributed to backlash from women voters. So, women got a high-profile conversation about rape victims deserving credibility and respect, galvanization of women across the political spectrum who stood up for their gender on op-ed pages and at the ballot box, and the election of Claire McCaskill as one of the record number of female senators who emerged victorious in 2012. What about that doesn't suggest forward motion for the feminist movement?

Speaking of election of female leaders, the statistics Valenti cites from EMILY's List—90 percent of voters in battleground states prepared to vote for a qualified female candidate, 86 percent believing that America is ready for a female president—suggest that attitudes are actually changing, which is perhaps the real measure of feminism's impact. The same could be said of the bestseller popularity of Sheryl Sandberg's, which according to Valenti demonstrates that women are "champing at the bit" to see themselves in positions of power. Yet those massive, hard-won cultural shifts do not need to be channeled onto a single inadequate figurehead.

After all, the counterfactual is readily available. Obama's presidency has hardly been a bonanza for African-Americans, as noted by Frederick C. Harris in *The New York Times* in 2012:

has not been a triumph for African-Americans in the aggregate. It has failed to arrest the growing chasm of income and wealth inequality; to improve prospects for social and economic mobility; to halt the re-segregation of public schools.... Mr. Obama, in his first two years in office, talked about race less than any Democratic president had since 1961. From racial profiling to mass incarceration to affirmative action, his comments have been sparse and halting...when it comes to the Obama presidency and black America, symbols and substance have too often been assumed to be one and the same.

Harris also quoted Representative Emanuel Cleaver, then-chairman of the Congressional Black Caucus, saying "The president knows we are going to act in deference to him in a way we wouldn't to someone white."

A woman in the Oval Office would not result in greater motivation for feminist action—it may actually dampen it. Obama's presidency has demonstrated that pioneering holders of that office are cautious about protecting their political capital. Their identity constituency is left with heartening optics, but no special advocacy when it comes to policy. The very evidence Valenti summons to justify her "jaded orneriness" proves the opposite—that feminists have no need for a heroine to swoop in and save the Republic. In fact, the remedy she would pursue for this alleged nadir would only weaken the energy that the movement is steadily building, day by day.

Valenti admits that "intractable problems would [not] magically disappear if we had a woman president." But, she writes, "it just might make the relentless sexism easier to bear." Easier to bear—for whom? Are we so detached from the reality of sexism that we can honestly be content with shallow symbolism? No thank you. Better to have urgency and outrage than resigned complacency.

I understand Valenti's exhaustion. I have my share of weary days. But I'm pretty sure that feminists two or three generations ahead of Valenti and me are *really* tired. The way we honor their determination, and the work of all feminists whether they run for office, shelter survivors of domestic violence, write insightful articles, or report and prosecute rapes, is not to throw up our hands and go for a feel-good fix—especially one that may be no fix at all. ❖

It's Not Her Turn

RICHARD KIM, OCTOBER 21, 2013

ecause there are only 824 days to go before the 2016 Iowa caucus, it's time to start thinking about who should win the Democratic Party's nomination— Hillary or Not Hillary? Before you roll your eyes and turn the page, allow me to note that all the talk about the next, next national election isn't just the idle chatter of bored, twitchy journalists. The world may still be waiting for that white plume of smoke to rise above Chappaqua, but Clinton's supporters are not. They've already started a Ready for Hillary PAC, which has raised over a million dollars in its first six months and secured the services of two key former Obama campaigners, Jeremy Bird and Organizing for America director Mitch Stewart. EMILY's List has launched the Madam President project, which coyly pretends to agitate for a woman president, but which recently hosted town halls in Iowa and New Hampshire that became de facto Clinton rallies. "Go to the Ready for Hillary website!" urged former Michigan governor Jennifer Granholm in Manchester. And a slew of prominent women—from minority leader Nancy Pelosi to Missouri Senator Claire McCaskill to *Vogue* editor Anna Wintour—have pre-emptively pledged their allegiance to HRC. All of which produces the impression that Clinton's nomination is more than just a likely outcome; it's an inexorable ascension. As Donna Brazile put it, "If Hillary Clinton gets in the race, there will be a coronation of her."

Can we please hold the crown for at least another day? Or 824 of them? I'm totally behind the idea of electing a woman president in 2016, and I also understand the wellspring of buyer's remorse that attaches to Obama's oft-dispiriting presidency. But anointing Clinton now isn't just anti-democratic; it paints a big sign on the party's door: No New Ideas Here.

Here's how I see it: America has a lot of problems, the most acute of which is the yawning gap between the rich and everyone else. According to Berkeley economist Emmanuel Saez, the top 1 percent captured 95 percent of all income gains in the so-called recovery, while the bottom 99 percent barely gained at all. And the chances of anyone breaking into that uppermost echelon are dwindling. As a slew of recent studies have shown, America has less class mobility than it used to and less than Canada or Western Europe; an American child born in the lowest quintile has just a 6 percent chance of rising to the top quintile—42 percent will stay at the bottom.

These grim data are more than just an abstraction; they are, as Peter Beinart argues in a Daily Beast article on "The Rise of the

New New Left," the defining condition of the millennial generation, who face scarcer job prospects, lower wages, fewer benefits
and a weaker social safety net than those before them. All that
anger and discontent that boiled up at Occupy Wall Street two
years ago wasn't swept away with the encampments. It's simmer-
ing, waiting, and even if elections aren't always the conduit for
youth insurrections, it's hard to see a whole cohort sitting the next
big one out as the American dream crumbles around them.

It's also hard to imagine a Democrat of national stature more
ill-equipped to speak to this populist mood than Hillary Clinton.
Yes, her tenure at State gave her the rehabilitating Texts From Hillary Clinton Tumblr and the thickest diplomatic passport the world
has ever known, but a taste for class warfare it most certainly did
not. To wit: her decision to house her post-cabinet, pre-campaign
apparatus at the foundation her husband started, now rechristened
the Bill, Hillary and Chelsea Clinton Foundation. The organization, and the related Clinton Global Initiative, carries some lofty
intentions—planting trees in sub-Saharan Africa, empowering
women and girls, treating HIV and malaria, and saving endangered
elephants. But as Alec MacGillis captured in a devastating feature
for *The New Republic*, it also serves as a kind of global plutocrats'
social club—a Davos on the Hudson where corporate executives
pledge millions for the privilege of rubbing elbows with celebrities
and world leaders. They also, according to MacGillis, throw some
lucre back to the Clinton apparatchiks who greased the wheels, like

Doug Band, Bill's former body man, who managed to turn his lowly position as jacket holder and BlackBerry keeper into a consulting business that afforded him $8.8 million in Manhattan real estate.

In glittering Clintonland, Band is now on the outs, but he was always small fry. The foundation counts among its major partners billionaires and corporate giants like Walmart, Goldman Sachs' Lloyd Blankfein, Mike Bloomberg, Hollywood mogul Steve Bing and Paychex chairman Tom Golisano, who habitually ran for New York governor until he moved to Florida in 2009 because, as he explained in a pique-filled op-ed, he'd save "$13,800 every single day" on taxes. Maybe HRC won't solicit the advice of all these folks, but she surely will solicit their donations. And once she does, how keen will she be to tell them that their gains are ill gotten, that they'll need to pay more, not in tax-deductible charitable contributions, but in taxes?

If Hillary wins, it will likely be because she scared off potential insurgents and shut down the debate early. If her campaign gets hold of the Obama small-donor list, the only credible countervailing force to Clinton's unmatchable war chest and elite connections, it's game over. And once in office, how can she not reward the loyalists who helped her out? The prospect of a Clinton restoration, frankly, fills me with dread. I want Terry McAuliffe to beat Ken Cuccinelli, because Virginia is for lovers, not cavemen, but can he please stay on the other side of the Potomac? And just how many horcruxes need to be destroyed before Larry Summers is forever vanquished from public life?

It's certainly possible that in an uninspired field that consists of Joe Biden, Andrew Cuomo and Martin O'Malley, Clinton would emerge as the least-worst choice. But at this point, can't we aspire to do better? Senator Warren, your country calls. ❖

Hillary Already?

EDITORIAL, DECEMBER 15, 2014

fter the dispiriting midterm elections, with the highest spending in history and the lowest turnout in the postwar era, there is a heightened sense of urgency about the 2016 presidential election. Senator Bernie Sanders feels it acutely. "This country faces more serious problems today than at any time since the Great Depression. We have already, in the midterms, gone through an election where there was no substantive debate about the most important issues, which is why you have, I think, the lowest voter turnout since 1942," says the independent from Vermont. "The idea that we could go through a presidential election where you have all these right-wing Republicans on one side talking about their issues, and then, within the progressive community, not to discuss issues like the collapse of the middle class, the growth in poverty, the fact that we're the only country in the industrialized world without a national healthcare program...to discuss climate change when the scientific community tells us that we have a short window in which to address it; not to discuss these and other issues would, I think, be horrendous for this country. Absolutely horrendous."

Horrendous, yes, but not beyond the realm of possibility.

In February, *The Nation* launched Project 45, a multiyear examination of the process by which the forty-fifth president will be chosen, with a "commitment to encourage those who will fight to prevent the hijacking of the 2016 campaign by high-powered strategists, well-heeled donors and big media outlets that are more interested in cash, and a vapid politics of personality, than in a genuine clash of ideas."

Many will argue that in today's politics, shaped by mega-rich donors and an intellectually disengaged punditocracy, the best we can hope for is a contest between candidates who are acceptable to the money and media elites. The first test of whether this is the case comes in the next few months, as potential challengers to former Secretary of State Hillary Clinton—characterized by a Wall Street executive in a Politico article as the "relatively tolerable" Democrat—must decide whether to try to displace a front-runner who leads national polls and key-state surveys by more than 40 percent.

Sanders is one prospect. Former Virginia Senator Jim Webb is another; he has launched an exploratory committee to determine whether there's room for a "nobody owns me" populist run. Outgoing Maryland Governor Martin O'Malley would also like to be considered, despite suffering a setback when his designated successor unexpectedly lost on November 4. And the group Ready for Warren just launched a three-month drive to get Massachusetts Senator Elizabeth Warren to rethink her steady refusal to run. The desire for an alternative to Clinton is real: a November survey of Democracy for America members found 42 percent favored a Warren run, while 24 percent were for Sanders. Clinton was at 23 percent.

We share that desire. As we argued in February, even the most ardent Hillary supporters should acknowledge that the Democratic Party, and the country, will be better served if she has real competition in the primaries. This is not an anti-Hillary message; it's a pro-democracy one. It is about whether the party will speak to the real concerns of voters. We need a Democratic presidential candidate with a smart, populist program untethered to Wall Street and committed to dismantling a rigged system that enriches the very few at the expense of everyone else. The appeal of progressive values and issues in the midterm elections—in which voters in red and blue states overwhelmingly endorsed referendums calling for increases in the minimum wage, paid sick leave and Medicaid expansion—demonstrates the public's hunger for such a message, and the promise of such a politics.

The Democratic Party's challenge today is that, in the minds of many voters, it is no longer linked with the issues it says are important. In part, that's because big money and bad media warp our politics. But it's also because the party is too close to corporate funders and too frequently fails to speak to the tens of millions still struggling in a weak recovery. One of the core understandings of

Project 45 is that, in the process of nominating a presidential candidate, parties define themselves not merely as a reflection of the candidate, but as a reflection of the demands raised in primaries and platform fights. For this process to work, however, there must be challenges both to the front-runners and to assumptions about what is possible and what is necessary.

Bernie Sanders is right when he says there is "a desperate need" for candidates who will challenge those assumptions. But he is also right that it can't just be about candidates; it has to be about movements. Activists must be willing to do the hard work—inside and outside the Democratic Party—of building a powerful progressive movement that can redefine our politics. Only organized people can counter organized money, and because organizing takes time, the point at which to make that commitment is not in 2016. It is now. ❖

A Hawk Named Hillary

ANATOL LIEVEN, DECEMBER 15, 2014

Hillary Clinton is running for president not only on her record as secretary of state, but also by presenting herself as tougher than Barack Obama on foreign-policy issues. With this stance, she presumably plans to distance herself from a president increasingly branded as "weak" in his approach to international issues, and to appeal to the supposedly more hawkish instincts of much of the electorate.

It is therefore necessary to ask a number of related questions, the answers to which are of crucial importance not just to the likely course of a hypothetical Clinton administration, but to the future of the United States in the world. These questions concern her record as secretary of state and her attitudes, as well as those of the US foreign-policy and national-security elites as a whole. They are also linked to an even deeper and more worrying question: whether the country's political elites are still capable of learning from their mistakes and changing their policies accordingly. I was brought up to believe that this is a key advantage of democracy over other systems. But it can't happen without a public debate—and hence mass media—founded on rational argument, a respect for facts, and an insistence that officials take responsibility for evidently disastrous decisions.

The difficulties that a Democratic politician must overcome in designing a foreign and security policy capable of meeting the needs of the age are admittedly legion. These include US foreign-policy and national-security institutions that are bloated beyond measure and spend most of their time administering themselves and quarreling with one another; the weakness of the cabinet system, which encourages these institutions and means that decisions are constantly thrown in the lap of the president and a White House staff principally obsessed with the next election; an increasing political dysfunction at home, partly as a result of the unrelenting American electoral cycle; a Republican opposition that is positively feral in its readiness to use any weapon against a Democratic White House; a corporate media that, when not working for the Republicans directly, is all too willing to help turn minor issues into perceived crises; and problems in some parts of the world (notably the Middle East and Afghanistan) that are indeed of a hideous complexity.

Even more important and difficult than any of these problems may be the fact that designing a truly new and adequate strategy would require breaking with some fundamental American myths—myths that have been strengthened by many years of superpower status but that go back much further, to the very roots of American civic nationalism. These myths, above all, depict the United States as—in one of Clinton's favorite phrases—the "indispensable nation," innately good (if sometimes misguided), with the right and duty to lead humankind and therefore, when necessary, to crush any opposition.

It is the strength and centrality of these nationalist myths that have prevented our elites and the American public from learning or remembering the lessons of Vietnam—a failure that helped pave the way for the disaster of the 2003 Iraq invasion, the consequences of which are still unfolding in the Middle East today. And as Clinton's entire record—all her writings and all the writings about her—show she has made herself a captive of those nationalist myths beyond any possibility of escape. As she asserts in her new book, *Hard Choices*:

> Everything that I have done and seen has convinced me that America remains the "indispensable nation." I am just as convinced, however, that our leadership is not a birthright. It must be earned by every generation.

And it will be—so long as we stay true to our values and remember that, before we are Republicans or Democrats, liberals or conservatives, or any of the other labels that divide us as often as define us, we are Americans, all with a personal stake in our country.

It's the same old nationalist solipsism: all we have to do is stick together and talk more loudly to ourselves about how wonderful we are, and the rest of the world will automatically accept our "leadership." This is not a case—as has sometimes appeared with Obama—of a naturally cool and skeptical intellect forced to bow to the emotions of the masses. To all appearances, Clinton's nationalism is a matter of profound conviction.

And let us be fair: this may help to get her elected president. Once she is, however, it is likely to constrain drastically her ability to shape a foreign policy appropriate to the new circumstances of the United States and the world. Above all, perhaps, it hampers her ability to learn from the past, and from her own and America's mistakes—a defect blazingly on display in her latest memoir. Instead, even when (on very rare occasions) she does make the briefest and most formal acknowledgment of a US crime or error, it is immediately followed by the infamous statement that we must put this behind us and "move on." This phrase is dear not only to Clinton, but to the foreign-policy establishment as a whole. It makes any serious analysis of the past impossible.

Of course, one hardly looks for great honesty or candor in what is, in effect, election propaganda—and one must always keep in mind the presence of a Republican Party and media ready to tear into even the slightest appearance of "apologizing for America." Nonetheless, a passage early in the book did give me hope that it would contain at least some serious discussion of past US mistakes and their lessons for future policy. It concerned what

Clinton acknowledges as her own greatest error—the decision to vote for the Iraq War:

> As much as I might have wanted to, I could never change my vote on Iraq. But I could try to help us learn the right lessons from that war and apply them to Afghanistan and other challenges where we had fundamental security interests. I was determined to do exactly that when facing future hard choices, with more experience, wisdom, skepticism, and humility.

Neither in her book nor in her policy is there even the slightest evidence that she has, in fact, tried to learn from Iraq beyond the most obvious lesson—the undesirability of US ground invasions and occupations, which even the Republicans have managed to learn. For Clinton herself helped to launch US airpower to topple another regime, this one in Libya—and, as in Iraq, the results have been anarchy, sectarian conflict and opportunities for Islamist extremists that have destabilized the entire region. She then helped lead the United States quite far down the road of doing the same thing in Syria.

Clinton tries to argue in the book that she took a long, hard look at the Libyan opposition before reporting to the president her belief that "there was a reasonable chance the rebels would turn out to be credible partners"—but however long she looked, it is now obvious that she got it wrong. She has simply not understood the fragility of states—states, not regimes—in many parts of the world, the risk that "humanitarian intervention" will bring about state collapse, and the inadequacy of a crude and simplistic version of democracy promotion as a basis for state reconstruction. It does not help that the US record on democracy promotion and the rule of law—including Clinton's own record—is so spotted that very few people outside the country take it seriously anymore.

Her book manages simultaneously to repeat the claim that the United States and its allies were only enforcing a no-fly zone in Libya and to try to take personal credit for destroying the Libyan regime. And she wonders why other countries do not entirely trust her or America's honesty! There is also no recognition whatsoever in her book that those who opposed US military action were in fact right and not "despicable," to use her phrase about Russian opposition to the US military intervention in Syria. Nor has her disastrous record on Iraq led her to take a more sensible stance toward Iran. On the contrary, in her anxiety to appear more hawkish than Obama, she has clearly aligned with those who would make a nuclear deal with Iran impossible and therefore leave the United States in the ridiculous and unsustainable position of trying to contain all the major forces in the Middle East simultaneously.

This kind of nationalist faith in American strength and American righteousness is no longer adequate to the challenges the country faces. Above all, such a faith makes it impossible to deal with other nations on a basis of equality—not only on global issues or those of great interest to Washington, but on issues that other countries regard as vital to their own interests.

This also makes it far more difficult for US officials to do what Hans Morgenthau declared is both a practical and moral duty of statesmen: through close study, to develop a capacity to put themselves in the shoes of the representatives of other countries—not in order to agree with them but to understand what is really important to them, the interests on which they will be able to compromise and those for which they will feel compelled to fight. Clinton displays not a shred of this ability in her book.

The greatest future challenge in this respect is our relations with China. The arrogance with which Washington treats other countries is at least understandable given that none of them are or are likely to be equals of the United States—though some, like Russia, can often compete successfully in their own regions. China is another matter. If, as now seems all but certain, its economy will soon surpass that of the United States, then on issues of interest to Beijing, it will indeed demand to be treated as an equal—and if Washington fails to do so, it will propel the two sides toward terrifying confrontations.

In terms of the day-to-day conduct of relations with Beijing, Clinton had a generally good record as secretary of state—though in this, she was following what has generally been a restrained policy by both political parties. But if Clinton's day-to-day record was pragmatic, her long-term strategy may prove disastrous. This was the Obama administration's decision—in which she was instrumental—to "pivot to Asia." As Clinton's writings make clear, "pivot" means the containment of China through the enhancement of existing military alliances in East Asia and the development of new ones (especially with India). This strategy is at present reasonably cautious and somewhat veiled, but if Chinese power continues to grow, and if collisions between China and some of its neighbors intensify, then a containment strategy will inevitably become harsher—with potentially catastrophic consequences.

This is not simply a case of a knee-jerk US reaction to the rise of a potential peer competitor. Some of China's policies have helped to provoke the new strategy and also enabled it by driving China's neighbors into America's arms. This is above all true of Beijing's territorial claims to various groups of uninhabited islands in the East and South China seas. While some of its claims seem reasonably well founded, others have no basis in international law or tradition; and by pushing all of them at once, Beijing has frightened most of its neighbors and created real fears that in East Asia, at least, its "peaceful rise" strategy has been abandoned.

But if aspects of China's strategy have been aggressive, that does not necessarily make the US response to them wise—especially since Obama and Clinton's announcement of the pivot to Asia, at least in part, *preceded* the new aggressiveness of Chinese policy. In particular, Clinton appears to have forgotten that a key difference between the Cold War with the USSR and the current relationship with China is that during the Cold War, Washington was careful never to involve itself in any claims by neighbors on Russian territory. In consequence (as I can testify from my work as a British journalist in the USSR during the years of its collapse), there was no successful mobilization of Russian nationalism against the United States. That has come later, when with monumental folly the United States (under the Clinton, Bush and Obama administrations) involved itself in the quarrels of the post-Soviet successor states.

As a senator, Clinton was entirely complicit in the disastrous strategy of offering NATO membership to Georgia and Ukraine, which led to the Russo-Georgian war of 2008 (and a de facto US strategic defeat) and helped set the scene for the Ukraine crisis of this year. This is not to excuse Russia's mistaken and criminal reactions to US policy; but to judge by her book, Clinton never bothered to try to understand or predict likely Russian reactions— let alone, once again, to acknowledge or learn from her mistakes. On the Georgia War, she simply repeats the lie (which, to be fair, she may actually believe) that this was deliberately started by Putin and not by Georgia's president at the time, Mikheil Saakashvili.

In her policy toward China, Clinton and the administration in which she served have embroiled the United States in the islands disputes. Formally, Washington has not taken sides concerning ownership of the islands. Informally, though, by emphasizing the US military alliance with Japan and its extensive character, it has done so—at least in the case of the Diaoyu/Senkaku islands. As a result, Clinton may have helped put her country in a position where it will one day feel compelled to launch a devastating war to defend Japanese claims to uninhabited rocks, and at a time dictated by Tokyo.

As the Australian realist scholar Hugh White has suggested, underlying the other disputes between the United States and China is Washington's refusal to accord legitimacy to China's system of government, something repeatedly demonstrated in Clinton's book. White argues that such recognition is essential if the two countries are to share power and influence in East Asia and avoid conflict.

This is admittedly a very difficult moral and political issue, given China's human-rights abuses. Clinton made human-rights advocacy a hallmark of her tenure at the State Department (without, it seems, understanding the disastrous effects on this advocacy of the US international record). More substantial has been her contribution to raising global awareness of women's rights; and perhaps most praiseworthy of all (because it is deeply unpopular with many Americans as well as others around the world) is her staunch defense of gay rights.

It would be an immense help, however, if American representatives could recognize the degree to which the US model at home and abroad is now questioned by enemies as well as concerned friends—at home due to political paralysis and the increasing and obvious inadequacy of an eighteenth-century Constitution to deal with a twenty-first-century world; abroad due to a series of criminal actions carried out in defiance of the international community, as well as the catastrophic failure of the US war and state-building effort in Iraq—and very likely in Afghanistan, too. There is not the slightest indication of such a recognition in Clinton's book.

When it comes to the Obama administration's dysfunctional policy toward Afghanistan, Clinton cannot be held chiefly responsible. As her work and books by others make clear (notably Vali Nasr's *The Dispensable Nation: American Foreign Policy in Retreat*), this was a policy driven chiefly by the White House, and for domestic political reasons. Nonetheless, she can hardly evade all responsibility, since on issues that can in any way be presented as successes, she is so anxious to claim responsibility.

At the core of the administration's failure (leaving aside the horribly intractable nature of the Afghan War itself) was the combination of a military surge with the announcement of early US military withdrawal. As far as hardline Taliban elements were concerned, this meant they only had to wait. As far as actual or potential moderates were concerned, Washington failed to accompany the surge with any serious attempt at a peace settlement.

For this failure, opposition by the US military and Afghanistan's then-president, Hamid Karzai, was chiefly responsible, together with the fear of a political backlash in the United States. But as Clinton makes clear, there was no way that she would have supported any peace offer that even the most moderate Taliban elements would have discussed. In her words, "To be reconciled, insurgents would have to lay down their arms, reject al Qaeda and accept the Afghan Constitution." In other words, not a settlement but surrender.

Such an offer should indeed have been made by the Bush administration in 2002 and 2003; it probably would have been accepted by many Taliban commanders, since at the time the Taliban appeared to have been thoroughly defeated. That opportunity was missed, and today—with the United States withdrawing, the Afghan "constitution" deep in crisis, and the Taliban conquering more and more of the east and south—it will not even be looked at. And this syndrome, of either pretending or genuinely believing that Washington is offering compromise when it is actually demanding surrender, is a leitmotif of Clinton's work. It is very sensible to make such offers if you are winning, not so if you are retreating.

This is not to say that in Afghanistan or the Middle East there are easy answers that Clinton has somehow missed. In both cases, there are no real "solutions," only better or worse management of crises based on a choice of lesser evils. Perhaps as president, Clinton would prove to be a competent manager of these crises; but on the basis of her record and writings so far, the verdict on this must at best be "unproven." So far, her actions and those of the United States have succeeded only in making things worse.

Can the United States escape the trap created by its belief in its own supreme morality and right to lead? To do this would require its leaders to tell the American people a number of things that a majority of the country's political classes (which on foreign policy can generally manage to impersonate the people) really do not want to hear: about the relative decline of US power and the need to adjust both policy and rhetoric to accommodate this development; about the consequent need to seek compromises with a number of countries that Americans have been taught to hate; about the insufficiency of the American ideology as a universal path for the progress of humankind; and, most important of all, about the long-term unsustainability of the US economic model and the absolute need to take action against climate change.

In an ideal world, an astute president with popular support should be able to reach past the elites to appeal to the generally sensible and generous instincts of the majority of Americans. As recent polls have demonstrated, on the question of arming Syrian rebels and of seeking a reasonable compromise with Iran, large majorities have shown much more cautious and pragmatic instincts than Clinton, let alone the Republicans. Only 8 percent of Americans want Washington to attempt to lead the world unilaterally compared with overwhelming majorities in favor of seeking cooperation (and cost-sharing) with other powers.

But as Peter Beinart has shown in a recent essay in *The Atlantic*, there is a yawning gap on these issues between the American public and the political and media elites—and, most crucial of all, the big donors on whom candidates increasingly depend. If, as many now believe, the United States is heading toward a de facto oligarchy, then the views of that oligarchy on foreign-policy and security issues are clear—and they're close to those of Hillary Clinton.

There is certainly little basis for the belief that she would be prepared to challenge the oligarchy on these issues. Thus, on the crucial question of climate change, she has indeed taken a rhetorical stand sharply different from the Republicans and a number of conservative Democrats. On the other hand, the chapter on it in *Hard Choices* begins with an extended passage in which Clinton crows about a tactical victory over China at the 2009 Copenhagen summit—a victory that did nothing to combat climate change and only managed to alienate further the Chinese, Indians and Brazilians. Clinton's verbal commitment to this central issue is impressive and commendable, her actual record much less so. But again, the real question is whether any US statesman could do better, given that most Republicans—who now dominate Congress and control federal legislation on this issue—have managed to convince themselves that the problem does not even exist. How is it possible to implement rational policies if much of the political class has abandoned respect for facts and evidence?

Given the US record of the past dozen years, there is a great deal to be said in principle for a long period in which Washington simply pulls back from involvement in international crises. In practice, though, as several administrations have found, international affairs will not leave a US president alone. Crises blow up suddenly, and to craft an appropriate response requires a consistent philosophy, deep local knowledge, a firm grip on the US foreign-policy apparatus, and the ability to frame that response in ways that will gain the necessary support from the policy establishment, media and population. These are sufficiently great challenges in themselves. To expect in addition that a statesman will display originality, moral courage and a willingness to challenge national shibboleths is probably too much to ask of anyone. On the evidence to date, it is certainly too much to ask of Hillary Rodham Clinton. ❖

Forum: Who's Ready for Hillary?

DECEMBER 15, 2014

Hillary Clinton's 2016 candidacy casts a bright light on every fissure within the modern Democratic Party. From domestic policy during the first Clinton presidency to foreign policy under Obama, from the Senate to the West Wing, Clinton has been involved with the most fraught political issues of the last two decades. Her team never ceases to remind the public of her experience, and to trumpet the "inevitability" of her presidency. So why can't we make up our minds about her? Here, seven Nation *contributors gave it their best shot.*

KATHLEEN GEIER

hen I contemplate the presidential candidacy of Hillary Clinton, my heart sinks. "Inevitable" though she may be, she's the wrong woman for the job. Voters just handed the Democrats a resounding defeat at the polls in the 2014 midterm elections, and the reason is clear: it's the economy, stupid.

Voters told pollsters that the economy was their top concern: 70 percent believe the economy is in bad shape, and fully half say they "expect life for the next generation of Americans to be worse."

Their growing discontent is well-founded. Though the economy is improving, 72 percent of Americans believe we're still in a recession. The bottom 90 percent actually experienced negative income growth during the recent "recovery"; all the gains went to the top 10 percent. The richest 0.1 percent controls a stunning 22 percent of our nation's wealth. Such dizzying levels of inequality have not been seen in nearly a century.

Frustrated voters are demanding change, but nothing in Hillary Clinton's history suggests that she is capable of delivering it. Clinton has far more in common with the Rahm Emanuel/Andrew Cuomo wing of the party than with Elizabeth Warren or Sherrod Brown. Not only is she Wall Street's favorite Democrat, drawing hefty donations from the finance industry, but she has supported many of the destructive neoliberal economic policies that ushered in the crisis, such as financial deregulation and free trade. She spent years on the board of the most viciously anti-labor employer in the country, Walmart, and never once spoke up in favor of unions. She voted for the odious 2001 bankruptcy bill, which made it harder for Americans to shed impossible debt. She not only supported welfare "reform" but advocated tougher work requirements—a position that put her at odds with most Democrats.

And that's just her domestic policy. Clinton's neocon-friendly foreign-policy record is even worse—not only her vote in favor of the Iraq War, but her advocacy of drone strikes and her saber rattling over Syria. There are also serious concerns about her executive competence: her leadership in the 1993 healthcare-reform effort and her own 2008 presidential campaign does not exactly inspire confidence.

There is one fresh and exciting thing about Clinton as a presidential candidate, of course, and that would be her gender. Even a Hillary skeptic like me has to admit that the prospect of the first woman president is pretty freaking awesome. But while President Hillary Clinton would be an important symbolic breakthrough, there is little evidence that she is enthusiastic about enacting the feminist economic policies that women need to jump-start our stalled gender revolution—Clinton doesn't even support national paid family leave!

Many on the left are too preoccupied with presidential politics; a more productive channel for activist energies would be organizing on the state and local levels. But while grassroots organizing is the key to a stronger left, presidential politics are still extraordinarily important. From Jimmy Carter through Barack Obama, Democratic presidents have too often been complicit in the neoliberal policies that have devastated so many working Americans. It is the job of those of us on the left to point this out, and to put forward an alternative political vision and accompanying strategy. This is no time for the politics of complacency that Hillary Clinton represents. To the extent that the left falls in line for Hillary, we enable neoliberalism. Meanwhile, the dream of a social-democratic America is borne back ceaselessly into the past.

Joan Walsh

I f Hillary Clinton runs and wins, she will be a good enough president. Not progressive enough for me, by any means, but as progressive as anyone currently electable. I expect to vote for her—if not in the Democratic primary, then later, in November 2016. That's it. That's my endorsement.

With some weariness, I have agreed to write another piece defending Clinton from the charge that she's a neocon in a pant-suit who shares the blame for all of her husband's triangulating compromises in bringing centrist, pro-business policies from the Democratic Leadership Council to the White House. My will-ingness to accept Clinton as a Democratic presidential nominee doesn't stem from any great passion for Hillary herself—though I respect her—but from my aversion to the impotent game of "Let's find an insurgent candidate who will topple a centrist front-runner!" played by the left every four to eight years. It's a colossal waste of political time and energy.

Now, you might say this game worked in 2008. The man embraced by progressives, Barack Obama, who seemed to have little chance either of toppling Clinton or of being elected president at the campaign's start, did both. That wasn't a victory for progressive politics, however, but for progressives' wishful thinking. Obama was never to the left of Clinton, as their subsequent partnership proved. That he put her in charge of diplomacy only further undermined the notion that their foreign-policy views were very far apart.

The most important thing that the left can do to elect a more progressive president would be to give her (or him) a more progressive Congress. But fantasizing over primary challenges is a lot easier, and apparently a lot more fun.

All of that said, if Clinton gets a genuine primary challenger from her left, so be it. Senator Bernie Sanders could run an inspiring campaign, and I might even vote for him. I'm more skeptical of the efforts to draft Senator Elizabeth Warren, who I think could play a huge role in the Senate, but would only break progressive hearts—witness the disappointment over her support for Israel and new military moves in Iraq—and waste her time with a presidential campaign. (I'm distinguishing here between a sincere challenge from Warren and a desperate "anybody but Hillary" draft-Warren campaign from the left.) And don't even try peddling Jim Webb as a progressive alternative.

Finally, I recoil at the Hillary hate because it seems so gendered. I don't mean to accuse my Clinton-critical colleagues of sexism, exactly. It's just that, in my experience, it's never enough for critics of a female leader to say that she isn't qualified, or that she's the wrong choice, or that she's made this or that mistake. A woman has to be described as the absolute worst, and she has to be destroyed.

Whether from the left or the right—and there's remarkable overlap in the story lines offered by Clinton-haters across the political spectrum—headlines that blare Stop Hillary! always make me think they're talking about Glenn Close in *Fatal Attraction*. They depict Clinton as not merely a bad choice, but a dangerous one. There are valid policy reasons to oppose a Clinton candidacy. It's too bad so much of the rhetoric and imagery used against her traffics in an unconscious discomfort with the power of women.

JAMELLE BOUIE

e shouldn't understate the unique position of Hillary Clinton in the world of modern American politics. A former first lady turned US senator (a first in American history) and then secretary of state, she came close to making history—again—as the first woman to win a major party's nomination for the presidency. When President Obama finishes his term in two years, she will stand as his most obvious successor and as a strong candidate for president: even now, in an era of hyperpolarization, she retains more public support than Elizabeth Warren, Paul Ryan, Marco Rubio, Chris Christie or Joe Biden.

This is all to say that if Clinton is the Democratic presidential nominee in 2016, we shouldn't call it a "coronation." The 2000 Republican primary *was* a coronation, when party leaders all but cleared the field for George W. Bush, the undistinguished governor of Texas whose chief advantage was his deep roots in party politics by way of his father. By contrast, if it's Hillary Clinton in two years, it will come eight years after a hard-fought campaign against one of the most electrifying Democratic candidates in recent memory—in which Clinton nevertheless won nearly half the votes—and four years of loyal service in his administration. Put another way, if Clinton has the support of a large cross section of Democratic voters, including single women, educated urbanites, Latinos and—most important for a primary—black Americans, it's because she's earned it.

The problem with Clinton has nothing to do with process and everything to do with substance. As others in this forum have noted, Hillary Clinton is a triangulating corporate Democrat who forged her political identity against a relentless, ideologically driven GOP and built her core support among the wealthy elites of the Democratic Party. The former makes her suspicious of (if not hostile to) the left on foreign and domestic policy, while the latter—coupled with her time as New York senator—makes her receptive to the failed ideas and expertise of Wall Street.

Now, in the absence of a strong left-wing base that can determine elections on the local and state levels—and thus the long-term direction of the Democratic Party as a whole—some of this is baked in the cake. Any Democratic presidential nominee, including an Elizabeth Warren or Bernie Sanders, would have to trade influence with the corporate wing of the party; that's what leading a party means. But it also means responding to the present anxieties of American voters. At her best, that's what Warren does: articulate the frustrations of everyday people at this moment and offer plausible solutions to their problems.

The question for Clinton, should she stand as the Democrats' leader in 2016, is whether she is too stuck in the politics of the past to do this. If she is willing to chart a new course, she has the political strength to offer voters the clear solutions they crave to wage stagnation and economic malaise.

If Clinton sticks to the small-ball approach that defined her husband's time in office, however, then we should remember this: presidential nominees reflect their party as much as they lead them, and a Hillary Clinton who doesn't see space for a more muscular liberalism is reflecting a Democratic Party with the same blind spot. The task for liberals—and the left more broadly—is to correct that blind spot in the party and, in the process, force Clinton to see that the 1990s are over, and the public is more than primed for a big swing.

DOUG HENWOOD

O h, no—not another Clinton. Please. Is there anything that symbolizes the exhaustion of American life like the view that Hillary Clinton is the inevitable Democratic nominee for president in 2016? Or, worse yet, the possibility that she could be running against yet another Bush? It's like our entire culture is operating under some compulsion to repeat. In psychiatry, that's considered a mental disorder. It should be in politics as well.

The positive case for Hillary Clinton's candidacy is remarkably thin. She's a woman, yes, but so was Margaret Thatcher. She's experienced in some sense, but it would be hard to make a list of her accomplishments. As first lady, she ran healthcare reform, which turned out to be a disaster. After that, she retreated to symbolic politics for the rest of her husband's term, allegedly promoting the interests of women and children despite supporting Bill's ending of welfare as we knew it: an act that did more damage to women and children than all the photo ops in the world can undo. In the Senate—where she made a beeline for the Armed Services Committee, stopping only to attend Republican prayer breakfasts—she concentrated her legislative attentions on things like naming post offices in New York after local worthies. Her major accomplishment as secretary of state was traveling almost a million miles. She contributed hawkish advice at cabinet meetings but not much else, since Obama runs foreign policy within his own tight inner circle, delegating little to the diplomatic corps. And her preference for secrecy, first demonstrated in her handling of healthcare reform in the 1990s, is the last thing we need after more than a decade of intensified government lying and spying.

Hillary (and she has clearly rebranded herself as just a first name) embodies the "New Democrat" politics of the 1990s that now seem hopelessly obsolete, no match for a world of chronic economic stagnation, polarization and climate catastrophe. She was very much a partner in inventing that ideology—business-friendly, hawkish, tough on unions and the poor—with her husband. The Clintonites purged the Democrats of their social-democratic wing, consolidating the victories of the Reagan Revolution. At this point, it's hard to say what Hillary or the Democrats stand for, other than being protectors of the status quo. But even that isn't so clear, given that some neocons—worried by the possible ascendancy of Rand Paul–style neo-isolationism in the GOP—have been making very pro-Clinton sounds over the past few months. She does, after all, love a good military intervention.

As I said at the top, though, Clinton's alleged inevitability is about much more than her own story: it's about American society's loss of dynamism in general and the decline of the left as well. We've been so poisoned by decades of neoliberalism and military adventurism that we seem to have lost the capacity to imagine a more peaceful and egalitarian world. Changing that is a longer-term project than a single presidential election cycle, but we've got to get working on it. Next to that, Hillary Clinton is a distraction.

HEATHER DIGBY PARTON

Even though lively primary campaigns often feel like bloody civil wars, they are among the few times that voters get a chance to express their wishes to party elites. Unfortunately, it looks as if that memorably tumultuous primary campaign of 2008 between Senators Clinton and Obama also determined the Democratic nominee through 2016, possibly 2020. This is regrettable. The voters deserve to have big national issues fully aired and argued before the campaign degenerates into the sickening partisan slime fest it's destined to be.

Many on the left end of the party would be happy to see Senator Bernie Sanders join the fray, and they'd be positively giddy if Senator Elizabeth Warren decided to give Clinton a run for her money. The more the merrier, in my book.

With or without an energetic challenge, many liberals doubt that Hillary Clinton will be able to reassemble the Obama coalition if she is nominated, and they worry that she won't turn out Democratic voters. I have to disagree: Clinton victories in deep-red states like Arkansas or Georgia may be a pipe dream, but there's little reason to doubt that she will be able to kindle excitement among the Democratic faithful. Lest we forget, she would be the first woman nominated for president by a major political party in the United States. Half the population has never seen a president who looks like them—*half*.

On the night Clinton spoke to the Democratic convention in 2008, exhorting her followers to get behind Barack Obama, I found myself watching with a group of young African-American women who were strong Obama supporters. They were not exactly Hillary fans in that moment, but I felt a shift in the room's mood as she started to speak eloquently and passionately about the long struggle for women's rights. When she said, "My mother was born before women could vote—but in this election, my daughter got to vote for her mother for president," those young Obama-supporting women next to me all spontaneously stood and cheered, one of them exclaiming, "There's the Hillary I know! There she is!" I was reminded that both Clintons were always more popular among the rank and file than they were among the liberal cognoscenti.

Democratic women will be excited to vote for Clinton in 2016, and I think the rest of the Obama coalition will be as well. All other considerations aside, the first woman president is a big deal. I plan to criticize her without restraint when she takes positions with which I disagree. I fully expect to be frustrated and often angry—as I have been with every president in my lifetime— and I'll call it like I see it. But if she wins, I will also allow myself at least a few moments to feel the pleasure and pride of finally seeing a woman elected to the top job. It's been a long time coming.

STEVEN TELES

The beginning of wisdom in thinking about the 2016 presidential race is that no serious candidate for the nomination will diverge from the personnel and positions of the generic Democrat. The pool of potential judges and executive-branch nominees that any Democratic president will choose from is roughly similar. On most of the issues, almost all plausible Democrats running in 2016 will be positioned where the major interest groups that make up the party base, and its sources of funding, want them to be. Hillary Clinton may have her vices and virtues, but political polarization means that she's unlikely to be different in office from her challengers.

Clinton is certainly the most widely recognized potential candidate for president in 2016. And she has her virtues, in particular a great breadth of experience, both in domestic and foreign policy. I do not trust all of her instincts where national security is concerned, but she won't have to be trained for the job. Having spent her time in the Senate doing constituent service for Wall Street, Clinton is far too close to the bloated financial sector than I am comfortable with. As an advocate of school choice, I'm distressed that she has voiced much more hostility to charter schools than Barack Obama or Bill Clinton, both of whom were strong supporters. A fixture in Washington DC since the early 1990s, Hillary Clinton is unlikely to expect more from the politics of the nation's capital than it can deliver. And while it may seem like grudge-bearing, I still cannot quite forgive her role in the effort to pass universal healthcare during her husband's administration, which was one of the most astounding organizational screw-ups in recent times.

These are important distinguishing features of Clinton, but she is, in fact, the most generic of Democrats. I wish that the Democrats had a candidate who was willing to make a central issue of attacking regulation where it serves the interests of the wealthy—in finance, medicine, urban development and occupational licensing. I wish we had a candidate who would run on fundamentally rethinking our system of criminal justice, making the changes necessary to dramatically reduce our incredible rate of incarceration. I wish there was a Democrat who would attack what I have called "klugeocracy"—unnecessarily complicated policy—by, for example, eliminating all tax-advantaged savings and increasing Social Security. And I wish there was a Democrat willing to fundamentally unshackle American education from the archaic boundaries of local control and unjust local finance, putting in place instead a system of progressive, national vouchers. But we do not have such a candidate, because that is not where the party—as represented by its donors, activists and major interest groups—is.

So we will probably be stuck with Hillary. If so, well, we could do worse. But we should not fool ourselves, when speaking to each other, that we are doing anything other than settling because of the absence of plausible alternatives. I wish that Jim Webb, for instance, did not have a biography that disqualifies him from getting the support of the party's feminists, or have too much published that suggests more sympathy than I can stomach for the Confederacy. He could run in parts of the country where few other Democrats can, could plausibly run against plutocracy, mass incarceration and an excessively adventuresome foreign policy—a very attractive issue mix not likely to be embraced by Hillary Clinton. But his biography makes him a protest candidate—albeit a protest worth supporting.

I will dutifully support Clinton or whichever other Democrat the party in its infinite wisdom nominates in 2016. To do otherwise, especially with the possibility of a unified Republican government in prospect, would be absolute lunacy. But I fear that the Democrats are ill served by the mix of positions the party will straitjacket a nominee into, which are unlikely to slow the growth of plutocracy at the top, the stagnation of social mobility further down, and the decline in the nimbleness of government. We must focus on changing that straitjacket, rather than imagining that it matters a great deal whether Hillary Clinton or someone else wears it.

RICH YESELSON

How you feel about Hillary Clinton's inevitability depends a lot on how alarmed you are that the GOP—the most radically extreme major party formation since the Southern "Slave Democrats" of the 1850s—might take full control of the federal government in 2016. (Evaluating her candidacy shouldn't, by the way, have much to do with imagining that Clinton will be a great candidate who will "expand the electoral map." Anybody who thinks that she is going to carry Arkansas or Missouri or Arizona is a fool—or else her flack.) In most respects, except the salient one of gender, Clinton is exactly the kind of candidate one would expect the Democrats to nominate in 2016. She has the typical political credentials of a modern presidential candidate: eight years in the Senate, followed by a high cabinet post. She has 100 percent name recognition. She has a powerful fundraising apparatus. And her policy positions are broadly aligned with the vast majority of Democratic Party elites and much of its electorate, too. In this, she is the embodiment of what, in a useful phrase, *The New Republic*'s Noam Scheiber has described as "boardroom liberalism."

The phrase connotes, as Scheiber says, both ideology and political method. The ideology contains the basic litany of Democratic economic and social policy—the lineaments of the mixed economy—with a deep commitment to racial and gender diversity. It barely addresses wage stagnation and its concern about the gigantic role of finance capital in the economy is, to be kind, tentative. The method is to get meritocratic elites—government, academic and business—in a room to hash out the policy. Social justice movements (and leftist intellectuals, too) are viewed not as the foundation that drives the party's mission, but as nagging impediments to technocratic efficiency.

Clinton is a quintessential boardroom liberal. And yet her policy proposals—and much more important, her executive and judicial appointments—will be infinitely superior to those of whatever candidate represents the revanchist, ethno-nationalist GOP. This matters: the US governing system grants enormous authority to federal judicial review and the Federal Reserve. If the Supreme Court and the Fed frighten or disappoint you now, imagine what they will look like under the aegis of a President Paul Ryan or Ted Cruz or Scott Walker.

I'm a social democrat and feminist, so Clinton doesn't look that good to me compared to an imaginary candidate to her left on many economic issues—say, Elizabeth Warren or Sherrod Brown. But not only is she a far superior choice to any Republican, it is also clear that, under the current conditions of asymmetrical partisan and ideological polarization, it's impossible for our presidential system of separation of powers to function, i.e., engender bipartisan legislative policy.

So I'd argue that in this election of 2016, party trumps differences between given intra-Democratic candidates by a wide margin. Any generic Democrat is far superior to any generic Republican. Any Democrat, including Clinton, will sustain the Affordable Care Act and climate-change remedies; no Republican will. Obama initially encouraged a post-partisan fantasy of party cooperation that American political culture can no longer afford to entertain.

In summary, the state of the Democratic Party is that it is porous, somewhat center-left, but ideologically constrained by its fealty to its Wall Street donor class. The state of American democracy is that it is catastrophically hamstrung by an anachronistic governing outline composed in the late eighteenth century that did not anticipate that political parties would exist, let alone become highly adversarial. And the state of the left is that it has a very strong intellectual/academic/media infrastructure, but it needs many more rank-and-file adherents and a movement culture if it is to accomplish what the right of Barry Goldwater/William F. Buckley/Strom Thurmond/Newt Gingrich managed—the seizing of a major party. For now, Clinton is more likely than anybody else to be elected the next Democratic president. If this happens, it will be at once historic and banal. ❖

Can Hillary Win Over the Left?

Michelle Goldberg, September 14, 2015

Earlier this year, Buzzfeed uncovered a 1979 television interview with Hillary Clinton—then Hillary Rodham—who had just become first lady of Arkansas. In the half-hour video, we see a young woman in oversize glasses, calm and smiling as the host grills her about whether she's too liberal, too feminist, too career-oriented to fit into her new role. The host tells her that she probably cost her husband votes by keeping her last name. (She would later give in and change it.) "You're not a native," he says. "You've been educated in liberal Eastern universities. You're less than 40. You don't have any children.... You practice law." (She assures him that she and Bill plan to have children and adds, "I'm not 40, but that hopefully will be cured by age.") After nearly twenty minutes of this sort of thing, the host asks Clinton what she finds attractive about Arkansas—a place to which, her biographers have made clear, she moved with great reluctance to further her husband's political career. Outsiders, he notes, complain that "we're so unprogressive here. We're just not as progressive as they are up North." Appearing eager to finally ingratiate herself, she replies by pouring scorn on urban America: "You know, if it's progress to default on your bond obligations so that your city's going into bankruptcy, or if it's progress to have such an incredible crime rate that people don't venture outside their doors, or if it's progress to live in a city whose air you can't breathe, well, then I hope we are unprogressive, and I hope we never get to the point where that's our definition of progress."

This exchange exemplifies a dynamic we would observe over and over for more than two decades. For the first half of her political life, Hillary Clinton was consistently painted as so far left—so feminist—that it threatened her husband's political viability. Whenever that viability was in doubt, she would overcorrect, trying to convince a skeptical mainstream press that she wasn't nearly as liberal as she seemed. Eventually, the strategy of triangulation—using the left as a foil to prove her moderate bona fides—became nearly reflexive.

In recent years, however, America's political context has been transformed. With the white South becoming solidly Republican—something that happened during Bill Clinton's administration—the Democratic Party has become more reliant on the votes of women, people of color and those who wear the "liberal" label proudly. This means that elections have become less about wooing swing voters than about turning out the base. Meanwhile, policies once supported by a smug centrist consensus—from Wall Street deregulation to military adventurism in the Middle East—have proved themselves failures, pushing the center of gravity in the Democratic Party to the left. Triangulation has become passé.

This means that, in a historical irony, Hillary Clinton now needs to convince progressives that she really is who she was once widely believed to be. She is running for president as a progressive feminist, something that would have been utterly quixotic when she entered public life. In a major address on the economy in July, Clinton emphasized the importance of women's equality in a way that no mainstream candidate has done before, describing equal pay, accessible childcare and fair scheduling as key to economic growth. She's making paid leave a signature issue. "I am well aware that for far too long, these challenges have been dismissed by some as 'women's issues,'" she said. "Well, those days are over."

It was thrilling language. Yet after spending so many decades trying to shed her reputation for liberalism, Clinton has amassed a record that many on the left find troubling, if not unforgivable. The wildfire growth of Bernie Sanders's campaign suggests that a large part of the grassroots is dissatisfied with her. She will almost certainly be the Democratic nominee, but "the X factor is enthusiasm, which is going to be a real challenge," says Rashad Robinson, executive director of ColorOfChange, the online civil rights organization. "The question will be, for all of us: How will Hillary speak to the issues of the left?"

Whatever Clinton says, some will remain unconvinced. But

in attempting to court progressive voters, Clinton isn't adopting new positions; rather, she's coming full circle. "I think her progressive résumé and her progressive roots are very, very strong," says Congresswoman Jan Schakowsky, a progressive stalwart who backed Barack Obama eight years ago but is now an enthusiastic Clinton supporter. "Not only has she decided to go back to her roots, but the time is different. This is a progressive moment, I believe." What remains to be seen is whether Clinton, after all the ideological maneuvering required to climb in US politics during a very different time, will be able to seize it.

Hillary Clinton was never a radical, but her formative political years were spent on the left. She did her undergraduate thesis on organizer Saul Alinsky, to whom she once wrote (in a letter unearthed by the right-wing *Washington Free Beacon*), "The more I've seen of places like Yale Law School and the people who haunt them, the more convinced I am that we have the serious business and joy of much work ahead—if the commitment to a free and open society is ever going to mean more than eloquence and frustration." During law school, Clinton interned at Treuhaft, Walker & Burnstein, a radical law firm whose clients included the Black Panthers. In *A Woman in Charge*, Carl Bernstein's 2007 biography of Clinton, he quotes Robert Treuhaft, the firm's senior partner, as saying that Clinton was "in sympathy with all the left causes, and there was a sharp dividing line at the time. We still weren't very far out of the McCarthy era." After graduating, Clinton would eschew corporate law to work for Marian Wright Edelman's Children's Defense Fund, where she focused on the needs of migrant farmworkers.

Years later, when Clinton did enter corporate law, it was in order to provide her family with some economic stability amid the vicissitudes of her husband's political career, which she saw as a vehicle for the sort of progressive change she longed for. Even then, she remained socially engaged: President Jimmy Carter appointed her to chair the Legal Services Corporation, the politically embattled organization providing free legal services to poor defendants. She was the first woman to hold the position.

When her husband became president, Hillary was solidly on the left of his administration's ideological spectrum. During Bill Clinton's first term, the White House was divided between those who wanted to prioritize healthcare reform, like Hillary, and deficit hawks like Robert Rubin, the former co-chairman of Goldman Sachs, who cared most about balancing the budget. At one point, Bernstein describes her snapping at her husband: "You didn't get elected to do Wall Street economics."

When Clinton testified about healthcare before Congress in 1993, her disciplined passion mesmerized *New York Times* columnist Maureen Dowd, who would later become one of her most merciless critics. "Her bravura in back-to-back appearances today before two House committees carried a sense of wonder," Dowd wrote. But the first lady's crusading spirit was far from universally appreciated in the early days of the Clinton administration. In her biography *Hillary's Choice*, Gail Sheehy quotes an exchange between Dick Morris, the mercenary pollster who had worked with the Clintons in Arkansas, and Clinton strategist James Carville, about Hillary's plans for healthcare:

Mystified, he went to James Carville: "What's with all this liberalism?"

"These fuckin' liberals are all over the place!" exploded Carville. "They are like water damage. They seep in."

After the Clintons' attempt at healthcare reform went down in flames, the economic centrists in the White House got the upper hand. Hillary was widely blamed for the catastrophic 1994 midterms, in which Republicans, led by Newt Gingrich, won the House for the first time in forty years. "My view is Hillary Clinton destroyed the Democratic Party," Lawrence O'Donnell, the former aide to Senator Patrick Moynihan and current MSNBC host, told Bernstein. Personally shattered, Hillary threw herself into her husband's strategy of triangulation, a word she uses approvingly in her own memoir, *Living History*. She even brought Morris into the White House, despite the fact that, during the midterms, he'd been working for Republicans. "Morris's specialty," Hillary wrote, "was identifying the swing voters who seesawed between the two parties." The Clintons re-dedicated themselves to winning those voters over.

In his memoir, *In an Uncertain World*, Robert Rubin describes a conversation he had with Hillary and her ideological ally, Labor Secretary Robert Reich, after the midterm elections. According to Rubin, Reich believed that the Democratic base had been unmotivated and prescribed a more populist economic stance. Rubin, however, blanched at language like "corporate welfare," arguing that it would "adversely affect business confidence" and be politically ineffective. Hillary, he wrote, agreed with him: "The polls and political intelligence we have say that the people we need to reach don't respond well to that kind of populist approach," she told Reich.

This was a typical pattern. Faced with a humiliating public rebuke for being too far to the left, she retreated to the safer center. "There's this human quality of, when you are that buffeted and that challenged, you go back to the more conservative stuff," says a former Clinton White House staffer. "What has been instrumental for her as a political person was also a survival mechanism for her as a human being. She had her identity publicly dismantled twice"—first during the 1992 campaign, and then during the Monica Lewinsky scandal. "She invests very heavily in American progressivism as a younger woman," the staffer adds, "and it sort of hangs her out to dry."

This doesn't mean that Clinton abandoned progressivism entirely. According to Melanne Verveer, her former chief of staff, after healthcare reform failed, Hillary pleaded with her husband to expand the coverage for children, which he did through the State Children's Health Insurance Program, passed in 1997. And

Hillary remained particularly strong on women's issues. In 1995, as the head of the American delegation to the United Nations' Fourth World Conference on Women, held that year in Beijing, Clinton gave a speech that is widely seen as a watershed moment in the history of the global women's rights movement. "Twenty years later, you can see it really did begin this massive shift on how we look at gender and development," says Heather Hurlburt, a former White House and State Department speechwriter who served as a consultant to Clinton when she was a US senator. "You have a dramatic change in the degree to which development is focused on women and women's health and reproduction."

Domestically, however, Clinton stopped sticking her neck out. Though uneasy about welfare reform, she didn't oppose her husband signing it; according to Bernstein, "She accepted the decision as inevitable." Nor did she try to distance herself from it later: In her Senate run in 2000, she made her support for the death penalty, welfare restrictions and a balanced budget clear.

Yet once Clinton became a senator and had the opportunity to carve out her own political identity, she moved left once again. According to the vote-ranking system DW-Nominate, which is used by political scientists, Clinton is one of the more liberal senators when all her votes are tabulated, consistently to the left of Barack Obama, Joe Biden and John Kerry. She voted against the Central American Free Trade Agreement, which her husband publicly supported, as well as Bush's energy bill, which included $14.5

billion in tax breaks for the energy industry, and which Obama voted for. She attempted to establish a 9/11-style commission to investigate the federal response to Hurricane Katrina.

"I think she had a great record in the Senate," says Larry Cohen, the recently retired president of the Communications Workers of America, who is volunteering for the Sanders campaign. According to Wade Rathke, founder of ACORN, the now-defunct community-organizing association, when Clinton was senator, "We couldn't have asked for a better friend on any issue we had that involved ACORN in New York." She advocated for the group's housing pro-grams and defended the Community Reinvestment Act, a 1977 law encouraging banks to make loans to people in low-income neigh-borhoods, when it was under fire by Republicans.

For most of the left, however, Clinton's generally progressive Senate record was eclipsed by her vote authorizing the war in Iraq, her biggest overcorrection of all. Her observers are still debat-ing whether the vote was one of misguided principle or political expedience. Most likely, it was both: Clinton is more hawkish than other Democrats, but also often responsive to political pressure. "I do believe there's a good bit of ideology" behind the vote, says Rashid Khalidi, a professor of Middle Eastern Studies at Colum-bia University and the author, most recently, of *Sowing Crisis: The Cold War and American Dominance in the Middle East.* "On the other hand, she's mainly a political operative; she will go with the wind, within the limits of her party."

It's easy to forget now, but when Hillary first ran for president, much of her platform was to Obama's left, particularly on domestic economic issues. She called for a cabinet-level position "solely and fully devoted to ending poverty as we know it, that will focus the attention of our nation on this issue and never let it go." Her health-care plan was more far-reaching than the one Obama initially proposed. "We did a speech in Iowa in November of 2007 calling for regulation of derivatives," says Neera Tanden, who worked on Hillary's presidential campaign and now heads the Center for American Progress. "No one was talking about those issues."

Yet the Iraq debacle haunted her—and though voting for it had been a disastrous mistake, it didn't convince Hillary to stop triangulating in an effort to appear tough. Faced with Obama's insurgent candidacy, Clinton resorted to Dick Morris–style tactics, painting her challenger as weak and radical and seeking to remake herself as the champion of the very sort of blue-collar white men who reviled her during her husband's presidency. A particular low point was an interview she gave to *USA Today*, in which she said that "Senator Obama's support among working, hardworking Americans, white Americans, is weakening again."

This is the Hillary Clinton that many of today's young activists remember. "We can't pretend like that didn't happen," says ColorOfChange's Rashad Robinson. Although she healed some of the wounds of that campaign when she became Obama's secretary of state, he adds, "I don't think it's about the hard feelings—I think it's about how much people sign up on the Love Train."

Of course, during her tenure as head of the State Department, Clinton alienated the left in other ways. She was a major supporter of American intervention in Libya, and, if she'd had her way, the United States would have gotten more involved in the war in Syria. She also supported an escalation of the war in Afghanistan. "Hillary Clinton has many virtues," says Juan Cole, a professor of Middle Eastern history at the University of Michigan. "I think she would stand up in important ways for labor; I think she'd be good on many domestic issues that progressives care about. But on foreign policy, she has been a hawk, and in that regard more hawkish than President Obama, whose hawkishness has disappointed a lot of progressives."

Yet her hawkishness isn't the whole story. As secretary of state, Clinton also brought the awareness of global women's issues that she'd developed as first lady. At the United Nations, she led the push for Security Council Resolution 1888, which requires the UN to take steps to protect women and children from wartime sexual violence. She made sure that women's concerns were represented in forums where they had traditionally been absent. Verveer, who served as the US ambassador for global women's issues under Clinton, describes how she put women's economic participation on the agenda at the twenty-one-nation Asia Pacific Economic Cooperation forum. "There are aspects of her foreign policy record that are profoundly progressive, and she's done things that nobody else could do," Hurlburt adds. "I think people miss that."

Further, Clinton has defended President Obama's nuclear deal with Iran, the most significant foreign policy issue of the day, despite the misgivings of some of her pro-Israel donors, particularly billionaire Haim Saban. "You have to give her credit," says Khalidi. "Saban is one of the biggest funders of the campaign against the Iran deal, and she has taken a clear position on that."

Indeed, most of the positions she's taken in her current run should please progressives: Clinton has generally been more liberal than either she or Obama was in 2008. After her searing loss eight years ago, she appears to be fully cognizant of the way that American politics have changed since the 1990s. "The path to winning requires the Democratic presidential candidates to understand that the center of power in this country is no longer Third Way corporate 'centrism,'" says Anna Galland, executive director of MoveOn.org Civic Action, one wing of the progressive organizing behemoth originally founded to oppose Bill Clinton's impeachment. "The political center of gravity is now a populist center of gravity, and everyone needs to reckon with that. I think her campaign is savvy, and they will."

Not everyone buys Clinton's born-again progressivism. Bill McKibben, the founder of the activist environmental group 350.org, is scathing about her record on the environment at the

State Department. "She mishandled, at best, Keystone, which became the greatest environmental cause of recent decades in the United States," he says. Clinton once said she was "inclined" to approve the pipeline, and as a presidential candidate has refused to take a position on it. As secretary of state, McKibben points out, she attempted to promote fracking overseas, and the 2009 Copenhagen Climate Conference "completely collapsed" on her watch and never reached binding targets on emissions reductions.

Now, McKibben continues, nearly all of the lobbyists bundling donations for Clinton have ties to the fossil-fuel industry. "If you're going to deal with climate change, there's no way to avoid squaring off with the fossil-fuel industry at some point," he says. "It's not one of these things where you can have everybody happy with you in the end, because we're going to have to strand huge quantities of carbon, gas and oil under the ground. The [Republicans] know this, which is why the Koch brothers are willing to invest immense amounts of money in the campaign."

Still, in one of Clinton's first public appearances in this campaign, she called for getting the money out of politics—"once and for all, even if it takes a constitutional amendment"—and she has pledged to appoint Supreme Court justices who will overturn *Citizens United*. Until that happens, Clinton defenders argue, it's impossible to run a viable political campaign without cultivating powerful allies and raising a lot of money. Already, Clinton is far behind the GOP in that regard: The largest Super PAC backing Clinton,

Priorities USA Action, has raised $15.7 million, while Jeb Bush's Super PAC has drummed up $103 million; Scott Walker's has raised $20 million. Even, the AP pointed out, Rick Perry, who didn't qualify for the first Republican debate, has raised more in Super PAC funds than Clinton. "There is no hypocrisy in saying you can run a campaign according to the rules of the road while also saying that you want to change the system," Lawrence Lessig, a Harvard professor who has launched a number of campaign-finance-reform efforts, told *The New York Times* about Clinton's fundraising.

Is Hillary Clinton uniquely or even particularly objectionable, then, for taking Wall Street and K Street money? After all, the single most common adjective that people attach to her is "pragmatic." For example, Ellen Chesler, a longtime friend of both Clintons and director of the Women and Girls Rising Initiative at the Roosevelt Institute, describes her as "a genuine progressive, in terms of her thinking, who is also pragmatic, in terms of understanding the exigencies or requirements of moving forward in a two-party system or a federal government."

In many ways, the progressive debate over Hillary Clinton is all about the limits of pragmatism: How much compromise can be excused by good intentions? When does realism become a complacent acceptance of the status quo? Cohen, for his part, refuses to call Clinton "pragmatic." He prefers the word "practical," arguing: "Pragmatic people believe in problem solving. Practical people often tell us why we can't solve problems that we care deeply about."

It is easy to overstate how widespread this sort of disillusionment with Clinton is. A recent survey by Public Policy Polling found that while 69 percent of Democrats view her favorably, 82 percent of those who describe themselves as "very liberal" do. But there is a fear among many activists that Clinton's long history of cautious positioning has made it hard for the base to muster much enthusiasm. "This is going to be a stretch for a lot of people—to believe that this is where they should put their $20, that they should go down and volunteer and make phone calls," Rathke observes. "There's no heart beating; there's no excitement."

Saru Jayaraman, co-founder of the Restaurant Opportunities Centers United, a group seeking fair wages for restaurant workers, suggests that the lack of passion stems from a broader disenchantment with electoral politics, at least among the people she represents. "The real energy in my community isn't actually around presidential elections at all," she says. "It's not around voting at all. Right now, it really feels like a moment of social upheaval. People are feeling like their form of democratic representation is taking to the street, taking action. Honestly, it's not like my people are any more excited about Bernie Sanders."

Jayaraman's constituency is mostly female, and if they're as disengaged as she says, it's bad news for the Clinton campaign, which will need working-class women and women of color to turn out en masse. (A recent *Wall Street Journal*/NBC News poll showed that while 66 percent of black Americans have a positive view of Clinton, only 34 percent of white women do.) Yet Jayaraman is more sanguine about the Clinton campaign than Cohen is—and that's largely because there's one very big way a Clinton presidency would not be business as usual at all. It matters, Jayaraman says, that Clinton is a woman. It's led her to pay attention to working-class issues that others miss, such as the plight of tipped workers, two-thirds of whom are women. "Every time the minimum wage has gone up in forty-three states across the country, tipped workers have pretty much entirely been left out and stuck at $2 wages," Jayaraman says. "Which means minimum-wage advocates themselves—people on the left—have left out half of the women in the minimum-wage population every time the minimum wage has gone up."

At least in her rhetoric, Clinton isn't leaving these women out. "The fact that she's a woman, the fact that gender equality and income inequality are going to be two of the key issues of this campaign—[wages for tipped workers] really fits in the nexus of those two issues," Jayaraman says.

Sixteen years ago, the late Barbara Olson, who served as chief investigative counsel to one of the House committees that investigated the Clintons in the 1990s, wrote *Hell to Pay: The Unfolding Story of Hillary Rodham Clinton*. In it, Olson warned: "Hillary is a woman animated by a lifelong ambition. That ambition is to make the world accept the ideas she embraced in the sanctuaries of liberation theology, radical feminism, and the hard left." These were the words of a paranoid fanatic. Yet if, after all these years, Clinton were elected on a pro-childcare, pro-healthcare, pro-family-leave platform, it would represent a profound historical victory over the right-wing reaction that has dogged her for most of her life. Whether that's enough of a victory to excite today's ascendant left remains to be seen. ✤

Contributors

Ari Berman is a senior contributing writer for *The Nation* and the author of *Herding Donkeys: The Fight to Rebuild the Democratic Party and Reshape American Politics* (2010) and *Give Us the Ballot: The Modern Struggle for Voting Rights in America* (2015).

Andrea Bernstein is a Peabody award–winning journalist senior editor for politics and policy at WNYC News.

Jamelle Bouie is a staff writer at Slate covering policy, politics and race.

Lakshmi Chaudhry is the former executive editor of FirstPost .com and a contributor to *The Nation*, Alternet, and *In These Times*.

Ellen Chesler is a senior fellow at the Roosevelt Institute, the author of *Woman of Valor: Margaret Sanger and the Birth Control Movement in America* (1992; republished in 2007) and, most recently, the editor, with Terry McGovern, of *Women and Girls Rising: Progress and Resistance Around the World* (2015).

David Corn, the Washington bureau chief of *Mother Jones* and the former Washington bureau chief of *The Nation* for many years. His most recent book is *Showdown: The Inside Story of How Obama Fought Back Against Boehner, Cantor, and the Tea Party* (2012).

Barbara Crossette, the United Nations correspondent for *The Nation*, is a former foreign correspondent for *The New York Times*. She is the author of *India: Old Civilization in a New World* (2000) and co-author of a chapter in *Powers and Principles: International Leadership in a Shrinking World* (2009).

Bob Dreyfuss is a longtime journalist and a contributing editor for *The Nation*. For the past twenty-five years, he's written frequently for *Rolling Stone*, *Mother Jones*, *The American Prospect*, *The New Republic* and other magazines. His most recent book is *Devil's Game: How the United States Helped Unleash Fundamentalist Islam* (2005).

Barbara Ehrenreich has contributed regularly to *The Nation* since 1982 and has been a member of the editorial board since 2007. Her most recent book is *Living With a Wild God: A Nonbeliever's Search for the Truth About Everything* (2014).

Michelle Goldberg is a columnist for Slate and a former senior contributing writer to *The Nation*. Her most recent book is

The Goddess Pose: The Audacious Life of Indra Devi, the Woman Who Helped Bring Yoga to the West (2015).

Kathleen Geier is a Chicago-based writer and researcher. Her work has appeared in *The Baffler*, *The Washington Monthly*, *In These Times*, Salon and other publications.

William Greider is *The Nation*'s national affairs correspondent and a longtime journalist. His most recent book is *Come Home, America: The Rise and Fall (And Redeeming Promise) of Our Country* (2009).

Doug Henwood is a contributing editor for *The Nation* and the editor and publisher of *Left Business Observer*. His most recent book is *After the New Economy* (2003), and his book on Hillary Clinton, *Her Turn*, is forthcoming from OR Books.

Christopher Hitchens wrote *The Nation*'s "Minority Report" column for almost twenty years. He was the author of numerous books, including *No One Left to Lie To: The Values of the Worst Family* (1997) and *Hitch-22: A Memoir* (2010). Hitchens died in 2011.

Sam Husseini is the communications director of the Institute for Public Accuracy in Washington, DC.

Doug Ireland was a longtime *Nation* contributor and investigative journalist. He died in 2013.

Wendy Kaminer is a lawyer and the author of *A Fearful Freedom: Women's Flight from Equality* (1990) and *Worst Instincts: Cowardice, Conformity and the ACLU* (2009).

Elaine Lafferty (www.ElaineLafferty.com) is a former staff correspondent for *Time* magazine, former editor in chief of *Ms.* magazine and former war correspondent for *The Irish Times*. She volunteered for Hillary Clinton's 2008 primary campaign and later worked as an adviser for the McCain-Palin campaign in the 2008 general election. She has also written for The Daily Beast and the *New York Observer.*

Anatol Lieven is an award-winning journalist and a senior researcher at the New America Foundation. He has been a foreign correspondent for the *Financial Times* and the *Times* of London. He is the author, most recently, of *Pakistan: A Hard Country* (2011).

Tara McKelvey is the White House reporter for BBC News and a recipient of a 2011 Guggenheim fellowship. She is the author of *Monstering: Inside America's Policy of Secret Interrogations and Torture in the Terror War* (2008).

Heather Digby Parton has been observing politics and culture at her blog Hullabaloo since 2003 and writes regularly at Salon. She was the recipient of the 2014 Hillman Prize for opinion and analysis.

Katha Pollitt, a winner of two National Magazine Awards, has contributed to *The Nation* since 1975—first as a poet and later as literary editor, film reviewer, contributing editor, associate editor and, since 1994, "Subject to Debate" columnist. Her most recent book is *Pro: Reclaiming Abortion Rights* (2014).

Betsy Reed, a *Nation* senior editor from 1998 to 2006, was executive editor until 2014. She is now editor in chief of the Intercept.

Greg Sargent writes The Plum Line blog at *The Washington Post*.

Robert Scheer is the editor in chief of Truthdig, a former editor of *Ramparts*, and a former correspondent and columnist for the *Los Angeles Times*. His most recent book is *They Know Everything About You: How Data-Collecting Corporations and Snooping Government Agencies Are Destroying Democracy* (2015).

Amy Schiller is a writer focused on feminism, politics, philanthropy and culture who has contributed to *The Atlantic*, *The Nation*, The Daily Beast, *The American Prospect* and Salon.

Steven Teles, associate professor of political science at Johns Hopkins University, is the author of *The Rise of the Conservative Legal Movement* (2008) and co-editor of *Conservatism and American Political Development* (2009).

Michael Tomasky, a former *Nation* intern, is a special correspondent for the Daily Beast, a contributor to *The New York Review of Books* and editor of the journal *Democracy*. He is also the author of *Hillary's Turn: Inside Her Improbable, Victorious Senate Campaign* (2001).

Jessica Valenti is a columnist for *The Guardian* and a founder of the website Feministing. Her most recent book is *Why Have Kids?: A New Mom Explores the Truth about Parenting and Happiness* (2012).

Joan Walsh is a national affairs correspondent for *The Nation* and a former editor at large at Salon. She is the author of *What's the Matter With White People? Finding Our Way in the Next America* (2012).

Rich Yeselson, a contributing editor to *Dissent*, is a former labor strategist who writes about politics and history. He lives in Washington, DC.